日英対訳

日本の歴史

A HISTORY OF JAPAN :
FROM THE ANCIENT PAST TO THE PRESENT

西海コエン＝著
竹森ジニー＝訳

IBCパブリッシング

装幀・岩目地 英樹（コムデザイン）

●写真協力●

芥川龍之介・有島武郎・板垣退助・伊藤博文・犬養毅・岩倉具視・内村鑑三・大隈重信・
勝海舟・桂太郎・木戸孝允・西園寺公望・西郷隆盛・坂本龍馬・高杉晋作・坪内逍遥・
徳川慶喜・福沢諭吉・二葉亭四迷・夏目漱石・与謝野晶子・森鷗外・鹿鳴館
以上、「国立国会図書館」webサイト http://www.ndl.go.jp/

ウィリアム・アダムス像
「写真で見る日本の歴史」webサイト　http://www.pict-history.com

平塚雷鳥
http://www.cc.matsuyama-u.ac.jp/~tamura/

はじめに

　本書は、2010年に英文版として出版された「日本の歴史100」の完全対訳版を、さらに現代の事情に合わせて再度改訂したものです。

　対訳版の刊行を決めたのは、今後ますます増えることが予測される海外との交流の機会、訪日する外国人の増加にあたって、日本をしっかりと英語で説明したいという声が日本の津々浦々からあがっているためです。自国を語ることができなければ、海外との深い交流は不可能です。しかし、英語で日本史を語るには、その独特の文化背景や外国人には語られていない歴史的背景などが多すぎ、相当な工夫が必要になることは言うまでもありません。

　本書は、英語の勉強のために、最初から完読を目指していただく真摯な読者の方々にもお薦めしたい一冊です。そのため逐語訳ではなく、意訳になっている箇所があることもここに記しておきたいと思います。また、日本史や国の背景を英語でというニーズに直面している方々が、もしその特定の部分を探し出し、そこに記載されている歴史上の解説を参考にしていただくためにも、本書を活用していただければと思っています。

　海外からのお客さまを鎌倉や京都に案内しようとか、夕食の席での話題のために参考にしようなどというニーズにもぜひ利用していただきたいのです。

　本書は時代を追って5つのパートにわけて解説を進めています。各パートの冒頭にはその時代背景を英語でどのように説明すればいいか、そのコツについて日本語で解説をいれてあります。また、索引から検索することで、より簡便に求める事象の英語での解説が可能になるはずです。そうした活用法も駆使しながら、外国人とつき合うときの座右の書としてご活用いただきたく、お願いいたします。今回はコロナウイルスやロシアのウクライナ侵攻に翻弄される世界の中での最新の日本の事情にも触れました。

　もちろん、日本史の解説、解釈にはさまざまなものがあります。ここに記されている解釈は一つの視点であるに過ぎないはずです。読者の方々のご意見こそが、そこに付加され海外の方に伝われば、海外の方々とのより活き活きした交流が促進されるはずです。そうした意味で、ぜひ本書を手にしたことを契機に、日本史そのものを自らの心で理解しなおしてみるのも一案かと思います。

　本書を通し、より深い異文化交流を進めていただければ幸いです。

2023年1月吉日　西海コエン

CONTENTS 目次

Part 1 Ancient Japan

古代日本とは

Part 2 | Medieval Japan

Part 3 | Feudal Japan

中世日本のあらまし

幕藩体制下の日本

Part 4 Imperial Japan

大日本帝国の興亡

Part **5** Postwar Japan to the Present

戦後から現代へ

Part **1**

Ancient Japan
古代日本とは

古代日本とは

　外国人が日本について質問するとき、日本の歴史はどこまで遡れるのかというテーマがつねに浮上します。

　歴史とは、文字で記された時代のことを意味します。日本で文字が活用され、国家としてまとまりだしたころといえば、2世紀から3世紀ごろかもしれません。

　ただ、それ以前にも、中国の歴史書に日本のことがしばしば記されていることも理解しておきましょう。そうなれば、日本の国としての紀元はもっと古くまで遡れるはずです。

　ここでは、歴史時代以前の日本の太古の状況にふれ、日本人の起源を語ることからはじめ、そこを起点に黎明期の日本、さらに国風文化が花開いた平安時代へと読者をいざないます。

　また、最初に日本の歴史の特徴についてふれています。この項では古代現代にかかわらず、日本そのものの特徴に通じる事柄にふれています。それは、海外の人との交流の中で最もよく話題になる部分かもしれません。

　さらに、平安時代初期までの、古代史前半は中国や朝鮮半島との交流がさかんだった時代でもあります。日本で日本史や世界史を学習するとき、わたしたちはよく大陸の国などの名前を日本風の漢字読みにして学びます。しかし、英語で表記するときは、オリジナルに近い発音で表記することが

常識です。例えば大和朝廷と深いつながりがあった朝鮮半島南部の王国
百済は、日本では「くだら」と学びますが、英語ではより韓国語の発音に
近い「Baekche」と表記し、「ベクチェ」という風に発音します。

　実は、世界史や世界地理で、カタカナで学んだ事柄の多くの表記が、
英語では異なることが多々あります。これは日本人の多くにとっての頭痛の
種となるはずです。本書でも、古代史や現代史でのこうした表記の違いに
は特に注意しておくことをおすすめします。

　また、日本史の背骨ともいえる天皇制の起源でもある古代史において、
日本がいつから自国のことを empire（帝国）としたかはさまざまな議論が
あります。そうした意味では、大和朝廷はその過渡期にある政権として、
あえて Yamato Court と表記しました。こうした歴史の機微もぜひ楽しん
でいただければ幸いです。

1 Japan's Distinguishing Features

Japan faces the Pacific Ocean, where the Kuroshio Current brings in warm, humid air and associated benefits, including abundant marine resources.

Geologically, the Japanese archipelago is located around the border of Pacific Plate. Due to the impact of this plate colliding with the Eurasian Continental Plate, the country is volcanically active and experiences frequent earthquakes. However, the mineral-rich volcanic soil and warm, humid air create an environment extremely well suited to farming.

In addition, Japan's position on the easternmost edge of the Eurasian continent, separated from the mainland by sea, has impeded any unwelcome influx of people and culture and protected it from the territorial expansionism of the continental nations.

In other words, it is both possible for Japan to be self-sufficient and difficult for outsiders to invade, which has made it one of the world's richest, most peaceful environments.

At the same time, unlike the American continent Japan is not physically isolated. It is within easy reach of China, one of the four great ancient civilizations, and traveling south on the Kuroshio Current enables contact with Southeast Asia and even further afield.

In summer Japan is covered by high atmospheric pressure from the Pacific Ocean, while in winter it borders the continental high pressure

日本の特徴は？

　日本は太平洋に面しています。そこには黒潮が流れ、湿った暖かい空気が流れ込みます。豊かな海洋資源とともに、この湿った暖かい空気は様々なメリットを日本にもたらします。

　地質学的には、日本は太平洋プレートの境界線あたりにある島国です。そのプレートがユーラシア大陸のプレートと衝突する衝撃から火山が活動し、時には地震がおこります。しかし、この火山による日本列島のミネラル豊富な土壌は、そこを巡る暖かい湿った空気の恵みが加わり、耕作にきわめて適した環境を育みます。

　また、日本はユーラシア大陸の最東端にあります。ユーラシア大陸で成長した民族は、まず地続きに拡大します。従って、海によって隔てられた日本は、自らが求めない限り、人や文明が流入しにくい地勢にあったのです。

　すなわち、日本は自給自足が可能で、同時に他者からは侵略の意図を持たれにくい、豊かで平和な環境を約束された世界でも稀な場所なのです。

　しかも、南北アメリカ大陸のように、文明の大勢から隔絶された場所にあるわけでもありません。ちょっと手を伸ばせば、**四大文明**の一つである中国と交流ができ、さらに南からは黒潮に乗って、東南アジアやさらに遠方からの文明が到達することも可能でした。

　日本は、夏は太平洋の**高気圧**に覆われ、冬は大陸の高気圧の縁に位置します。従って、夏と冬の気象の違いが

🔍 **ひとくちメモ**
四大文明
エジプト（ナイル川）、メソポタミア（チグリス－ユーフラテス川）、インド（インダス川）、中国（黄河）の流域で起こった文明

system. There is thus a pronounced difference between summer and winter weather, with abundant rainfall in spring and autumn, and at the changes in season. Lifestyle customs have developed around the four distinct seasons and comparatively straight forward harvest.

Britain is another island nation, but the sea separating Japan from the continent is wider than the Dover Straits and, given the changes wrought by the Roman and Norman invasions in Britain, Japan has clearly been the more stable of the two nations. Japan's topography means that it is apt to be left alone and runs the risk of being forgotten, although it has on occasion been contentious and aggressive when it has felt the need to assert its existence.

These are Japan's distinguishing features, and the history and culture of this island nation from ancient times to the present have been shaped by the behavioral patterns of people raised in such an environment.

顕著で、その中間にある春と秋、そして季節の変わり目には大量の雨にも見舞われます。他の土地に比べ、労苦少なく収穫が可能な四季の変化があり、その変化に沿った生活習慣が培われます。

　日本と同じ島国であるイギリスと比較しても、日本と大陸との間には、**ドーバー海峡**よりは広い海があり、イギリスがローマやノルマン人によって国体が変わるまでに侵略されたことと比較すれば、日本がいかに安全な島であったかは一目瞭然です。日本は、自分からアピールしない限り、ともすれば忘れ去られる国であり、そっとしておいてくれる**地勢**にある国なのです。ただ、その存在を誇示することが必要だと思うとき、日本という国家はときに挑発的、挑戦的になることもありました。

　これらが日本という島国の特徴です。この特徴によって育まれた日本人の行動様式が、日本の歴史を形作り、太古から現在までの様々な出来事や文化活動が綴られてゆくのです。

2 The Origins of the Japanese People

It has been claimed that Japanese people are a single race.

However, it is known that in fact many peoples historically intermixed to become today's Japanese. In the Paleolithic period, before Japan even existed, what is now the Japanese archipelago was attached to the continent. All over Japan there is evidence from the Paleolithic era that continental people had already moved here a hundred thousand years ago. At the end of the Ice Age, people managed to travel overland from what is now Russia via Sakhalin as far as Hokkaido. It is thought that although the Tsugaru Strait did exist at that time, due to the lower temperatures the Strait was narrower and frozen over in winter. The northern people were able to migrate without difficulty to present-day Honshu and down as far as Kyushu.

The Korean peninsula and Kyushu were not connected by land, but the sea between them at that time was perfectly crossable by small boats. Furthermore, the early seafaring Lapithes traveled far and wide, and it is thought that some of them even reached Japan. Such people were major players in Japan's Paleolithic era.

At the close of the Paleolithic era around twelve thousand years ago, the Ice Age came to an end and there was sudden warming. Sea levels rose, and migrants from the north, west, and south were stranded in the Japanese archipelago. They lived by hunting and fishing, and settled throughout the territory. They made the unique cord-marked earthenware known as Jōmon pottery, and formed communities. This marked the start

日本人の起源とは？

　日本人は、**単一民族**といわれます。

　しかし、その起源をたどれば、実に多様な人々が入り交じって、今の日本人へと変化してきたことがわかります。**旧石器時代**、日本がまだ日本となる前、日本列島は大陸とつながっていました。10万年以前に、既に人々は大陸から日本に移住し、日本各地に旧石器時代の痕跡を残しました。**氷河期**の末期、人々は現在のロシアから樺太を経由し、**陸路**で北海道までやってくることができました。津軽海峡には海があったとされていますが、現在よりも低温だった当時、海峡は狭く、同時に冬には結氷します。北方から人々が現在の本州へ、さらに九州へと容易に移動できたのです。

　また、**朝鮮半島**と九州とは陸続きではありませんが、そこにあったのは、当時の小さな舟でも充分に横断できるほどの海でした。さらに、ポリネシアや東南アジアには、原始の海洋民族である**ラピタ人**などが広く活動し、その一部が日本にやってきたのではとも考えられています。こうした人々が日本の旧石器時代の担い手だったのです。

　旧石器時代はおおよそ1万2千年前に終了します。その頃、氷河期が終わり、急激な温暖化がはじまります。海面は上昇し、北から、西から、そして南からやってきた人々は日本列島に取り残されます。彼らは狩猟や漁労により生活をし、各地に定住します。そして、**縄文土器**と呼ばれる**縄目のついた**独特の土器を生産し、集落を形成します。

ひとくちメモ
ラピタ人の土器は縄文土器と似ていることからも、日本とのつながりを示すとする説もある

ひとくちメモ
縄文土器
縄でつけたような文様があることで縄文土器と称された

of what is known as the Jōmon period.

For the next ten thousand years, people within the isolated archipelago gradually mixed and became the ancestors of today's Japanese.

Towards the end of the Jōmon period, around 1000 BC there was another cold period. It is thought that farming was started at around the time of this environmental change.

But another influx from the continent also contributed to the Japanese people of today. These were the highly cultured people from the Chinese mainland and the Korean peninsula, who are thought to have merged with the indigenous Jōmon people. The Japanese people are therefore not a single race, but a mixed race from varied backgrounds.

土偶
縄文時代末期につくられ、東日本側で多くが発
掘されている

いわゆる縄文時代の始まりです。

　日本はこの縄文人の時に孤立した島国で、約1万年の長い年月の中で、次第に混ざり、日本人の**先祖**になっていったのでしょう。

　縄文時代の後期である紀元前1000年前後には、再び寒冷期がおとずれます。この環境が変化した頃に、農耕も始まったといわれています。

　しかし、現在の日本人が形成されるには、さらに大陸から新たな人々が流入してこなければなりません。それは、中国大陸、そして朝鮮半島からの、より**高度な文明をもった人々**のことを意味します。この新たな移民と、先住民であった縄文人との確執と融合の中から、現在の日本人が生まれてきたのではないかと思われます。単一民族とされてきた日本人は、実は多様な背景を持つ、混血民族だったのです。

縄文土器

3 The Yayoi Period

In Japan's long history, there have been many exceptional periods that have all had a major influence on the subsequent direction of history.

The first occurred in about 200 BC.

On the continent, a unified dynasty was coming to the fore in China as the prosperous Qin extended their power eastwards. The numerous eastern states were not only blocked from expanding westwards, but were subjugated and driven out by the Qin. This was achieved within barely ten years from 230 BC. In this brief period, the territories of the Han, Wei, Zhao, Qi, Chu, and the Yan were overthrown one by one.

Of course many must have opted to leave their homeland and go into exile. These would have traveled through the Korean peninsula or crossed by sea directly to Japan. With their excellent skills, they must have reached Japan and either mixed with or subjugated the Jōmon people.

There are many cases around the world where a small number of immigrants have ousted a much larger indigenous population. Just as 168 Spanish troops crushed the Incan empire in southern America in the sixteenth century, the Chinese and Korean immigrants into Japan brought not just overwhelmingly advanced weaponry, but also contagious diseases into an area that lacked immunity, which was probably just as powerful a weapon. It cannot have been all that difficult for the incomers to eradicate the Jōmon people and their culture.

弥生時代とは？

　日本は、その長い歴史の中で、外から強い影響を受けた例外的な時期が何度かありました。しかも、その全ての「例外」が、その後の歴史の方向に大きな影響を与えています。

　最初の例外は、紀元前 200 年前後にありました。

　その頃大陸では、中国に統一**王朝**が生まれようとしていました。西に興った**秦**が勢力を東に拡大したのです。東にあった多くの国が西への拡大の道を閉ざされるどころか、圧迫され、秦によって駆逐されます。これは、紀元前 230 年あたりから 10 年にも満たない短期間に起きたことなのです。そんな短期間に**韓**、**魏**、**趙**、**斉**、**楚**、**燕**といった文化の発達した国が次々と滅びました。

　当然多くの人々が祖国を離れ亡命をはかったに違いありません。彼らは朝鮮半島を経由し、あるいは直接海を渡って、日本にもやってきました。卓越した技術をもって日本に上陸し、縄文人とも混ざり、時には**駆逐して**ゆきます。

　少数の民族が大多数の先住民を駆逐した事例は、世界のあちこちにあります。16 世紀の南米で、たった 168 名の兵力で**インカ帝国**を打ち破ったスペイン人のように、圧倒的に進んだ兵器のみならず、その土地にはない免疫力をもった他の大陸からの渡来人がもたらした**伝染病**も強力な武器であったかもしれません。少数の渡来人が、縄文人とその文化を駆逐することは、さほど困難なことではなかったはずです。

🔍 ひとくちメモ
秦 《BC778–BC206》
韓 《BC403–BC230》
魏 《BC403–BC225》
趙 《BC403–BC228》
斉 《BC386–BC221》
楚 《?–BC223》
燕 《BC11世紀-BC222》

These immigrants, their bloodlines and cultural influences, eventually merged with the indigenous Jōmon people to create a new population and farming culture. This was the Yayoi period.

The immigrants brought bronze and ironware with them. For four hundred years from about 200 BC, the new tools, weapons, and farming implements led to the development of wet rice cultivation and associated formation of villages, and eventually a nation-state was created in Japan.

In China, the Qin were followed by the Han dynasty that took control of China. The Han were once destroyed and later revived, their respective kingdoms being referred to as the Earlier Han and the Later Han. The rulers of the new nation-state in Japan would sometimes visit the Han and receive the Han Emperor's official approval for their rule. That is, the immigrants from the continent who became rulers would regale the homeland of their ancestors with Japanese brocades. The Yayoi period marked Japan's first exchange of this kind with the outside world.

　この**渡来人**、渡来人と縄文人の混血、そして渡来人の
もたらした文化の影響を受けた縄文人の3者が一体となっ
て、日本に新たな**農耕文化**を拓くのです。それが弥生時
代でした。

　渡来人は、日本に**青銅器**や**鉄器**を持ち込みます。紀元
前200年頃から400年の間に、こうした新しい工具や武
器、農工具に支えられ、**稲作**が発展し、日本のあちこちで
村ができ、やがて国家を形成します。

　中国では秦のあと**漢**が興り、中国の広大な地域を版図
にもちます。漢は一度滅びた後に再興されるので、最初の
王朝を**前漢**、後の王朝を**後漢**と呼びます。日本に新たに
生まれた国家の王は、時には漢を訪ね、漢の皇帝からそ
の国を統治するための「おすみつき」をもらいます。国王
が渡来人であれば、まさに先祖のいた故郷に錦を飾ったわ
けです。弥生時代にはそうした日本初の外交活動も行われ
ていたのです。

🔍 **ひとくちメモ**
漢
《前漢BC206–8、
　後漢25–220》
前漢
《BC206–8》
後漢
《25–220》

弥生土器

4 The Formation of a Nation-state in Japan

Numerous nations were formed during the Yayoi period, and these repeatedly merged and divided until gradually they were unified under a greater authority.

Visits to China from envoys from these states are recorded in the Book of Han, the historical record of the Earlier Han dynasty, while according to the Book of the Later Han, in 57 CE, an emissary sent by the Nakoku state (present-day Fukuoka) was granted a gold seal by Emperor Guangwu, founder of the Later Han. This seal was later found on the island of Shikanoshima, thus verifying this written record. Later, in 107 CE, a King Suishō is recorded as having paid tribute.

Having unified China, the Han extended their power into Korea, establishing the Lelang Commandery in the northern part of the peninsula. Of course Lelang also became a base for exporting Chinese culture to the Korean peninsula and the northeastern regions of China, and its influence extended as far as Japan.

Towards the end of the Later Han as disorder spread through China, Gongsun, a member of the Wei dynasty that eventually overthrew the Han, became the effective ruler of Lelang and northeastern China and held power there for many years. Around this time Gongsun separated off the southern part of Lelang and ruled this as the Daifang Commandery, which he made his base for his role in military foreign affairs in the southern part of the Korean peninsula and Japan.

日本での国家形成の
過程とは？

　弥生時代に形成された無数の国家は、融合と分離を繰り返しながら、次第により大きな権力によって統合されてゆきます。

　前漢の歴史書である漢書には、それらの国の使節が漢を訪ねてきていることが記されており、後漢の歴史書である後漢書にも、西暦57年に**奴国**という国が、日本から使節を送り、後漢の初代の皇帝である光武帝は、その使節に**金印**を与えたと記しています。この金印は、後に福岡の志賀島で発見され、その歴史書の記述が事実であることが証明されました。その後、西暦107年には**帥升**という王も朝貢してきたと記されています。

　漢は、中国を統一すると、朝鮮半島にも勢力を伸ばし、朝鮮半島北部に**楽浪郡**という行政区を設置しました。当然、楽浪郡は、中国文明の朝鮮半島や中国東北地方への輸出拠点にもなり、その影響は日本へも届きます。

　やがて、後漢も終わりに近づき、中国の国内が混乱してくると、楽浪郡も当時中国東北部で権勢をふるっていた**公孫**氏が実質上統治することになり、公孫氏は後漢を滅ぼした魏に帰属しながらも、そこで長年にわたって権勢を振るいます。公孫氏は、そのころ楽浪郡の南部を分けて、**帯方郡**として統治していました。魏に帰属した公孫氏は、この帯方郡を拠点として、朝鮮半島南部や日本に向けた軍事外交の役割を担ってゆきます。

 ひとくちメモ
奴国
弥生時代、北九州にあった小国

◀ 志賀島（福岡県）で発見された「漢倭奴国王」という金印

 ひとくちメモ
帥升
弥生時代中〜後期の倭国の王。外国史書に名の残る最初の人物

楽浪郡
朝鮮半島北部に存在した中国王朝の郡県。BC108–313

 ひとくちメモ
公孫
中国後漢末から三国時代の武将。?–238

帯方郡
朝鮮半島中西部に存在した中国王朝の郡県。204–313

An emissary from Japan visited Daifang in 239 CE. This was Queen Himiko of Yamatai-koku, who was accepted as the emissary of the state representing Japan and was accordingly presented with a gold seal and bronze mirror. The following year an envoy made a return visit to Queen Himiko, thus establishing formal diplomatic relations, as recorded in a Chinese historical document known as The Record of Japan in the History of Wei. According to the earlier Book of Later Han, before Himiko's time there had been widespread disturbances in Japan. What this means exactly is unclear, but it suggests that amidst various power struggles Japan was gradually unified into the large nation-state Yamatai-koku under Himiko's leadership.

Opinion is divided as to whether Yamatai-koku signified the later unified kingdom of the Yamato Court or whether it was a different nation-state, or also whether it was located in Kyushu not far from the mainland or near present-day Kyoto. However, major structural remains thought to be from Yamatai-koku have recently been discovered in Nara prefecture, and it has thus been surmised that Yamatai-koku was the kingdom directly linked to the unification of Japan. It was the birth of the Japanese nation.

そんな帯方郡にやってきた日本の使節がありました。西暦239年のことです。その使節は邪馬台国の卑弥呼という女帝の使節で、日本を代表する国の使節として待遇され、金印と銅鏡が授けられました。そして、翌年には返礼使が卑弥呼の元を訪ねます。正式な外交関係が樹立されたわけです。この記録は、**魏志倭人伝**という中国の歴史書の中に記されています。それ以前の後漢書によれば、卑弥呼が出現する以前、日本は大乱があったようです。それが何を意味するのかは不明ですが、様々な権力闘争の中で、次第に日本が卑弥呼に率いられる邪馬台国のような大きな国家に統合されてきたことを暗示しているようです。

邪馬台国が、その後の統一王朝である**大和朝廷**を意味するのか、それとも別の国家なのか、また邪馬台国が大陸に近い九州にあったのか、畿内にあったのか意見が分かれます。しかし、最近奈良県で邪馬台国の遺跡ではと思われる大きな遺構がみつかり、邪馬台国が日本の統一にそのままつながる王朝であったのではと推測されるようになりました。日本を代表する国家の誕生です。

ひとくちメモ
魏志倭人伝
中国の「三国志・魏志」にある「東夷伝ー倭」の項に、邪馬台国など日本の風俗、地理などについてまとめて記したもの

5 The People of Wa

The Wajin, or people of Wa, are often construed to be Japanese, but this is not necessarily the case. The Chinese seemed to have used this as a generic name for the people who were expanding into Japan and the surrounding areas. Nevertheless, the Country of Wa was used to indicate the various states that existed in Japan in the Yayoi and Kofun periods.

There is evidence that in ancient times, Northern Kyushu and the Izumo area had close ties and trade with Korea. Later, when the unified Yamato Court appeared in the Kinai area, Wajin actively advanced into the Korean Peninsula.

In the second century, the Lelang and Daifang Commanderies were administered by Gongsun under China's Wei Dynasty. However, the Korean Peninsula was affected by the strife on the Chinese mainland occasioned by the rift between Gongsun and the Wei, and the overthrow of first Gongsun then the Wei, and conflicts broke out between various ethnic groups.

The Wajin had a strong trading base in southern Korea from early on, although this base may originally have been created by the Chinese and Korean immigrants to Japan who assimilated into Wa culture from the Yayoi period onwards. The Wajin in the Korean peninsula were gradually caught up in the political conflict there.

Chinese history is just like a balloon. When the balloon loses air, the territory shrinks and the surrounding peoples expand, desirous of the rich Chinese culture. And when new air is injected into China, the balloon

倭人とはどんな人？

🔍 ひとくちメモ
倭人（和人とも）
中国人が日本人を呼んだ呼
称

　よく**倭人**はそのまま日本人と解釈されますが、日本に住んでいる人々のみが倭人であるかと言えば、必ずしもそうではありません。日本列島とその周辺に展開していた人々を総称して、中国人が倭人と呼んでいたようです。ただ、倭国といえば、日本に弥生時代から古墳時代にかけてあった国々を指しています。

　古代、九州北部や出雲地方は朝鮮半島と密接に交易し、交流していた形跡があります。その後、畿内に統一王朝である**大和朝廷**が出現すると、倭人は積極的に朝鮮半島に進出しました。

　朝鮮半島では、2世紀には中国の魏王朝のもと、楽浪郡、帯方郡が公孫氏によって運営されていました。しかし、公孫氏と魏との間に亀裂が生まれ、公孫氏が滅び、その後魏も265年に晋に滅ぼされるというように、中国本土の混乱に影響され、朝鮮半島でも様々な民族が入り乱れた抗争が始まります。

　倭人は、早くから朝鮮半島南部に交易の拠点をもっていたのでしょう。あるいは、弥生時代から日本に進出して倭人となった中国や朝鮮半島の人々の拠点が半島南部にも残っていたのかもしれません。そうした朝鮮半島の倭人も、半島の政治の混乱に巻き込まれてゆきます。

　中国の歴史はちょうど風船のようなものです。中の空気が少なくなればその版図は縮小し、豊かな中国の文物を求めた周辺民族が伸長します。そして、中国に新しい空気

regains its momentum and conversely subjugates the surrounding peoples. During the third and fourth centuries the Chinese balloon shrank, and the people of Wa actively advanced into the Korean peninsula. They strengthened their base in the southern Gaya Confederacy and proceeded to advance into Silla to the north.

At that time, the Tungusic peoples from present-day Russia and across Northern Asia who had established the Goguryeo kingdom in the northern part of the Korean peninsula, began extending their empire southwards as far as the center of the peninsula. The inscription on a monument in Jilin Province, China, to their leader Gwanggaeto the Great, has proved key to solving some major historical puzzles.

The Wajin in Silla and Baekche in the southeast resisted the Goguryeo advance southwards, but were gradually subjugated and eventually driven out and confined within the Gaya Confederacy. Subsequently events on the Korean peninsula became a diplomatic issue of utmost importance for the Yamato court established around that time.

This is because the Wajin also played a major role in the vicissitudes of East Asian history.

が注入されれば、その風船は勢いを取り戻し、逆に周辺民族を従えます。3世紀から4世紀にかけては、まさに中国という風船が縮小した時代です。倭人もそんな中で積極的に朝鮮半島に進出しました。朝鮮半島の南部にある伽耶（かや）の国周辺で力を蓄え、その北にあった新羅（しらぎ）へも進出をもくろみます。

　その頃、朝鮮半島北部では、現在のロシアを中心とした北アジア一帯に拡散していたツングース系の民族によって建国された高句麗（こうくり）が南下し、半島の中央部までを版図とする大帝国を築きました。その中心となった好太王の碑文が現在の中国吉林省に残っていて、古代史の謎を解く大きな鍵となっています。

　倭人は、そんな高句麗の南下を恐れ、抵抗します。しかし、次第に高句麗に押され、新羅や半島の南東にあった百済（くだら）の倭人の勢力も駆逐され、伽邪の国周辺に閉じ込められます。それ以来、朝鮮半島の時事は、当時成立した大和朝廷にとっての最も重要な外交課題となるのです。

　倭人も東アジアの興亡の歴史の担い手の一つだったわけです。

🔍 **ひとくちメモ**

伽耶
3世紀から6世紀中頃にかけて朝鮮半島の中南部に散在していた小国家群。日本では「任那」とも表記された

新羅
古代の朝鮮半島南東部にあった国家。356-935

高句麗
ツングース民族による国家。最盛期は朝鮮半島のほとんどを領土とした

好太王
（374-413）高句麗の第19代王、高句麗の最盛期を築く。広開土王

百済
古代の朝鮮半島南西部にあったツングース系国家。BC18-660

6 The Formation of the Yamato Court

Yamato is written with the characters. The name has existed since ancient times to refer to the area around the Nara Basin, but was probably first written with these characters when the court was established. The kanji used to write Wa (ancient Japan) is homonymous with another reading of (which is also used to signify Japan, but which has wider meanings of peace and harmony), and the People of Wa probably added (which means "great") before it in emulation of the Chinese style at the time they named the court. In any case, Chinese historical records refer to ancient Japan as (the country of Wa).

The connection between Yamatai-koku (a state that existed in ancient Japan) and Yamato is unclear. There is a theory that Yamatai-koku was a precursor of the Yamato Court, although other theories reject this and it is by no means definite.

To begin with, the Yamato Court was probably a federation of various clans. It is thought that the clan that most successfully dealt with the common interests in southern Korea, military needs, and diplomatic affairs predominated over the others to become the supreme ruler in charge of the Yamato government.

There is no written record of this period, and it is only possible to guess at the conditions at that time from the myths and legends recorded in the later Nara period works the *Kojiki* (Record of Ancient Matters) and *Nihon shoki* (Chronicles of Japan), along with Chinese documentary records and excavated materials. Indeed, the period is shrouded in mystery given that all accounts of Japan disappear from the Chinese history books for a

大和朝廷はどのようにして
成立した？

　倭人の「倭」は、大和の「和」に通じます。倭が朝廷をもった
とき、中国にまねて倭（和）の前に「大」の字をつけて、
大和としたのかもしれません。ただ読み方の「やまと」は、
古くから奈良盆地周辺にあった名前で、それにこの漢字を
あてて表記したわけです。いずれにしろ、中国側は、古代
日本を記述するときに常に倭の文字を使い、倭国とか倭
国王というふうに表現しています。

🔍 ひとくちメモ
大和朝廷
古代日本の最初の統一国家。
４世紀の中ごろまでには中
部から北九州までを統一し、
その後、関東・東北へと勢力
をのばしたと考えられる

　邪馬台国と**大和朝廷**との関連は不明です。邪馬台国が
大和朝廷の前身であるという説と、そうでないという説と、
どちらにも軍配はあがっていません。

　実際は、豪族たちの共通の利権である朝鮮半島南部へ
の対応や、対外的な軍事や外交の必要性にあたって、最
も有力な豪族が覇王として彼らを従え、その覇王が大和の
政権を担ったのではないかと思われます。初期の大和朝廷
は、豪族の連合体だったのでしょう。

　この時代は、神話の時代です。『**古事記**』や『**日本書紀**』
といった奈良時代に記された**神話**や**伝説**に、中国の文献
や発掘された資料を加え、当時の状況を推理するしか方
法はありません。特に、西暦 266 年以降、150 年にわたっ
て、中国の史書から日本の記述が消えていることが、ます
ますこの時代を闇の中に閉じ込めます。しかし、３世紀か

period of 150 years from the year 266 CE. However, from the third to fifth centuries, burial mounds known as *kofun* were constructed all over Japan, and some of the larger of these remain today, the best known being that of Emperor Nintoku in Osaka. It is therefore thought that the Yamato Court rapidly consolidated its power during this period.

Immigrants from the Korean peninsula and China must have played a major role in the formation of the state, contributing their knowledge of the advanced systems and laws in China, as well as military affairs and engineering technology. There were many immigrants at this time due to the political instability of the Korean peninsula, as well as the north-south split in China and suppression of the northern peoples. And by the fifth century, the power of the Yamato Court extended all the way from Kyushu to eastern Japan (Kanto). According to the *Nihon shoki*, military force was apparently used to oust some of the powerful regional clans.

At around this time, the Chinese historical records state that the Five Kings of Wa brought tribute once more. Furthermore, in the Korean peninsula Goguryeo was increasingly oppressing the south, threatening the interests of the Wajin in the peninsula. The Yamato regime, built on the balance of the regional clan rulers, was facing leadership problems at home and abroad.

ら5世紀にかけて、日本各地で古墳が建造され、特に畿内では仁徳天皇陵に代表されるような、巨大な**古墳**が残っていることから、この時期に急速に大和朝廷の権限が強化されてきたのではないかと思われます。

彼らの国家形成に大きな役割を担ったのが、朝鮮半島から、あるいは中国から移住し帰化した渡来人、すなわち帰化人たちでした。彼らのもたらす中国などの進んだ制度や法律についての知識、そして軍事や土木技術などが国家建設に大きな役割を担ったことはいうまでもありません。朝鮮半島の不安定な政治状況に加え、中国も国が南北に分断され、北方民族に蹂躙されていた時代が、こうした大量の帰化人をうみだしたのです。そして5世紀ごろには、大和朝廷の力は九州から関東一円に及ぶようになっていました。時には武力で豪族を駆逐していた様子が、日本書紀などの記述からも推測できます。

そしてその頃、再び中国の歴史書に、**倭の五王**が朝貢してきたことが記されています。当時は、朝鮮半島では高句麗がますます南部の国々を圧迫し、半島での倭人の利権も脅かされていた時代です。豪族とのバランスの上に成立した**大和の政権**は、内外に向けた困難なかじとりに直面していたのです。

仁徳天皇陵

🔍ひとくちメモ
倭の五王とは
讃、珍、済、興、武の5人を指す

Politics in the Yamato Court

The protodynastic Yamato Court started from a coalition of regional clan leaders, so naturally it was politically unstable.

Furthermore, the rise of Goguryeo in the Korean peninsula had created a critical situation for the Wajin resident there, and was a serious economic blow for the clans in Kyushu that traded with them. There must also have been a need for the Yamato Court to assert their power by taking a lead in cooperation with Silla and Baekche, the southern Korean states under threat from Goguryeo. There was a particularly pressing need to defend Imna, a stronghold for the Wajin in Gaya, in the south, who had close relations with Baekche. However, the relationship with Baekche and Silla was not solid, and the opposition of many clans to the Yamato Court's support of Baekche on occasion caused internal conflicts.

Meanwhile, an emissary from the King of Baekche came to request the support of the Yamato Court, and presented Emperor Kinmei (or, according to some accounts, Emperor Senka) with a Buddhist statue and sutras. This was in the year 552 (or in the case of Emperor Senka, 538).

At that time, the most powerful clans were the Ōtomo, the Mononobe, and the Soga. The Ōtomo eventually fell from power, but the Mononobe and Soga clashed over the question of whether or not to accept Buddhism, a dispute that may have split the Court. The Mononobe apparently insisted that accepting Buddhism would be sacrilege to Japan's gods.

大和朝廷の政治課題は？

　大和朝廷は、**豪族**の連合政権からはじまった原始王朝のため、当然政治的には不安定な状態であったと思われます。

　しかも、朝鮮半島での高句麗の台頭は、現地の倭人の危機であり、その倭人と交流していた九州などの豪族にとっては経済的な痛手でもありました。大和朝廷は、同じく高句麗におびえる朝鮮半島南部の新羅や百済との連携をリードし、覇王としての力を見せる必要もあったはずです。特に百済と密に交流し、半島南端の伽耶の中に存在した倭人の拠点である**任那**を防衛することは急務でした。しかし、百済と新羅とは決して一枚岩ではなく、百済と連携する大和朝廷に反抗する豪族も多く、それが内乱の原因となったこともありました。

　そんな中、大和朝廷との強い連携を求める百済の王からの**使者**が、仏像や経典を欽明天皇（あるいは宣化天皇という説もあり）に届けました。552 年 (宣化天皇の場合は 538 年) のことでした。

　当時、数ある豪族の中で、大伴氏、**物部氏**、そして蘇我氏は最も有力な豪族でした。大伴氏はやがて失脚しましたが、仏教を受け入れるかどうかを巡り、物部氏と蘇我氏とが激しく対立したのです。豪族の対立は、朝廷の分断へと繋がりかねません。物部氏は、仏教を受け入れることは、日本の神々への冒涜となると主張したといわれています。

🔍 **ひとくちメモ**
任那
朝鮮半島に、4〜6世紀頃あった伽耶諸国のこと。大和朝廷の支配下に入り、軍政府をおいたとされる

🔍 **ひとくちメモ**
物部氏
古代の大豪族で、天皇の親衛軍を率い、大伴氏とともに最有力となる。仏教の受け入れに反対した物部守屋は蘇我馬子および皇族の連合軍と戦い死亡

Shinto, Japan's ancient religion, has only ever been a state religion in modern times. At that time, individual clans worshipped their own gods and the emperor accepted the authority of those gods, although the god worshipped by the imperial family was probably held in the highest esteem. As well as being syncretic, Shinto was animistic, revering the soul and spirits of the natural world, and shamanistic, seeking to communicate with the spirits of the elemental gods, such as the Sun. Buddhism, however, was closer to philosophy than religion as such, and also encompassed various further fields of study. The Mononobe probably feared that the adoption of Buddhism by the state would threaten the religious rites behind their own traditions and authority.

At the time that the Mononobe and the Soga started their fierce standoff, finally in Imna the local Wajin were attacked by Silla and destroyed in 562, cutting off the economic base of the powerful clans.

Could the Yamato Court become a strong centralized state? From this time they were put to the test.

　神道という日本古来の宗教が、**国家神道**として統率されたのは、近代になってからのことです。むしろ、当時はそれぞれの豪族が自らの神を奉じ、そうした神々の権威を天皇がみとめ、天皇家の信奉する神の儀式が最も尊重されていたのかもしれません。そうした多様な宗教の総合体である神道は、自然界の精霊や魂を敬う**アニミズム**であり、太陽などの絶対なる自然との魂の交流を求める**シャーマニズム**でもありました。しかし、仏教はそれ自体が宗教というよりは、哲学に近く、さらに仏教とともに様々な学問が伝来します。物部氏は、そんな仏教が国家と結びつくことにより、自らの伝統や権力の母体となる宗教儀式が脅かされると思ったのかもしれません。

　物部氏と蘇我氏とが激しく**対立**をはじめたころ、ついに任那では、倭の出先機関が新羅に攻められ、滅亡します。562年のことでした。この事件は、そのまま、一部の有力な豪族の経済基盤を奪うことにも繋がります。

　大和朝廷が強力な**中央集権国家**となりうるのか。試練がここに始まるのです。

🔍 **ひとくちメモ**

アニミズム
生物・無機物を問わないすべてのものの中に霊魂や霊が宿っているという考え方

シャーマニズム
シャーマン（巫人・祈祷師）の能力により成立している宗教や宗教現象の総称

8 The Asuka Culture

Asuka is Japan's oldest Buddhist culture.

China was emerging from a long period of disorder, and in 589 CE finally drew a line under more than three turbulent centuries. China's balloon was beginning to swell once again.

This meant that the surrounding countries were under threat from the Sui, which had become a powerful unified kingdom.

Japan, at that time still called Wakoku, actively sought engagement with the Sui, perhaps perceiving their opposition to Goguryeo. In 607 Emperor Kinmei's grandson, Prince Shōtoku, dispatched Ono no Imoko as Japan's official envoy to Sui Dynasty China to request friendly relations.

This was seen as victory to the Soga in their dispute with the Mononobe over the introduction of Buddhism. There is also a theory that the Soga were the descendants of immigrants originally from Baekche, and that it was for this reason too that they had opposed the Mononobe who stressed the importance of the domestic tradition and following Shinto rites at Court. After winning the dispute with the Mononobe, the Soga assassinated Emperor Sushun who had opposed them, and installed their own candidate Empress Suiko, thus placing the court under their sole control. Prince Shōtoku governed as Empress Suiko's regent.

Recently doubts have been expressed as to how far Prince Shōtoku was

飛鳥文化とは？

飛鳥文化は日本最古の仏教文化です。

中国が長い混乱から蘇生し、300 年以上の乱世に終止符を打ったのは西暦 589 年のことでした。**隋**の中国統一です。中国の風船は再び膨らみはじめました。

周辺の国々は、強大な統一王朝となった隋の脅威を受けることになります。そんな隋と積極的に交流しようとしたのが日本でした。

飛鳥寺の飛鳥大仏（奈良県）

当時まだ日本は倭国と呼ばれていました。倭国は、隋が高句麗と対立していることを察知したのか、すぐに隋に**遣隋使**を送り、友好関係を求めようとしました。607 年に小野妹子を大使として、遣隋使を送ったのが、欽明天皇の孫にあたる聖徳太子です。

物部氏と蘇我氏との仏教の取り扱いを巡る争いは、蘇我氏が物部氏を抑え、落着したかにみえました。元々蘇我氏は、渡来人の子孫ではという説もあるほど、百済からの帰化した人々とつながりが深く、そうした意味からも朝廷の**祭祀**を司り、**国内の伝統**を重んじる物部氏などと対立していたわけです。物部氏との紛争に勝利したあと、蘇我氏は彼らと対立した崇峻天皇を暗殺し、自らの息のかかった推古天皇を**擁立する**など、一族による朝廷支配を進めます。その時代に推古天皇の**摂政**として政務をみたのが聖徳太子でした。

彼が実際にどこまで多くの仕事をしたかは、最近になっ

🔍 **ひとくちメモ**
隋
中国の王朝、581–618

遣隋使
日本の記録では、推古天皇時代607、608、614の3回送られている

actually responsible for carrying out many of the works credited to him. However it is well known that, having a strong blood connection with the Soga clan, he encouraged the propagation of Buddhism, introduced a system of ranks at court, and established the Seventeen-article Constitution, Japan's oldest law. According to the official story, Prince Shōtoku lived in Ikaruga (Nara) and immersed himself in contemplation of Buddhist teachings, but it is not known how true this is. What is known for sure is that one reason Prince Shōtoku was so venerated was that he enabled the subsequent regime to make Buddhism a pillar of the centralized state.

Hōryūji temple in Ikaruga, which Prince Shōtoku built in 607, includes the world's oldest group of wooden buildings. The style of entasis, derived from Greek architecture, can be seen in its columns, a vestige of the Western civilization that reached China along the Silk Road. It is also thought that the smiles of the Shaka Triad enshrined in the Golden Hall were influenced by Greek sculpture.

The vestiges of Greek culture in Central Asia from Alexander the Great's invasion of India eventually reached Japan via China. Asuka was an unusual culture attuned to the flow of the ancient world.

て疑問とする見解も多く発表されています。しかし、蘇我氏と血縁もある強いつながりの中で、仏教の伝搬に努め、**位階の制度**を整え、日本最古の法令である**十七条憲法**を設定したことはよく知られています。聖徳太子は、斑鳩に住み、仏教の教えについての思索に耽ったと後世には伝えられていますが、その真偽はわかりません。ただ、後の政権が、仏教を柱に中央集権国家を造ろうとしたことで、聖徳太子を聖人としなければならない理由があったことは事実でしょう。

聖徳太子が607年に斑鳩に建立した法隆寺には、世界最古の木造建築群が含まれています。そこの柱にはギリシャ建築の名残ともいえる**エンタシス**様式がみられ、遠くシルクロードを経由して中国に至った西洋文明の一部をここに見ることができるのです。金堂に安置される**釈迦三尊像**の笑みにも、ギリシャ彫刻の影響があるとされています。

これらは、アレキサンダー大王のインドへの遠征のあと、中央アジアに残ったギリシャ文化がその後中国を経由して渡来人によって日本にもたらされたものです。**飛鳥文化**は、古代世界の流れを呼吸した、希有な文化なのです。

法隆寺（奈良県）

飛鳥寺（奈良県）

🔍 **ひとくちメモ**
十七条憲法
聖徳太子が作ったとされる日本で初めての成文法。604

冠位十二階
冠の種類で位階を示す制度

🔍 **ひとくちメモ**
エンタシス
古代ギリシャの建築方法。円柱を下部から上部にかけて徐々に細くすることで、柱を下から見上げるとまっすぐに安定して見える

釈迦三尊像
仏教における仏像安置の形式の一つ。釈迦如来を中尊として、左に文殊菩薩、右に普賢菩薩を配置するのが一般的

飛鳥文化
7世紀の聖徳太子時代が中心の、法隆寺に代表される日本で最初の仏教文化

9 The Taika Reform

Prince Shōtoku passed away in 622. He was a blood relative of the highly influential Soga Clan. After Prince Shōtoku's death, the issue of the succession of his son Prince Yamashiro arose. It appears that there was some support for Prince Yamashiro within the Soga Clan, but Soga no Iruka, heir to the clan's most powerful member, Soga no Emishi, opposed the prince and eventually forced him to commit suicide.

Prince Naka-no-Ōe, who later became Emperor Tenji, together with some associates staged a coup d'état that resulted in the deaths of Soga no Iruka and his father. The Taika Reform is the major reform he instigated in 645 after seizing power.

However, this account is based on the *Nihon shoki*, the historical record written later at the instigation of the government, and some doubts remain as to the backgrounds and roles played by the people involved in the Taika Reform, or even whether the account of the Imperial family's struggle to eliminate the tyrannical Soga Clan is necessarily correct. Nevertheless, following the Taika Reform, the country's governmental system is clearly more in line with that of China than before.

First, the Emperor took the name Taika (which means "great reform") to mark the start of a new era, and implemented a taxation system. In order to manage this effectively, all the land, including that belonging to the various clans, was held to be the property of the emperor, and then systems were established to either loan land back to its original owner

大化の改新とはどんな改革？

　聖徳太子は 622 年に世を去ります。聖徳太子は、蘇我氏の血縁の太子として、蘇我氏にも影響力がありました。彼の死後、聖徳太子の息子であるとされる山背大兄王の皇位継承問題が持ち上がります。蘇我氏の中でも、山背大兄王を支持する人もいたようですが、蘇我氏の最有力者であった蘇我蝦夷から家督をついだ蘇我入鹿が王子と対立し、ついに入鹿は王子を追いつめ自殺させます。

　そんな蘇我氏の横暴に対して、後の天智天皇である中大兄皇子が仲間と共にクーデターを起こし、蘇我蝦夷、入鹿親子を殺害します。そして政権を掌握した後に行われた大改革が、**大化の改新**です。西暦 645 年のことでした。

　しかし、この話は、後年に時の**政府の指示**で記された歴史書である『日本書紀』に基づいたもので、大化の改新に関わった人々の役割や背景がどうであったか、また専横の限りをつくした蘇我氏とそれを排除しようする皇族との争いという構図が、必ずしも正しくはなかったのではないかという疑問は残ります。ただ、大化の改新後の国の制度をみると、明らかにそれ以前より中国の政治制度が取り入れられていることが認められます。

　まず、大化という日本初の**元号**が使われ、租庸調という**租税制度**が制定されます。税制を運用するために、豪族の土地も含め、全ての土地を天皇の所有とし、**戸籍調査**の上で改めて元の所有者に貸し付ける公地公民制度、そして班田収受の制度が実施されます。国は、郡や県に分けられ、

🔍 ひとくちメモ
大化の改新
645（大化元年）年、中大兄皇子が中心となり蘇我氏を滅ぼして始めた改革

according to the family registry survey, or allot it to farmers for rice cultivation. The country was divided into counties and provinces collectively ruled by the emperor.

The reforms cannot have been easy for the coalition of clans at the imperial court, and had also been undeniably influenced by the envoy dispatched by Prince Shōtoku to Sui China. Minabuchi no Shōan and others who had witnessed at first hand the downfall of the Sui and subsequent establishment of the Tang nation in 618, had returned to Japan with what they had learned about the Chinese system, and the fledgling imperial family and powerful younger generation absorbed their lessons.

In a sense, the reforms were as far-reaching as the Meiji Restoration over a thousand years later.

At the time, Japan was exposed to the threat of China and Goguryeo. Up until this point, they must have thought that the power of the court would enable the Wajin to rival even China. However, a newly unified China with an advanced civilization must have driven home to them the importance of first consolidating the nation and of again studying continental culture.

The Taika Reform may well have been connected to this new political wave, and the once mighty Soga clan was probably a symbol of opposition to it.

天皇が一括して統治します。

　この制度改革は、豪族の連合体であった朝廷にとっては簡単なものではなかったはずです。そして、こうした改革の背景には、聖徳太子が派遣した遣隋使の影響が否めません。隋に渡って、隋が滅亡し、618年に**唐**が建国される様子を目の当たりにした、**南淵請安**などが帰国し、中国で学んだ合理的な制度を日本に伝えようとし、若き皇族や有力者の青年などがそこに学びました。

　これはある意味で、当時の**明治維新**ともいえるでしょう。

　その頃、日本は朝鮮半島を通した中国や高句麗の脅威に晒されていました。それまでは、朝廷の力で倭人として中国とも対抗できると思っていたはずです。しかし、中国に統一王朝が生まれ、その進んだ文明に触れた彼らは、まず国を整え、大陸文化を改めて学ぶことの重要性を直感したはずです。そうした、新しい政治の動きが大化の改新へと繋がったのではないでしょうか。

　そんな改革の障壁の象徴として、大豪族の蘇我氏がいたのかもしれません。

ひとくちメモ

唐
中国の王朝。618–690、705–907

南淵請安
飛鳥時代の学問僧で、隋へ留学。滞在中に隋の滅亡（618年）から唐の建国の様子を見る。640年に帰国

10 The Battle of Baekgang

With the Taika Reform, Japan began its transformation from a nation governed by a coalition of clans to a centralized government ruled by an emperor. It was the modernization of the times.

Also, around the time of the Reform, there were major changes in the areas around Japan. After unifying China in 589, the Sui dynasty carried out large-scale invasions of Goguryeo on at least three occasions, each time failing spectacularly. Exhausted by these military campaigns, the army and populace turned against the dynasty, and the Sui were defeated within less than thirty years of having unified the country.

The dynasty that took over from the Sui and again unified the country was the Tang. The Tang did not just attack Goguryeo, but formed an alliance with Silla, which was fearful of the threat from Baekche. In order to counter this, Goguryeo allied with Baekche. For Japan, the hostile power on the peninsula had changed from Goguryeo to the Tang and their ally Silla. This major change in diplomatic affairs would have an enormous influence on Japan.

Firstly, in order for Japan's centralizing government to establish its new system and introduce advanced technologies, the knowhow of China as well as those returning to Japan after many years in their ally Baekche had been absolutely essential. After the joint Tang and Silla forces eventually defeated Baekche in 660, in 663 Prince Naka-no-Ōe sent a large army to the Korean peninsula together with the Prince of Baekche who was in Japan at the time. However, the combined Japan and Baekche naval force was crushed by the Tang and Silla fleet at Baekgang to the

白村江の戦いとその後の日本は？

　大化の改新で、日本は豪族の**連合体**としての国家から、天皇を中心とした**集権国家**へと変貌をはじめます。当時で言えば、近代化のはじまりです。

　そして、大化の改新の前後、日本を取り巻く情勢も大きく変化しました。589年に中国を統一した隋は、高句麗と対立し、3度も大規模な**遠征**を実施しますがいずれも大失敗。そして、遠征に疲弊した軍隊や民衆が王朝を離反し、隋は中国を統一して30年にも満たずに滅びます。

　隋に変わって中国を統一したのが唐でした。唐は高句麗をただ攻めるのではなく、百済への脅威に悩んでいた新羅と**同盟**して、高句麗を圧迫します。高句麗は、それに対抗するために百済と**同盟**します。日本としては、半島の敵対勢力が、高句麗から唐へ、そして唐と同盟する新羅へと変わります。この外交上の一大変化が、日本に多大な影響を与えてゆきます。

　まず、**中央集権**を進める日本が、国の制度を整え、さらに様々な技術を進化させてゆくためには、長年の同盟国である百済からの帰化人に加え、中国からのノウハウが必要不可欠でした。日本は、その双方を失おうとしていたのです。660年、ついに唐と新羅の連合軍が百済を滅ぼすと、663年に日本に滞在中であった百済の王子と共に、中大兄皇子は大軍を朝鮮半島に送ります。しかし、日本と百済の遺臣による水軍が、韓国南西部の**白村江**で唐と新羅の

🔍 **ひとくちメモ**
白村江
現在の錦江近郊（韓国南西部）。663年、白村江で日本・百済軍と唐・新羅軍の間で戦いが起こった。日本軍は大敗し、百済王は日本に亡命し、百済も滅びた

south of the peninsula. As a result, the war took a turn for the worse and the Japanese army, together with the former Baekche retainers, withdrew from the Korean peninsula.

Due to the threat of invasion from the Tang and Silla, Prince Naka-no-Ōe, who had now acceded to the throne as Emperor Tenji, constructed a fortress to the north of Dazaifu in Kyushu, and also moved the seat of government inland to Otsu. This court was called Ōminomiya. At the same time, he stationed soldiers on permanent surveillance at strategic defensive positions in Kyushu.

Later, in 668, the Tang forces attacked and wiped out Goguryeo despite their stubborn resistance. Goguryeo's defeat brought stability to the northern part of the country, and the Tang subsequently focused on managing the Western Regions on the continent. Having lost its interests in the Korean peninsula, the Japanese Court changed its foreign policy and promoted exchange with the Tang. After this, for about nine hundred years up to the sixteenth century, Japan did not actively expand overseas but limited itself to conducting diplomatic relations and trade with neighboring countries from within its prosperous island nation.

艦隊に惨敗し、その結果、戦況が悪化し、日本軍は百済
の遺臣と共に朝鮮半島から**撤退した**のでした。

　唐が新羅と共に本土へ攻め入るのではという脅威のた
め、即位し天智天皇となった中大兄皇子は、太宰府の北
に水城という城壁を建造し、都も内陸の大津に移しました。
その都は近江京と呼ばれています。同時に、九州に防人と
いう防備の兵を常駐させ、監視にあたります。

　その後、あれほど頑強に抵抗していた高句麗もついに
668年には唐の攻撃で滅ぼされてしまいます。しかし、唐
は日本にはやってきませんでした。高句麗の滅亡で国の北
東部は安定。以後唐は、陸続きでもある西域の経営に注
力したのです。朝鮮半島への利権を喪失した朝廷は、外
交方針を転換し、唐との交流を進めます。以後、日本は
16世紀まで、およそ900年にわたって、自らが積極的に
海外に展開することなく、恵まれた島国の中から近郊の
国々との外交と交易に終始するようになったのです。

11 The Hakuhō Culture

Having assimilated Chinese civilization in the attempt to establish a political system, it was necessary to overcome some of the ancient customs and practices of the past.

For example, there was no custom of imperial succession, and various relatives could succeed to the position of emperor, so that often a younger brother would succeed an elder brother. The change to a Chinese-style system of accession is said to be partly due to the dispute over the right of succession between Emperor Tenji's younger brother Prince Ōama (later Emperor Tenmu) and Tenji's heir Prince Ōtomo (later Emperor Kōbun).

After the death of Emperor Tenji, who had designated Prince Ōtomo as his successor, Prince Ōama rebelled against Prince Ōtomo and in 672 the Jinshin War broke out. This was won by Prince Ōama, who acceded to the throne as Emperor Tenmu and continued with the centralization of government under the emperor. The full-blown legal system called Ritsuryō took control away from the clans and placed it within the framework of a government, with the entire populace and land under the emperor's control, along with obligatory taxation and military service.

It was also in this period that the word "emperor" (*tennō*) was first used. In addition, the power of the clans was reduced, ranks of office were set, and it was made possible to employ bureaucrats and military personnel. Furthermore, importance was placed on Shinto as the imperial faith, while Buddhism was preserved as the cornerstone of the regime.

A notable temple built at this time was the Yakushi-ji. The present-day

白鳳文化とは？

　中国から文明を吸収し、国家体制を整えようとすると、古来の土俗的な風習など、過去との様々なひずみを乗り越えなければなりません。

　例えば、天皇家には**嫡子相続**の風習は無く、天皇の地位はその時々によって様々な親族が継承し、兄から弟への継承も多くありました。それを中国風の相続に変更し、制度化しようとしたことが、天智天皇の弟の大海人皇子と嫡子であった大友皇子との皇位継承争いの一因であったといわれています。

　大友皇子を後継者に指名した天智天皇が他界すると、大海人皇子は大友皇子に叛旗を翻し、672年に**壬申の乱**がおこります。これに勝利した大海人皇子が即位して天武天皇となり、天皇を中心とした国家建設の取り組みを続けるのです。**律令制度**の本格的な導入です。律令制度とは、国民と土地を全て天皇の支配の元におき、そこに新たに**租税**や**兵役**などを義務づける制度で、今までの豪族の支配構造から脱却して、国家としての機構を整えるための制度です。

　天皇という言葉が生まれたのもこの時代でした。また、豪族支配ではなく、官位を定め、官僚や、軍人に対しては広く門戸を拓いた採用を行うように試みました。また、天皇の信奉する神として神道を重んじ、同時に治世の礎としては、仏教を保護しました。

　その頃建立された代表的な寺が薬師寺です。現在の薬

ひとくちメモ
壬申の乱
672年に起きた天智天皇の皇位継承をめぐる乱。天智天皇の皇子（大友皇子）と、弟（大海人皇子）の間で起きた古代最大の内乱

律令制度
租税、兵役の導入

薬師寺（奈良県）

Yakushi-ji was moved to the new capital of Nara during the Nara period, but many of the Buddhist images housed there are from the original temple.

The culture represented by these Buddhist images was called the Hakuhō culture. At the time of Emperor Tenmu, exchange with Tang China had ceased. However, the Buddhist teachings and architectural techniques brought to Japan by the envoys sent to Tang in its golden age, former retainers of Baekche, and Silla with whom diplomatic relations had resumed, all flourished in the cultural climate of the Hakuhō period.

Emperor Tenmu longed for the ideal of ancient China, and even appropriated part of his name from King Wu the founder of the Zhou Dynasty and held to be the ideal King of China. Together with his empress, who later became Empress Jitō, Tenmu constructed the capital city Fujiwara-kyō, which was larger than the later capitals of Heijō-kyō (Nara) and Heian-kyō (Kyoto) at 5.3 kilometers square. It is said that Fujiwara-kyō was planned during Emperor Tenmu's reign, and construction on it started after his death upon the accession of Empress Jitō.

The construction of a capital on the scale of Fujiwara-kyō indicated the completion of the imperial court system. It was also around this time that Japan, at that time still called Yamato, began to appear in Chinese historical documents as Wakoku, or the Country of Wa.

師寺は奈良時代になって移転したものですが、中にある仏像の多くは当時のものです。

　これらの仏像などに代表される当時の文化を、白鳳文化といいます。天武天皇の時は、唐との交流は途絶えていました。しかし、白鳳文化は、それ以前に最盛期の唐を訪ねた遣唐使や、百済の遺臣、さらには国交を再開した新羅などから伝わった仏教の教えや建築技術が日本の風土の中で開花した文化でした。

　天武天皇は、中国の理想的君主とされた周（しゅう）の創始者武王（ぶおう）の名前をとって天武としたと伝えられるほど、古代中国の理想にあこがれていた人物です。彼と後に持統天皇となる彼の后の二人で造営した藤原京は、後の平城京や平安京をしのぐ、5.3キロ四方の帝都でした。藤原京は天武天皇の治世に立案され、彼の死後、持統天皇の即位の頃に着工されたのではといわれています。

　藤原京という巨大な都を造営できたことは、天皇を中心とした古代王朝が完成したことを意味しています。中国などの歴史書に「日本（当時はヤマトと呼んでいました）」の名が、倭国に変わって登場し始めるのもこのころのことでした。

🔍 ひとくちメモ

周
中国の王朝。武王が建国した。BC11世紀-BC770

武王
在位 BC1023?- BC1021?
周王朝の創始者。父である文王とともに聖王としてあがめられている

薬師寺（奈良県）

12 The Relocation of the Capital to Nara

Japan occupies a unique position in the history of the Far East.

In the first half of the Yamato period, Japan followed the same foreign policy as all the surrounding countries by paying tribute to China and in return receiving China's seal of approval for their reign.

However, this began to change from Prince Shōtoku's rule in the Asuka period. Japan fought on equal terms with the Tang in the Battle of Baekgang, even though it ended in defeat, and did not visit China to curry favor. Even when Prince Shōtoku sent an envoy to Sui China, it is recorded that the Sui Emperor Yangdi was furious to read the message that started, "From the sovereign of the land of the rising sun to the sovereign of the land of the setting sun." The reason for this was that the Japanese ruler had referred to both himself and the Chinese emperor as "sovereign," thus putting them on an equal footing.

After this, in Emperor Tenmu's reign the word *tennō* for "emperor" was coined. This was a statement to the world, both within and outside Japan, that Japan's sovereign was not simply a monarch, but a ruler ordained by Heaven. This is particularly interesting considering that most other countries in the region continued to recognize China's superior position by sending tribute.

In 701 the Taihō Code was promulgated as Japan's first full-blown statute book. Of course, something close to a state had been enacted several times previously. However, the Taihō Code added to the criminal law with statutes covering not only administrative functions, various rituals and official ranks, but also provisions for the governance of the

奈良遷都とは？

極東の古代史での日本の位置づけはユニークです。

大和時代前半は、日本の王は、他の中国周辺諸国と同じく、中国に朝貢し、中国のお墨付きをもって王として認めてもらうという外交方針でした。

しかし、聖徳太子のいた**飛鳥時代**以降、そうした考え方への変化がみられます。敗戦であったとはいえ、白村江の戦いの頃、日本は唐と対等に渡り合い、いわゆる諂うための訪中は行っていません。聖徳太子が遣隋使を送ったときも、「**日出ずる国の天子が日没する国の天子に国書を届ける。恙無しや**」とした日本の国書をみて、隋の皇帝**煬帝**が立腹したと記録にあります。原因は、日本側が自ら「天子」を名乗り、中国の「天子」と対等な立場をとっていることです。

その後、天武天皇の時代に「**天皇**」という言葉が生まれました。これは日本の元首は王ではなく、皇帝と同格の天皇であると内外に表明したことになります。他の周辺諸国のほとんどが、中国を核に考え、元首を王とし、皇帝とせずに中国に**朝貢する**外交方針をとっていたことを考えれば、これは興味深い事実です。

701年に日本初の本格的な法令集である**大宝律令**が発布されました。もちろん、それ以前にも律令に近いものはいくつか制定されています。しかし大宝律令は、「律」にあたる刑法に加え、行政、さらには様々な儀式や官位についての法令から地方の統治についての定めまで網羅したもの

ひとくちメモ

大和時代
4世紀頃〜6世紀頃まで。古墳が盛んに作られたことから、古墳時代と呼ばれることも多い

飛鳥時代
大和（古墳）時代の終わりの時期と重なるが、592年から710年の間を指す

ひとくちメモ

煬帝
隋朝の第2代皇帝。在位604–618

「日出づる処の天子、書を日没する処の天子に致す。恙無きや（日出處天子致書日没處天子無恙）」の有名な一節

ひとくちメモ
大宝律令では、刑法、行政、儀式や官位、さらには地方統治についても定めていた

regions. The Taihō Code was initially enacted in Emperor Tenmu's reign, and over the following twenty years it was adapted to incorporate the Tang model, Confucian philosophy, and the state of affairs in Japan generally.

Japan stood out as an opulent island nation that had absorbed Chinese culture and had its own emperor, that wanted to be on an equal footing with China. In 708, seven years after the promulgation of the Taihō Code, Japan's first coinage of widespread currency, the Wadōkaichin, was minted. There had been coins in use previously, but this was the first to be completely under the management of the state. Until this time barter had been the norm in Japan, but now the fundamentals of a crude monetary economy began to be introduced.

At the time that the legal code, coinage, and government were completed, a new capital called Heijō-kyō was constructed. The new capital was better equipped than Fujiwara-kyō, and the court moved there in 710, during the reign of Empress Genmei. Until Fujiwara-kyō, the emperor's residence had always been considered the capital and there had been no real concept of a capital city. Heijō-kyō was constructed as Japan's first full-blown, permanent capital city and made up for the shortcomings of Fujiwara-kyō.

でした。大宝律令は、天武天皇の頃に制定が指示され、その後約 20 年をかけて、唐の事例の研究し、儒教などの考えを取り入れ、さらにそこに日本の国情を加味して作成したものです。

　中国と対等の意識を持ちながら、中国の文化を吸収し、独自の皇帝である天皇をもった国家、これが豊かな島国に育った日本という国の特徴だったのです。大宝律令の制定の 7 年後の 708 年には、日本ではじめて広範に流通した和同開珎という**貨幣**が鋳造されました。それ以前にも貨幣はありましたが、これは、本格的に国が管理して鋳造した最初の貨幣です。それまで**物々交換**が主体だった日本に、稚拙ながらも貨幣経済の原理が導入され始めたことになります。

　法律と貨幣、そしてそれを運用する朝廷という政府が完成した頃、藤原京よりもさらに整った日本の首都として造営されたのが平城京です。遷都は 710 年で、元明天皇の時のことでした。藤原京が造営される前は、天皇の居所を都としただけで、首都という概念はなかったのです。平城京は、藤原京の短所を補い、日本初の恒久的かつ本格的な首都として建設されたのです。

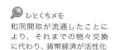
ひとくちメモ
和同開珎が流通したことにより、それまでの物々交換に代わり、貨幣経済が活性化

平城京（奈良県）
© I, KENPEI

13 The Tenpyō Culture

The Nara period is symbolized by the Tenpyō culture.

In East Asia the Tang Dynasty was at its peak and its territory comparable to that of Central Asia. To the west was the Islamic empire, another of the world's great empires. Free and safe transit through the individual countries in these great empires was guaranteed, and there was a lively exchange between civilizations.

Next to Japan, Silla had unified the Korean peninsula, and the people of the defeated Goguryeo had fled north and founded the Balhae kingdom in the coastal region of what is now Russia. Under the prosperity of the Tang, the entire East Asia region was experiencing its first period without war for a long time.

Japan at the time was conducting exchange with both Tang China and Balhae. Even though relations with Silla were strained, it appears there was brisk trade between the two countries. Prominent amidst this exchange were the frequent envoys sent by Japan to Tang China. The knowledge gained by these many scholars and Buddhist monks — not just about Tang culture, but about the Western Regions and the Islamic world beyond — was transmitted back to Japan. In the Shōsōin treasure house built in Nara at this time there are items from as far field as Persia. The ancient trade route connecting East and West known as the Silk Road is famous the world over, and Japan was on its eastern extremity. Tenpyō, from 729 to 749 under the rule of Emperor Shōmu, was the richest period of the Nara era. However, when we talk about the "Tenpyō culture" we are referring to the whole of the Nara period centered on the capital at Heijō-

古代日本とは

天平文化とはどんな文化？

奈良時代を象徴するものが、**天平文化**です。

当時、世界的にみれば、東アジアでは唐が最盛期を迎え、版図は中央アジアに及んでいます。その西にはもう一つの世界帝国であるイスラム帝国がありました。広大な版図をもつこの二つの帝国によって、国と国との通行に自由と安全が保障され、文物の行き来が旺盛になります。

日本のお隣では、新羅が朝鮮半島を統一し、滅亡した高句麗の人々は、北に逃れ、現在のロシア沿岸部に**渤海**を建国します。唐の繁栄のもと、東アジア一帯は久しぶりに戦争のない時代となったのです。

日本は、当時唐とも渤海とも交流していました。新羅とは緊張関係にありながらも、商業的な行き来は活発だったようです。こうした交流の中、際立っていたのが頻繁に派遣された遣唐使です。多くの学生や僧侶が唐に学び、唐のみならず、唐が吸収していた西域、さらに遠くイスラム世界などの知識が彼らと共に日本に伝わりました。奈良にその頃に建てられた**正倉院**には、当時日本にもたらされたペルシャの器などが保管されています。古代から中世にかけての東西交流の道は、シルクロードとして世界的に有名ですが、日本はその東の終点となっていたのです。天平とは、そんな奈良時代の最も充実した729年から749年までの元号です。時の天皇は、聖武天皇でした。しかし、天平文化は、平城京を中心とした奈良時代の文化全体を指して

ひとくちメモ
天平文化
平城京を中心に栄えた貴族・仏教文化。7世紀末〜8世紀中頃まで。聖武天皇のときの年号をとって天平文化と呼ぶ

ひとくちメモ
渤海
満州から朝鮮半島北部ロシアの沿海地方にかけて領域とした国家。698–926

ひとくちメモ
正倉院宝庫
木造校倉作りの倉庫で、宝物9000点以上を納めている

kyō.

Even in Japan's long history, this was an exceptional culture fully enriched by global trends and, from a world perspective, a jewel of the East Asian civilization of the time.

The rhythmical design of the East Pagoda of the Yakushi-ji temple, completed in the early Nara period and still extant today, was described as "Frozen Music" by the American scholar Ernest Fenollosa, who put much effort into preserving Japanese culture in the Meiji period. Emperor Shōmu went on to govern the country as a Buddhist state, establishing provincial temples known as *kokubunji*. He also built Tōdai-ji temple, which houses the large statue of the Buddha Vairocana, known as the Great Buddha of Nara, completed in 752. Many other temples, such as Kōfuku-ji were founded at this time, and it was also at this time that the Buddhist Master Ganjin (Chinese name Jianzhen), who had such a major influence on Buddhism in Japan, was brought to Japan by envoys to Tang, where he naturalized and established the Tōshōdai-ji temple.

The Tenpyō culture was one in which Buddhism and the state merged, and Buddhism was a pillar of the fledgling state. On the other hand, this affiliation with the power of Buddhism would be a political time bomb in later years.

いQ
ます。

　それは、長い日本の歴史の中でも、グローバルな風を
胸一杯呼吸した希有な文化であり、世界的に見れば、当
時の東アジア文明のひとつの結晶でした。

　現存する奈良時代前半に完成した薬師寺の**東塔**のリズ
ミカルなデザインを、明治時代に日本文化の保護に奔走
したアメリカの学者**フェノロサ**は、"凍れる音楽"と表現
しました。その後、日本中に国分寺という寺院をおき、仏
教をもって国を統治しようとした聖武天皇が東大寺を建立
しました。大仏として知られる盧舎那仏がその本尊です。
752年に大仏は完成したました。さらに、興福寺をはじめ
とした多くの寺院が当時創建され、日本の仏教界に大き
な影響を与えた**鑑真**和上が遣唐使とともに中国から帰化
し、唐招提寺を開いたのも当時のことです。

　天平文化は、仏教と国家とが融合し、仏教を国造りに
活用したことによる文化です。しかし、これは反面、仏教
の権力との融合という、その後の新たな政治的な火種にも
なったのです。

🔍 **ひとくちメモ**
アーネスト・フェノロサ
米哲学者、東洋美術研究家。
1878年に来日、岡倉天心と
東京美術学校を創設

🔍 **ひとくちメモ**
鑑真
奈良時代の帰化僧。日本にお
ける律宗の開祖。688-763

14 The *Kojiki, Nihon shoki, Fudoki*, and *Man'yōshū*

Cultural activity in the Nara period other than Buddhist-related activities involved the creation of Japan's first historical written records modeled on the official histories of China. The *Kojiki* in 712 recorded the myths and imperial line as passed down by the oral tradition from ancient times to the time of the imperial court, the *Nihon shoki* in 720 was compiled as a formal historical record, while the *Fudoki* was compiled on the orders of the imperial court in 713 for the provincial governors to gather the historical records and folklore from their region.

None of the original documents are now extant, so we can rely only later copies, and also they all reflect the political aims of the court at the time, so we cannot accept everything recorded in them as true.

However, the present Shinto faith is directly linked to the myths contained in the *Kojiki*, and by comparing many of the matters described in these historical documents to the historical records of China and Korea we can elucidate various facts of ancient history.

Amongst these written documents, the *Man'yōshū* is of particular interest.

One of its compilers is said to have been Ōtomo no Yakamochi, a powerful warrior of the time, and it was apparently completed in the late Nara period. It contains poems and songs composed by people from all ranks, from the emperor and clan leaders to the soldiers deployed in Kyushu to protect Japan's coastline. There are various forms of verse, but most are the Japanese poems known as *waka*, which follow the pattern

古事記、日本書紀、風土記、そして万葉集はどんなもの？

奈良時代の文化活動で仏教文化に関係すること以外に重要なことは、中国の正史の編纂にならい、日本で初めて歴史書などの本格的な文献資料が作成されたことにあります。太古から宮中などの語り部によって伝承されてきた神話や帝記などをまとめた『古事記』が 712 年に、正式な史書として編纂された『日本書紀』が 720 年に、朝廷が 713 年に地方の官吏に命じて収拾し、地方の歴史や伝承を集めた『風土記』がそれにあたります。

原典は現存しておらず、後世の写本などに頼るものがほとんどであること、そして当時の朝廷の政治的意図が反映されていることなどから、そこに記されている事柄の多くを鵜呑みにすることはできません。

しかし、古事記に書かれた神話が現在の神道の信仰に直結していることや、これらの歴史書に記述されている事柄の多くと、中国や朝鮮半島の史書とを比較することなどにより、古代史における様々な事実が解明されてきました。

文献資料の中で、さらに興味深いのが、『万葉集』の編纂です。

編纂には、当時の有力な武人であった大伴家持があたったといわれており、奈良時代後期に完成したといわれています。そこには、天皇や、豪族のみならず、九州にかり出されて守りにつく防人と呼ばれた兵士など、当時のあらゆる階層の人々が詠んだ歌や詩が集められています。様々な形式の詩歌が収拾されていますが、その中に和歌、すな

ひとくちメモ
奈良時代
710年〜794年、奈良に都（平城京）がおかれていた時代

ひとくちメモ
『古事記』
712年、Record of Ancient Matters
『日本書紀』
720年、Chronicles of Japan
『風土記』
713年、Records of culture and geography of provinces of Japan

ひとくちメモ
『万葉集』
防人など、あらゆる階層の人びとが詠んだ日本最古の文芸書。7〜8世紀の政治・社会を知る上での重要な文献

of 5-7-5-7-7 syllables. Even today waka is still the most popular form of poetry in Japan. Haiku, the most famous form of Japanese poetry worldwide, is derived from waka, limiting the composition to the first three lines of 5-7-5 syllables.

The *Man'yōshū* may therefore be considered Japan's earliest literary text. It is notable for its wide range of apparently uncensored poems, from serene love poems composed by people connected to the Imperial House, historically buffeted by political disputes, to songs written by poor peasants who had become soldiers. The *Man'yōshū* features simple poems from the provinces and by people from all levels of society, making it a valuable resource for historians and linguists.

These historical records can be considered an important legacy, informing us about the conditions within the country and the stories of its people quite apart from the brilliance of the Tenpyō culture and its international sensibilities.

わち日本語のシラブルで5-7-5-7-7という数を基準につくられる歌（詩）が多く登場しています。この和歌がその後受け継がれ、現在でも和歌は日本を代表する詩の制作方法となっています。世界的に有名な俳句も、この和歌を元に、前半の5-7-5だけで詠まれたものです。

　そうした意味で、万葉集は、日本最古の文芸書です。歴史的には幾多の政争に翻弄されていた皇室の関係者が、おおらかに詠む恋歌や、貧しい農民が兵士となって詠む歌など、検閲的な作為がないと思われるような詩歌が多くあることも注目されます。同時に、万葉集は地方の歌や、様々な階層の人々のつくった素朴な詩なども載っていることから、歴史や言語学上からも貴重な資料です。

　国際感覚のある天平文化の華やかな様相とは別に、日本の国内の状況や、そこで営まれた人の物語を知る上で、これらの記録は重要な遺産であるといえるでしょう。

柿本人麻呂像（奈良県）

15 The Transition from Nara to Heian

Nara appears to have been a brilliant period, with its Tenpyō culture and the compilation of the *Man'yōshū* and other records.

In reality, however, there were various contradictions and conflicts within the society. First, the radical centralization of government led to a power struggle. The Taika Reform saw the enactment of a national taxation system, including a rice tax, labor tax, product tax, and so forth. Furthermore, the defense forces had been stationed for a long time in Kyushu, and were also a burden on the rural communities. Consequently, discontent in society was evident. In 723 the government enacted the *Sanze isshin no hō*, or Three Generations Law, which stipulated that anyone cultivating newly reclaimed land would have the right to ownership for up to three generations, only to revise this in 743 to the *Konden einen shizaihō*, or Law Permitting Permanent Ownership of Newly Cultivated Land. While this lined the pockets of certain powerful people, it did little to improve the economic circumstances of the peasantry.

Also, the court had been threatened by the conflicts between prominent clans, but as the government underwent centralization, power struggles and factional infighting within the court gathered pace. Nakatomi no Kamatari, who had helped formulate the Taika Reform, was honored with the name Fujiwara. His power extended into the Nara period with his son, Fujiwara Fuhito, who was highly influential in the relocation of the capital, and who, along with subsequent descendents, made the Fujiwara one of the most powerful families in court politics. This met with opposition from the imperial family and other influential

奈良時代はどのように
平安時代へと推移した？

　天平文化や万葉集などの編纂の歴史をみると、奈良時代は一見とても華やかな時代にみえます。

　しかし、現実の社会には様々な矛盾や抗争がありました。まず、急激な**中央集権化**は権力闘争の火種にもなりました。大化の改新後、国が税制をもって全国から税金を徴収する制度として租庸調を制定した事は既に触れました。租は生産された穀物、庸は労役、調は特産物などに課せられた税金です。加えて防人など長期にわたる兵役が課せられることもあり、農村の負担は相当なものでした。これによる社会の混乱は顕著で、政府はその後開墾した田畑の３代にわたる所有を認める**三世一身の法**を723年に施行し、743年には**墾田永年私財法**によって、その永久的な所有を認めるなどして対応しましたが、一部の有力者の財布が潤うだけで、農民経済の活性化には至りません。

　また、以前は**豪族**の抗争が朝廷を脅かしていましたが、中央集権が進むにつれ、宮廷内の権力闘争、派閥争いに拍車がかかりました。大化の改新に功のあった中臣鎌足が起こした藤原氏が奈良時代になると伸長し、鎌足の次男で、奈良遷都にも大きな影響力をもった藤原不比等をはじめ、その一族、子孫がその後政界に進出します。それには、**皇族**や他の**有力貴族**の反発もあり、先に記した農村社会の混乱なども影響した政争が反乱に発展することもありました。

 ひとくちメモ
三世一身の法
開墾地についての土地所有方法。新しく開墾した土地は本人から３代にわたってその土地の保有を許可

墾田永年私財法
開墾地を永久に私財とすることを認めた。後の荘園制の前提となった

court nobles. Also, discontent over political issues within the farming community on occasion developed into insurgency.

Major examples of this include the rebellion led by the imperial family member Prince Nagaya, who resented the Fujiwara regime, and the revolt of Fujiwara no Hirotsugu that was caused by the rise to power of the Fujiwara's rivals, the Tachibana clan.

It was apparently in order to keep national peace following these bloody battles within the centralized government that Emperor Shōmu built Tōdaiji and the Great Buddha housed within it. However, temple priests were highly protected during the Nara period and temples became an extension of political power, with such characters as the monk Dōkyō, who enjoyed the political support of the imperial family and harbored his own ambitions to become emperor.

In order to flee the power of the clergy and reestablish the nation under the Ritsuryō Code, in 783 Emperor Kanmu constructed a new capital, Nagaoka-kyō, in Yamashiro province to the north of Nara. However, following the politically motivated assassination of Fujiwara no Tanetsugu, who was in charge of the project, this was suspended. In 794, the new imperial palace was completed in Heian-kyō, or present-day Kyoto.

Nevertheless, the labor force needed for the military and for the major engineering works occasioned by construction of successive capitals and Buddhist halls, not to mention the tax income, was probably supplied by the peasantry.

皇族が藤原体制に不満をもって起こした**長屋王の乱**や、藤原氏のライバル橘氏の台頭が原因でおきた**藤原広嗣の乱**などが代表的な例となります。

こうした中央政権での血なまぐさい争いから、国家鎮護を求め聖武天皇が建立したのが東大寺であり、そこにある**大仏**であるといわれています。しかし、奈良時代に手厚く保護された寺の僧の中で、皇族の寵愛を受け自らが皇位を狙う道鏡のような人物も現れるなど、時とともに仏教寺院も一つの政治勢力として伸長してきました。

東大寺盧舎那仏像（奈良県）

こうした寺社勢力から脱却し、律令国家を再編しようと、桓武天皇は奈良の北、山城の国に783年に長岡京を建設します。しかし、責任者である藤原種継が暗殺されるなどの政争があり、中断されました。そして改めて794年に完成した宮城が現在の京都にあたる平安京でした。

それにしても相次ぐ都や大仏殿の建設など、当時の大工事や兵役に働き手をかりだされ、さらに税務を課された農民の苦労は相当なものであったと思われます。

東大寺大仏殿（奈良県）

16 The Heian Period

When Emperor Kanmu moved the capital from Nagaoka-kyō to Heian-kyō, would he have been aware that it would remain the capital city for the next thousand years?

Surely he was not thinking beyond his own accession as emperor. At that time emperors were from the lines of either Emperor Tenji or Emperor Tenmu, and Kanmu was the third generation in Tenji's line. However, his mother was a descendent of a naturalized Baekche king and member of the Yamato clan, a status that precluded him from the accession.

Meanwhile, the four sons of Fujiwara Fuhito, of the Fujiwara clan that rose to prominence in the Nara period, were all in the line. One of these, Shikike, rose to prominence amidst the political struggles of the late Nara period, and eventually backed Emperor Kōnin who succeeded in 770. Until then, the succession had followed the line of descent from Emperor Tenmu, but Shikike managed to install Kōnin, who was from Emperor Tenji's line. Kōnin was Tenji's grandson and was already of advanced age so it would not be long before his son Osabe Shinnō was due to succeed him. However, Osabe Shinnō, together with his mother the empress, plotted rebellion against the emperor and was exiled, and met a violent death. Thus being the state of affairs, Emperor Kanmu was made crown prince. It is said that this, too, was part of Fujiwara Shikike's scheme.

Emperor Kanmu was aware that Heijō-kyō was the imperial capital

平安時代はどのように
はじまった？

　長岡京から平安京に都を遷したとき、桓武天皇はその
都がその後千年にわたって日本の都になると思っていたで
しょうか。

　それ以上に、桓武天皇自身も自らが皇位を継ぐようにな
るとは考えてもいなかったはずです。もともと当時の天皇
は、天智天皇の流れか天武天皇の流れかによるもので、
桓武天皇は天智天皇の３代後の系列に属します。しかし、
彼の母親は百済から**帰化した**王族の子孫である和氏の出
身で、身分の問題から皇位継承の対象からははずされて
いたのです。

　一方、奈良時代に台頭した藤原氏は、藤原不比等の４
人の子供によって、それぞれ引き継がれます。その中の一
つである式家とよばれる系列が、奈良時代の後半に政争
の中から台頭し、ついには光仁天皇を擁立するまでになり
ました。770 年のことです。それまでは、天武天皇の系列
が皇位を継承していましたが、式家は天智天皇の系列から
光仁天皇をたてたことになります。光仁天皇は、天智天皇
の孫にあたり、既に高齢でした。従って間もなく子供であ
る他戸王が後を継ぐはずでした。ところが、他戸親王は
光仁天皇の皇后と天皇への謀反を企てたとして追放され、
変死します。そうした経緯の中で、桓武天皇が皇太子とな
りました。ここにも、藤原式家の意図があったといわれて
います。

　桓武天皇は、平城京が天武天皇の系列による天皇の都

天皇系図

天武 40代 ── 天智 38代

持統 41代 　　弘文 39代
　　 42代
　　 43代
〜　　⋮
称徳 48代

　　　　　　持統 49代

　　　　　　桓武 50代

🔍 ひとくちメモ
藤原四家
不比等の４人の息子がおこ
した４つの家（南家、北家、
式家、京家）

from Tenmu's succession. With the support of Fujiwara Shikike, who since Emperor Shōmu's time had been had been ousting political rivals in his interests, he no doubt planned to strengthen his own powerbase by moving the capital to Heian-kyō. However, it appears that Emperor Kanmu and Shikike's directing faction was not invincible since Shikike's descendent Fujiwara Tanetsugu, who had actively backed the construction of the new capital at Nagaoka-kyō prior to Heian-kyō, was assassinated.

Originally, the Ritsuryō legal code underpinned the nation's political structure under the emperor's absolute authority, and this ideal appears to have been achieved during the times of Emperors Tenji and Tenmu. However, in the Nara period there was a conspicuous rise to power of nobles within the court, creating political conflicts that gradually began to change the emperor's role.

Emperor Kanmu attempted to reinstate the Ritsuryō structure and complete the centralization of government. However, in reality the emperor himself had come to power with the backing of the Fujiwara clan, and the Heian period thus started with the emperor as a and the real power concentrated in the influential persons below him.

であったことを意識し、その考え方と利害を一致させ、聖武天皇以来の**政敵を駆逐してきた**藤原式家の後押しもあり、自らの権力基盤を強化させるために平安京への遷都を企画したのでしょう。しかし、平安京の前に長岡京の造営を試みたとき、それを押し進めた式家の藤原種継が暗殺されたことからも、桓武天皇とそれを指示する派閥である式家の体制は決して盤石ではなかったようです。

　もともと律令国家は、天皇を頂点とした政治形態による国であったはずです。天皇の**絶対権力**が政治を動かすという理想は、天智天皇と天武天皇の時代には実現するかにみえました。しかし、奈良時代になると朝廷内の貴族の台頭が目立ち、その政争の中から次第に天皇のあり方も変わり始めたのです。

　桓武天皇は、律令体制を自らの手に取り戻し、中央集権国家を再度完成させようとしたのでしょう。しかし、天皇自身藤原氏の後押しで皇位についた事実からも、平安時代は、天皇が国の最高位にありながら権力の実態はその下にある実力者に集中する時代の始まりとなったのです。

17 The Kōnin-Jōgan Culture

If you divide up Japanese history simply according political power, then the Heian period was that of an ancient dynastic court under the supreme authority of the emperor. But you can define history in various ways. For example, if you consider scientific development and lifestyle, then there was a radical change in history before and after the invention of the internal combustion engine. There was also a major difference in social structure before and after democracy was established.

And so let's look here at another way to divide up Japanese history — namely, according to periods when Japan has been open to the outside world, and those when it has been closed. In ancient times, the Wajin actively sought relations with other countries. Wa society had an international mix, maintaining relations with the northern tribes and China, as well as vested interests in the Korean peninsula. There is even a theory that the Wajin had come from abroad to settle in Japan.

This influence continued until the Battle of Baekgang in the Yamato period prompted the withdrawal from the Korean peninsula. Even after this, diplomatic relations with China continued throughout the Nara period into the Heian period. Its final flowering occurred during the Kōnin and Jōgan eras in the early ninth century, when the Buddhist monks Saichō and Kūkai, who had been sent as emissaries to study in Tang China, returned to establish their respective esoteric sects Tendai and Shingon. This marked the arrival of Mahayana Buddhism, which had a lasting effect on Buddhism in Japan. Shingon and Tendai flourished as remote mountain sects, with monastery complexes on Mount Kōya and

弘仁・貞観文化とは？

　日本の歴史を単に政権だけで区切るのであれば、平安時代は一応天皇をトップとした**古代王朝**の時代であると言えるでしょう。しかし、歴史はいくつもの方法で区切ることができます。例えば、科学の発展と生活という区切り方をすれば、**内燃機関**の発明前後で歴史は大きく変化します。また、民主主義が確立する前と後の社会構造の違いで区分することも可能です。

　そしてここでは、もう一つの区切り方で日本の歴史をみてみます。それは、対外的に日本が開かれていた時代と、そうでない時代との区切り方です。日本が倭といわれていたころは、むしろ倭人は積極的に海外と関わっていました。倭人が海外から日本に来たという説もあるほどに、朝鮮半島の利権と関わりながら、**北方民族**や中国を交えた国際社会の中に倭はありました。

　その影響は、大和時代に**白村江の戦い**で朝鮮半島と隔絶するまで続き、さらにはその後の奈良時代における中国との外交関係へと引き継がれました。平安時代初期は、そうした影響が残る最後の時代でした。その最後に花開いたのが、当時の年号をとって**弘仁・貞観**と呼ばれる時代です。9世紀のことでした。遣唐使として中国に学び、後の仏教界に大きな影響を与えた最澄と空海が帰国し、それぞれ天台宗と真言宗という密教が日本にもたらされたのは、9世紀初めのことです。**大乗仏教**の到来です。真言宗が高野山に、天台宗が比叡山に寺社を開いたことからもわ

🔍 **ひとくちメモ**
白村江の戦い
朝鮮半島と隔絶するきっかけとなった

弘仁・貞観文化
平安遷都から、9世紀末までの文化

🔍 **ひとくちメモ**
桓武天皇は仏教勢力が政治に影響をもつことを避けるために、平城京の寺院を平安京に移さなかった

Mount Hiei respectively.

On the other hand, this was a period of political transition. At the beginning of Heian, the imperial household and the nobles were embroiled in political strife, with the Kusuko Revolt and other incidents, but the government stabilized from the time of Emperor Saga, three generations after Kanmu, due to the emperor's charisma. Subsequently, Fujiwara no Yoshifusa, a member of the Hokke branch of the Fujiwara clan, rose to prominence through various power struggles related to the imperial succession. Eventually the Fujiwara Hokke took center stage and brought the court to the height of prosperity.

Meanwhile the Tang's power was beginning to wane and China's balloon was deflating, while surrounding nations responded by becoming more active. Unlike the Wajin, however, Heian Japan did not participate in this. Having absorbed Tang culture at its zenith, they now began a period of internalizing it. The Kōnin-Jōgan culture was the last of the colorful eras of two hundred years of cultural exchange with the outside world since the Hakuhō (Asuka) period.

かるように、それらは山岳仏教として繁栄します。

　一方、この時代は政治の上でも過渡期にあたります。平安初期には**薬子の乱**など、皇室や貴族を巻き込んだ政争がありますが、桓武天皇から3代目の嵯峨天皇の時代には、天皇の求心力により一時的とはいえ、中央政界は安定しました。その後、皇位継承などに絡んだいくつかの抗争を経て台頭してきたのが藤原氏の北家に属する藤原良房でした。その後朝廷で栄華を極める藤原北家が本格的に表舞台に登場したことになります。

🔍 **ひとくちメモ**
薬子の乱
810年、藤原薬子が兄とともにおこした乱

　当時中国ではそろそろ唐の勢いも衰え始め、中国という風船が再びしぼみだし、周辺民族の活動がそれに応じるかのように活発なりまじめます。しかし、日本がその活動に以前の倭人のように参加することはもはやありませんでした。日本は、唐の最盛期に吸収した文化を、これから時間をかけて消化し始めます。弘仁・貞観文化は、飛鳥時代以来200年続いた世界と繋がった文化活動の最後を彩った文化だったのです。

🔍 **ひとくちメモ**
空海が大系化した密教とは、大日如来を中心に形成された仏・菩薩の世界に、秘密の呪法をもって接すれば、心身ともに仏と同一になり、現世利益をもらえるとする教え

18 The Fujiwara Clan

Emperor Saga was a powerful ruler who exercised absolute authority as emperor. However, the Ritsuryō system itself impoverished the rural communities and shook the foundations of government.

The excesses of compulsory labor and taxation were compounded by famine, and the continuous stream of displaced persons in rural areas led to reduced tax revenues. With the further provision of the law allowing permanent ownership of newly cultivated land in the Nara period, more and more terrain was being reclaimed, yet this proved ineffective and the court continued to be pressed for finance.

This same law had led to an increase in land ownership by the temples and nobles, who had the financial means to clear and prepare terrain for cultivation, and many of these used their relationship with the court and local officials to secure privileged exemption from taxes. The land eventually ended up under the ownership of clans like the Fujiwara, who grew rich on their holdings and even came to wield influence over the imperial succession. After the death of Emperor Saga, the issue of succession again flared up, and Michiyasu Shinnō acceded to the throne with the support of the powerful Fujiwara no Yoshifusa. This marked the rise of the Hokke branch of the Fujiwara, while the Shikike's power was on the wane.

Upon Michiyasu Shinnō's accession, Yoshifusa installed his own daughter as empress and then made his grandchild the Crown Prince, later to become Emperor Seiwa.

The Fujiwara clan's formula was to strengthen their family connections

藤原氏とは？

　嵯峨天皇は、天皇の権威を守った権力者ではありました。しかし、律令体制そのものは、当時の農村の疲弊でその根本的な土台が揺るいでいます。

　過剰な**賦役**や税金、それに**飢饉**がかさなり、農村では流民が続出し、税収は落ち込みます。奈良時代に制定した**墾田永年私財法**をさらに整備して、未開の地の開墾を促進しますがあまり効果はなく、朝廷の財政は逼迫します。

　逆に、墾田永代私財法は、開墾する資金力のある寺社や貴族の私有する土地を増やすことになり、中には現地の官吏や朝廷との関係を利用して、**免税の特権**を享受する者も現れました。こうした土地はやがて藤原氏などの私有する荘園となりました。藤原氏は、荘園経営での資金力をもって、皇位継承にも影響力を及ぼすようになります。嵯峨天皇の死後、皇位継承問題が再燃し、当時実権を握っていた藤原良房の押す道康親王が皇位を継ぎます。藤原北家の台頭です。その頃には権勢を振るった式家は**衰弱してい**ました。

　良房は、道康親王が皇位を継ぐと、自らの娘を皇后にし、産まれた子供を皇太子としました。後の清和天皇です。

　縁戚関係を利用し、朝廷で重職についてゆく方式を藤

through such successions to rise to positions of power at court. Through their political cunning they eliminated their rivals among the nobility and other powerful people, and in the tenth century used their relationship by marriage with the imperial line to hold successive posts as regent and other positions of power whereby they governed in place of the emperor.

Fujiwara no Michinaga's poem written in celebration of becoming the most powerful person at court is well known:

> This world, I think,
> Is indeed my world.
> Like the full moon
> I shine,
> Uncovered by any cloud.

(Translation by G. Cameron Hurst III in "Michinaga's Maladies," *Monumenta Nipponica* Vol. 31 No. 1, pp101-112)

Meanwhile on the continent, the Tang were finally overthrown in 907, and their empire came to an end. The practice of sending envoys to Tang China had already been stopped in 894 at the suggestion of Chancellor Sugawara no Michizane. Michizane himself was hounded from court by the Fujiwara clan and demoted to a minor position in Dazaifu in Kyushu.

Due to the prosperity of the Fujiwara, the arts flourished amongst the nobles at the court in Heian-kyō. The culture that had been brought across the sea to the island nation began to be gradually assimilated and transformed into a uniquely Japanese culture. A period started when Japan shut itself off from outside influence.

原氏がその後継承します。彼らは、巧みな政治力によってライバルとなる貴族や有力者を排除し、10世紀になれば、藤原氏は天皇家の縁者として、天皇に変わって政治をみる**摂政**などの重職を歴任するようになります。

当時、朝廷の最高権力者に上り詰めた藤原道長は、

「この世をば、
　我が世と思う望月の、
　かけたる事の、
　なしと思えば」

◀ 1018年、藤原道長が詠んだ即興の歌。
「この世は自分（道長）のためにあるものだ。だから満月が欠けることもない」の意

という和歌を詠み、自らの権勢を誇った事は有名な逸話です。

　その頃、大陸では、相次ぐ争乱の中で907年に唐が滅び、世界帝国が消滅しました。既に894年には、当時の太政大臣であった菅原道真の建議で遣唐使は取りやめられています。その菅原道真も藤原氏によって宮廷を追われ、九州の太宰府に左遷されました。

　藤原氏の繁栄のもと、平安京では宮中の貴族による文芸活動などが盛んになります。大陸と海を隔てた島国の中で、今まで取り入れた様々な大陸文化が次第に日本独自の文化へと変貌し始めるのはこの頃のことです。これからしばらく、日本は自ら積極的に海外を求めない時代にはいってゆきます。

19 The Culture of the Nobility in the Heian Period

The feature of Heian culture most worthy of mention is the adaptation of Chinese characters to create the written Japanese syllabaries called hiragana and katakana, used together with kanji in written Japanese to this day.

Just as in ancient and medieval Western Europe the Latin alphabet was used to write the various European languages, in East Asia many countries used Chinese characters to write their own languages. Japan's creation of a new alphabet is comparable to the way that Dante's Divine Comedy, written in his Tuscan dialect, heralded the Renaissance.

Previously the Japanese court had used Chinese characters to write in Classical Chinese, or phonetically to write Japanese words.

However, mixing hiragana and katakana with Chinese characters made it possible to easily write vernacular Japanese, which in turn allowed for more freedom and breadth in expression.

Just as youngsters these days communicate with emoticons and other pictorial symbols, so the nobles at the imperial court used the new syllabaries to compose and exchange the poems that formed the basis of the way they conducted love affairs. The practice of writing love poetry spread through the nobility, and the custom of expressing one's own feelings to an object of desire in a poem became widespread.

Ki no Tsurayuki included many poems of this nature in the

平安時代の貴族文化の意義と特徴は？

　平安時代の貴族文化で特筆されることは、漢字を使った日本独自の文字である**ひらがな**や**カタカナ**が生まれ、それが現在まで漢字とともに使用されるようになったことです。

　古代から中世にかけての文字であるラテン語が、西欧の国々では口語と分けて使用されていたように、東洋では多くの国が中国の漢字を国の文字として使用していました。日本で、新たな文字が産まれたことは、ちょうど**ダンテ**が**神曲**をトスカーナ語で著し、後の**文芸復興**のさきがけとなった現象に似ています。

　以前、日本では、漢字をそのまま日本の発音にあてて使用することもあれば、中国の書き方を漢文としてそのまま使用することもありました。

　しかし、ひらがなとカタカナを漢字に混ぜて使用することで、**口語文**もそのまま平易に文章化できるようになり、そのことから闊達で自由な表現活動ができるようになったのです。

　現在、若者が**絵文字**を使ってコミュニケーションするように、当時宮廷の貴族たちはこの新しい文字を使用して和歌を作り、それを交換することで恋をはじめとした様々な人の営みを語ります。恋歌は貴族の間に広がり、自らの思いを和歌で相手に伝え合う風習も盛んになりました。

　当時、紀貫之が 905 年に編纂した『**古今和歌集**』には、

ひとくちメモ
藤原氏全盛期の 10 〜 11 世紀の文化を国風文化と呼ぶ

ひとくちメモ
ダンテ・アリギエーリ
1265-1321　イタリア生まれ、トスカーナ語で長編叙事詩『神曲』を書いた

Kokinwakashū compiled in 905. The mature literary activity of the nobility was particularly evident among the women. The *Tale of Genji*, written in the early eleventh century by Murasaki Shikibu, a member of the Fujiwara clan, is well known as the world's earliest novel. The various love stories described in the *Tale of Genji* are a valuable resource for understanding how the nobility of the time conducted their lives.

There were many other woman writers besides Murasaki Shikibu who used these uniquely Japanese syllabaries. The *Makura no sōshi* (Pillow Book) by Murasaki Shikibu's contemporary, Sei Shōnagon is a collection of literary jottings, Fujiwara Michitsuna's mother (real name unknown) laid bare female jealousy and attitudes to life in *Kagerō nikki* (The Gossamer Years), while the author of *Sarashina nikki* (Sarashina Diary) described the life of one woman modeled on her own daughter, and so forth. Many of the works written at that time are still read today.

The direct expression of inner feelings and affections in poetry helped to foster the literary culture of the time. It is admirable that people were able to express their feelings through literature in the ninth century, when the concept of individual freedom was very weak.

そんな和歌がたくさん含まれています。貴族の円熟した文芸活動は、特に女性の間でもてはやされます。藤原氏の血縁である紫式部が11世紀初頭に著した『**源氏物語**』は、**世界最古の長編小説**として有名です。源氏物語に綴られる様々な恋愛物語は、当時の貴族の生活を知る上でも貴重な資料といえましょう。

　この日本独自の文字を使った女流作家は、紫式部の他にも多くいます。紫式部とほぼ同時代に著された清少納言の『**枕草子**』という随筆集、女性の嫉妬と生き様を赤裸々に描いた藤原道綱の母（実名不詳）の『蜻蛉日記』や、その娘が自らをモデルに女性の一生を描く『更級日記』など、今でも多くの人に読まれている作品は、その頃作られたものなのです。

　和歌により、自らの思いや恋愛感情を率直に表現することが、当時の文芸活動を育んでゆきました。自我や自由という概念の乏しい9世紀に、自らの思いを文芸にできたことは、驚嘆に値することといえましょう。

紫式部像（滋賀県）

🔍 **ひとくちメモ**
紫式部は『紫式部日記』の中で、清少納言の生き方を軽薄だと批判している

20 Warriors in the Heian Period

The Jōmon people had been forced northwards by the influx of people from the continent in the Yayoi period, but had maintained their own culture in chiefdoms from Tohoku up to Hokkaido. They were called the Emishi, later the Ezo, and their region was Ezochi. The first invasion of Ezochi by the imperial court was led by Abe no Hirafu in the mid-seventh century, and in 724 Taga Castle was built at north of present-day Sendai as a base for the advance into Tohoku. In the early ninth century, Sakanoue no Tamuramaro led forays into the region, constructing several more castles.

Originally, the Emishi were part of the people who spread into the Kamchatka peninsula, Kuril Islands, and further north. In the Tang period, it appears they even conducted trade with Balhae kingdom in the coastal area of Russia.

However, as the power of the imperial court expanded, they were gradually overwhelmed by the central government. It is conjectured that this was largely due to the *fushū*, Emishi who allied themselves to the court and systematically built a military force together with government soldiers. Especially in Kanto, where land reclamation was a relatively new process, the nobles and clans who had expanded their sphere of influence into an area where the prosperous Fujiwara were unpopular had to recruit soldiers to protect their own terrains. In the center, too, military force was necessary for the Fujiwara and powerful temples and shrines to protect their newly acquired lands.

More importantly, to compensate for the lack of funds at court, the

平安時代の関東・東北地方と、武士との関係は？

　弥生時代に大陸から流入してきた民族に追われた縄文人は、東北から北海道にかけて独自の文化を守ったまま、**首長国家**を維持していました。彼らは蝦夷（えみし→後にえぞ）と呼ばれ、その地域を蝦夷地と呼んでいました。最初に朝廷が蝦夷地へ侵入したのは、7世紀の中盤、阿部比羅夫によるものでした。その後724年には、現在の仙台の北方に、東北地方への進出の拠点として多賀城が置かれ、9世紀初頭には、坂上田村麻呂が同地に遠征し、さらにいくつか出城を築いています。

　もともと、蝦夷は日本から、カムチャッカ、千島列島やさらには北方地域を広く活動する民族の一部です。唐の時代には、ロシア沿岸部にあった渤海とも交易をしていたようです。

　しかし、日本の朝廷権力が拡大するにつれ、彼らは次第に中央勢力に取り込まれてゆきます。俘囚と呼ばれる朝廷側についた軍事勢力がそれにあたり、中央からきた兵士と共に、次第に組織的な武力集団になっていったのではと推測されます。特に比較的新しく開墾が進んだ関東では、藤原氏の中央での繁栄を嫌い地方で地盤を拡大した貴族や豪族が、自分たちの土地を守るために兵士を育成します。また、中央では藤原氏や有力寺社も、自らが開墾した土地を荘園として私有し、それを守るための武力が必要でした。

　さらに重要なことは、平安時代には朝廷が財政不足を

> **ひとくちメモ**
> 桓武天皇により征夷大将軍に任じられた坂上田村麻呂は北上川の中流域までを平定。ここに胆沢城を築き、鎮守府を多賀城から移した

collection of taxes in the Heian period was left to the provincial governors, who in return accepted responsibility for military affairs in their regions. Conflicts between the enormously powerful provincial governors and influential local landowners thus frequently developed into armed skirmishes. One of these conflicts in Kanto resulted in the rebellion by Taira no Masakado, which made the court realize for the first time the threat posed by the local militias. Taira no Masakado himself was a member of the Taira clan descended from Emperor Kanmu, but he was also a regional landowner and started the rebellion in order to protect himself and other local powers from the provincial governors.

Given these military needs, the warriors known as *bushi* were gradually organized into fighting forces. Bushi also guarded the imperial court in central Japan, but in the mid-Heian period they still had a relatively lower status.

The bushi rose to prominence at the end of the Heian period, and eventually formed the military government called the Bakufu.

補うために、租税の徴収を**国司**にまかせ、そのかわり国司は現地での軍事行政を担うことを容認しました。従って、地方で大きな権限をもった国司と、以前から下野していた地方の有力者との確執が武力闘争に発展することも多かったのです。関東では、そうした対立が元で**平将門の乱**が起こり、地場の**武士集団**の脅威を朝廷が初めて知ることになるのです。平将門自身、桓武天皇の血をひく平氏の一族でありながらも、地方で地盤を持つ豪族だったわけで、**乱**の発端は彼が同じ立場にある地方の実力者を国司から守ったことだったのです。

こうした軍事的なニーズの中で、**武士**という戦闘集団が組織化されます。武士は中央では朝廷の警護にもあたりますが、平安中期には、まだ身分は低い存在でした。

やがて、武士は平安時代の末期に台頭し、その後に幕府という軍事政権を開くことになるのです。

🔍 ひとくちメモ
平将門の乱
939年、将門は関東で国府を襲撃し、政府に逆らうようになる

21 The Rise of the Genji (Minamoto) and Heike (Taira)

Power at court in the eleventh century was monopolized by Fujiwara no Michinaga and his son Yorimichi, who ruled in the emperor's place through successive posts of *sesshō* (regent to a child emperor or empress) and kanpaku (regent to an adult emperor).

However, the Fujiwara clan was well versed in power struggles, and there were conflicts and bitter rivalries within the family. Emperor Go-Sanjō, who acceded in 1068, and his successor Emperor Shirakawa, managed to manipulate their internal disputes in order to return the authority to the emperor. Emperor Shirakawa in particular managed to keep hold of power even after retirement through the *insei* system of government by a retired emperor, ruling from a position that was out of reach of the power of the sesshō or kanpaku advisers. This was a strategy that slipped through the net of the Ritsuryō code legal system.

Meanwhile, the prelude to the next era was underway in the provinces, with the bushi rising to prominence in the conflicts in Kanto and Tohoku, particularly the Seiwa Genji, Minamoto descendants of Emperor Seiwa. From 1051, during the Early Nine-Years War and Later Three-Years War between the imperial court and the Tohoku clans, Genji clan head Minamoto no Yoshiie provided reinforcements from Kanto bushi in the rearguard, thereby increasing his own power.

The Heike, on the other hand, were descended from Emperor Kanmu, and from their power base in Ise gradually expanded throughout Western Japan. Both the Genji and the Heike were related to the imperial court, and both undertook to guard the court and conduct military operations

源氏と平家はどのように台頭した？

　11世紀には、藤原道長やその子頼通によって、朝廷の権力が独占され、彼らは天皇の代わりに政務をみる**摂政**や**関白**の要職を歴任していました。

　しかし、藤原氏は伝統的に権力闘争に長けている分、身内での紛争も熾烈でした。彼らの内紛をうまく利用しながら天皇に権力を戻していったのが、1068年に即位した後三条天皇とその後を継いだ白河天皇でした。特に白河天皇は、天皇を引退し上皇になったあとも、権力を握り続け、いわゆる**院政**をしくことによって、天皇の補佐役である摂政や関白の力の及ばない地位からの政治を断行しました。これは、律令制度での法制の網の目をくぐった戦略です。

　その頃、地方では次の時代への序章が始まります。関東や東北地方での争乱を通した武士の台頭です。特に清和天皇の子孫である源氏は、東北地方の豪族と朝廷とが対立し、地方豪族の争いが元で1051年から立て続けにおきた**前九年の役**や**後三年の役**を鎮圧します。この戦争を継続する中で、源氏の頭領であった源義家は、前線の後方である関東地方の武士を統率し、勢力を拡大します。

　一方の平家は桓武天皇の子孫ですが、伊勢を中心に地盤を築き、西国の豪族などを取り込んで、次第に膨張します。源氏も平家もともに朝廷と関わり、朝廷の警護や朝廷による軍事行動を代行しながら、次第に頭角をあらわし

ひとくちメモ
前九年の役 と後三年の役で、
源氏が東国に勢力を築いた

平家の紋 揚羽蝶

on its behalf, and they gradually rose to preeminence. However, it is also true that Minamoto no Yoshiie had been left without backup from the court in the Later Three-Years War, and this had conversely strengthened the Genji's connection with Kanto.

Meanwhile Fujiwara no Kiyohira, who secured the aid of the Minamoto to defeat his rivals in Ōshū province, expanded his territory across what is now Iwate prefecture and prospered as the head of the Fujiwara clan of Ōshū. Since he enjoyed the rights to Ōshū gold dust, he must have used part of the profits from this to strengthen his vassalage with Minamoto no Yoshiie.

In central Japan the imperial family had wrested power back to the retired emperor from the Fujiwara, known as the family of regents, but the infighting between ex-emperors and emperors continued in successive generations. The conflict over the succession between Emperors Sutoku and Go-Shirakawa in 1156 developed into rebellion, in which both sides depended on military support from the Genji and Heike. The Genji and Heike both split their clan allegiances with warriors from both clans fighting on both sides in the civil war known as the Hōgen Rebellion, which ended in victory for Emperor Go-Shirakawa.

The Hōgen Rebellion not only strengthened the central government, but was also a landmark event demonstrating how indispensable the bushi had become.

てゆくのです。ただし、後三年の役で活躍した源義家は、朝廷から勢力の伸長を疎まれますが、そのことが逆に源氏と関東の結びつきを強固にしたことも否めません。

源氏の紋 笹竜胆

🔍 **ひとくちメモ**
奥州藤原氏
初代清衡以降、4代泰衡まで平泉を拠点に栄えた。今も清衡創立の中尊寺が残る

一方、後三年の役で源氏側につき、ライバルとの戦いに勝利した奥州の豪族藤原清衡は、現在の岩手県一帯に自らの地盤を拡大し、**奥州藤原氏**として繁栄します。奥州には**砂金**がとれ、その権益を享受したわけで、当然その恩恵の一部を源義家も自らの家臣団の強化に使用したのではないでしょうか。

さて、中央では、院政によって**摂関家**とまで呼ばれた藤原氏から権力を奪還した天皇家も、その後歴代の上皇や天皇との確執が絶えません。そうした中で、1156年に崇徳上皇と後白河天皇との権力を巡る争いが乱に発展します。そして、どちら側も頼りにしたのは源氏と平家の兵力でした。源氏も平家も、家臣団が分裂し、上皇側と天皇側について戦い、最終的に後白河天皇が勝利します。この争乱を**保元の乱**といいます。

中尊寺（岩手県）

保元の乱は中央政権を維持してゆく上で、武士が必要不可欠であることを証明した画期的な出来事といえましょう。

22 Japanese Buddhism

The Heian period was the era of the nobility, who skillfully used the Ritsuryō system and the authority of the emperor to keep the splendor of the imperial court for themselves.

On the other hand, Buddhist institutions provided assistance to the court and, like the nobility, were also landowners and occasionally grew to form large pressure groups.

Relations with China had ceased, and the Buddhist statues made for temples no longer reflected the exoticism of an earlier age, with smooth, flowing robes and soft rounded bodies. The gods of the ancient Shinto religion were taken to be earthly manifestations of the buddhas and bodhisattvas in Japan, which led to the syncretic fusion of Shinto and Buddhism, with Shinto shrines being built in the precincts of Buddhist temples.

While the nobility was often deeply superstitious and particularly fastidious about time-honored practices and conventions, they also converted to Buddhism and prayed for supreme bliss in the afterlife. The teaching that appealed most to them was Amidism, or the faith in Amida (Amitabha) Buddha. According to Buddhist thought, there is not just one Buddha, but they exist everywhere in the universe. Amida is worshipped for leading his followers to the Buddhist Realm in the next world. Originally, people prayed to Amida for the happiness of their ancestors, and later came to pray to him to take care of their own afterlife. Monk Genshin, of Mount Hiei, in 985 wrote the *Ōjōyōshū* (Essentials of Rebirth in the Pure Land), which provides the best description of the

日本独自の仏教とは？

　平安時代はその大部分が**貴族の時代**でした。貴族は、律令制度と天皇の権力を巧みに利用し、朝廷での栄華を独占します。

　一方で、仏教界も朝廷を補佐する機関の一つとして捉えられ、貴族と同じく荘園を領有し、時には大きな圧力団体になることもありました。

　当時、中国との交流が途絶え、仏教寺院で制作される仏像からは、以前のエキゾチズムがとれ、衣服はなだらかな曲線をもって流れ、体系もやわらく丸みを帯びてきます。また、古来の宗教である神道の神々は、仏教の仏の化身として日本にやってきたものとする、**本地垂迹説**という考えのもと、寺院の中に神社が建立されるなどといった**神仏習合**が進んだのも当時のことでした。

　貴族は往々にして**迷信深く**、特に古来の様々な風習やしきたりにこだわりながら、同時に仏教に**帰依して**来世の至福をも祈念します。そうした彼らの意識に合致した教えが、**阿弥陀信仰**でした。仏陀は一人ではなく、宇宙の至る所に存在するという考え方が仏教にはあります。その中でうまれた阿弥陀仏は、特に来世での仏の世界に導く存在として崇拝されます。元々は、祖先を崇拝する中で、祖先の幸福を祈る対象であった阿弥陀仏が、自らの来世への願望への祈りの対象として重用視されるようになったのです。比叡山の僧源信が 985 年に描いた『往生要集』は、当時の天国と地獄に関する来世観を象徴した書籍として脚光を

阿弥陀如来坐像
（鎌倉大仏・神奈川県）

views of paradise and the hells of the afterlife at that time. In 1052, at the height of the prosperity of the Fujiwara clan, Fujiwara no Yorimichi built the famous Phoenix Hall at the Byōdōin Temple in Uji for the worship of Amida Buddha.

1052 is an important year in Buddhism. It marks 2000 years following the death of Buddha, and the year in which the world entered the "Latter Day of the Law" in which Buddha's influence wanes. This was taken to be the end of this world, and people became fervent about attaining salvation in the afterlife.

There were many famines, crops were failing, and people were especially fearful of this Buddhist age of decline. Some priests also rejected the cozy relationship of Buddhism with the government, and became sages intent on saving sentient beings, wandering the land and praying for the common people. A model tenth century example of these was Kūya, who is said to have wandered around devastated farming villages, reciting the Nenbutsu as he administered salvation. His Pure Land Buddhism, which taught that people at the mercy of fate should recite the Nenbutsu with all their heart and imagine the Pure Land in order to be guided to salvation, quickly spread throughout Japan.

The Heian period was an era of splendor at court, but also, of anxiety mixed with fear.

浴びました。また、1052年には、藤原氏の繁栄の頂点に
いた藤原頼通が、宇治の平等院に有名な**鳳凰堂**を建立し
て、阿弥陀仏を祀ります。

　1052年は、仏教では重要な年です。それは仏陀入滅
から2000年が経過し、以降仏陀の威光が遠ざかる**末法**
にはいるとされた年なのです。それは現世の終焉の時と捉
えられ、人々は迷信や**来世**での救済に熱心になります。

　当時は、飢饉も多く、農村は疲弊し、まさに人々は末
法におびえます。僧の中には中央と癒着した仏教を嫌い、
聖（ひじり）としてそんな衆生を救おうと、地方を歩き庶民のために
祈り、活動する例もみられました。10世紀を生きた空也
はその典型で、念仏を唱えながら、荒廃した農村を歩いて
は人々の救済に尽くしたといわれています。力のない巷の
人々に、一心に念仏を唱えながら来世を想い、救済へと導
く彼の考え方が浄土教として、その後急速に日本中に拡大
するのです。

　平安時代は、華麗な宮廷文化とは裏腹に官民共々に、
不安や恐れの入り交じった時代だったのです。

空也が創立した六波羅蜜寺
（京都府）

23 Enryaku-ji Temple

Enryaku-ji was founded on Mount Hiei by Monk Saichō in 788, and later established in the Heian Period. The Imperial Court was concerned about the increasing power wielded by the temples in Nara. The Chinese monk Ganjin had brought a formal system for training Buddhist priests and established the Kaidan-in, or ordination hall, at Tōdai-ji temple in Nara, with two more ordination halls, one to the west at Kanzeon-ji in Dazaifu, and one to the east at Yakushi-ji in present-day Tochigi prefecture.

The Kaidan-in had the privilege of training priests, and originally was intended to be an educational facility to enable the government to supervise the priesthood. Thus connected to the state, the Nara temples grew large. Even more than Tōdai-ji, the Fujiwara family temple, Kōfuku-ji, also increased its power under the patronage of the prosperous Fujiwara, and is said to have had grown so wealthy from managing its estate that its assets exceeded those of the state.

Partly to curb the power of the expanding Nara temples, in 822 the Imperial Court sanctioned the establishment of another Kaidan-in at Enryaku-ji. With the right to train priests, Enryaku-ji became a cornerstone for the spread of Mahayana Buddhism throughout Japan. The Kaidan-in at Enryaku-ji is known as the Mahayana Kaidan.

However, just like all the Nara temples, throughout the Heian period Enryaku-ji also turned to management of their extensive estates, and owned much land in which the state had no power to intervene. Due to factional conflicts within the temple, monks also carried arms and on occasion fought. These armed monks were known as warrior

延暦寺とは？

　延暦寺は、最澄によって奈良時代末期の788年に開か
れ、平安時代に整備された寺です。当時朝廷は、奈良にあっ
た寺院が肥大化し、圧力団体として君臨していたことに悩
んでいました。鑑真が日本に正式な僧侶育成制度を持ち
込み、いわゆる**戒壇院**が東大寺に設けられ、西には太宰
府の観世音寺、東には現在の栃木県の薬師寺に同様の戒
壇院が置かれました。

延暦寺釈迦堂（滋賀県）

　戒壇院は僧侶を育成する特権をもっていることを意味
し、元々は国家が僧侶を管理するための教育機関であっ
たはずです。このように奈良の寺院は、国と結びつきなが
ら大きくなりました。東大寺もさることながら、藤原氏の
菩提寺とされた興福寺は、その後繁栄した藤原氏の保護
のもとに勢力を増し、荘園経営による財力をもって一国の
規模を越える資産をもっていたといわれています。

　こうした奈良の寺院の肥大化から、その力を分散する思
惑もあり、朝廷は822年に延暦寺にも戒壇院を設ける勅
許をだしました。これによって、延暦寺でも僧が育成でき、
大乗仏教が本格的に日本に広がる礎となったのです。延
暦寺に開かれた戒壇院は大乗戒壇と呼ばれていました。

　しかし、平安時代を通して、延暦寺は奈良の寺々と同
様に荘園経営などを手がけ、国家権力が介入できない土
地を多く所有します。そして、寺内の派閥抗争の中から、
僧侶が武器をもって争うこともありました。武装した僧侶
を**僧兵**と呼びます。彼らは朝廷と利害の対立が産まれると、

monks. Whenever a conflict of interest arose between the court and their own interests, they would turn out in force, bearing a portable shrine to the capital and appealing directly to the court. Since everyone, from those in power to the common people, feared divine retribution, such highhandedness could not be suppressed by military force.

Much of the psychology of people in ancient and medieval times is unfathomable to people today, and religion is a prime example of this.

Since the Heian period, when the syncretic fusion of Buddhism and Shinto progressed and Buddhism spread to all of society, people must have felt that the afterlife, unfathomable natural phenomena, and the karma of people and living beings, were equally important, and sometimes more important than the mundane world and their own lives.

Together, Kōfuku-ji and Enryaku-ji are known as the Nanto-hokurei, or the Southern Capital-Northern Mountain (Nara being home to Kōfuku-ji and Mount Hiei home to Enryaku-ji), and Emperor Shirakawa famously grumbled about the "waters of the Kamo river [which regularly flooded], gambling, and the Mount Hiei monks" as things he could do nothing about.

Nevertheless, many of the priests produced by Mahayana Buddhism founded the religious sects that have subsequently been at the forefront of Japanese Buddhism.

延暦寺の**神輿**をもって都に繰り出し、強訴します。このような横暴を武力で鎮圧できなかったのは、当時、権力者から庶民まで、**仏罰や神罰**を恐れていたからに他なりません。

　古代や中世の人の心理を考えるときに、現代人の目をもってしては計り知れないものが多々あります。宗教観はその代表的なものでしょう。
　神仏習合が進み、仏教が広く一般に普及した平安時代以降、人々は世俗の生活と来世、そして人知で計り知れない様々な自然の活動、人や生き物の宿命を、同じ重みで、時には世俗以上に重要なものとして意識していたはずです。

　奈良の興福寺と京都の延暦寺は、南都北嶺と呼ばれ、白河法皇が鴨の水掻きと双六の賽、そして山法師（比叡山の僧兵）だけはどうにもならないとぼやいた話は有名です。

　とはいえ、大乗戒壇から輩出した多くの僧が、その後の日本の仏教を牽引する宗派を設立する人材であったこともまた事実なのです。

興福寺（奈良県）

24 The Heike Period

Monk Shinzei was a central figure in the push to return power to the emperor, and contributed to Emperor Go-Shirakawa's victory in the Hōgen Rebellion. He was from the southern branch of the Fujiwara clan, and after taking the tonsure achieved success as personal adviser to Emperor Go-Shirakawa.

However, the nobility opposed his aggressive tactics, and when Emperor Nijō acceded upon Emperor Go-Shirakawa's retirement, they organized a coup d'état in 1159. The military commander of the coup was the head of the Genji clan, Minamoto no Yoshitomo. Monk Shinzei was killed in the coup, but the head of the Taira clan, Taira no Kiyomori rushed to the scene upon hearing the emergency call and continued the battle. This series of disputes are known as the Heiji Rebellion. As a result, the Genji were driven out of the capital, Minamoto no Yoshitomo killed, and many of his family and other followers either executed or exiled.

Emperor Go-Shirakawa had originally not thought to willingly abdicate to Emperor Nijō, and had been actively plotting in the background of the rebellion. Afterwards, however, Emperor Nijō's position became more stable, and with it the Heike's position more prominent.

Emperor Nijō sought to retain power as emperor, but died young. Just before his death, as if to prevent the intervention of retired Emperor Go-Shirakawa, he abdicated in favor of his two-year-old son, Emperor Rokujō. This, however, gave Emperor Go-Shirakawa a reason to once again involve himself in the political arena. Within the year he had deposed the

平家の時代とは？

　保元の乱で地位を確立した後白河天皇を動かし、天皇親政を目指した立役者に信西という僧侶がいます。元々藤原氏南家の出身でその後出家し、後白河天皇の**知恵袋**として出世したのです。

🔍 **ひとくちメモ**
信西は藤原通憲の法名

　しかし、彼の目指す天皇親政への強引な手法に反感をもつ貴族は、やがて二条天皇が即位し、後白河が上皇となり院政をしくと、1159 年にクーデターを起こします。クーデターを軍事的に指揮したのが当時の源氏の頭領、源義朝でした。クーデターで信西は殺害されますが、逆にこの急報をきいて駆けつけた平家の頭領である平清盛と争い敗北します。この一連の騒動を**平治の乱**といいます。この結果、源氏が京都から一掃されてしまうのです。源義朝は、落ち行く途中で殺害され、多くの親族や関係者が処刑、あるいは**流罪**になりました。

平清盛日招像（広島県）

　後白河上皇は元々二条天皇への譲位を快く思っていず、乱の背景には彼が様々な策謀を練っていたことも伺えますが、乱の後は二条天皇の地位も**安泰し**、それと共に平家がみるみる昇進してゆきます。

　二条天皇は天皇親政を目指し政務をみますが、道半ばで崩御。死の直前に後白河上皇の介入を阻止するかのように、自らの2歳の子に譲位します。六条天皇です。しかし、これは却って後白河上皇が政治の表舞台に再登場する理由となります。彼は幼帝を1年で廃し、自らの子供を皇位

young emperor and instated his own child as Emperor Takakura. By this time the Heike had already built a firm foundation at court. Taira no Kiyomori made his own daughter empress to Emperor Takakura, and thus became deeply involved in governing.

The Heike, just like the Fujiwara before them, were now in control of politics at court. They were warriors, but behaved like nobility. In 1169 the retired Emperor Go-Shirakawa took the tonsure. Kiyomori was skillful in manipulating the powerful Fujiwara and people connected to Go-Shirakawa, and succeeded in winning the retired emperor over and keeping him in check.

The Heike owned large amounts of land, and monopolized trade with Song Dynasty China for their own means. The cities of Fukuoka and Fukuhara (present-day Kobe) that they established are still thriving ports today. However, as before, Japan was not actively engaged in exchange with East Asia.

At the height of their prosperity, Taira no Kiyomori and his family even said that "If you are not a Heike, you are nobody." The samurai would only gain true power after the downfall of the Heike.

につけます。高倉天皇です。既にこの頃、平家は朝廷に盤
石の地盤を築いていました。平清盛は自らの娘を高倉天皇
の后にして、政務に深く関わります。

　平家は、以前の藤原氏と同様に、自らが宮中にあって
政治を司ります。いわゆる武士でありながら貴族として振る
舞うわけです。1169年には、後白河上皇が**出家**して法皇
となりますが、清盛は藤原氏の有力者や後白河法皇との
関係もうまく**操る**政治手腕をもち、後白河法皇を時には**懐
柔**、時には牽制します。

　平家は大量の荘園を保有し、当時中国の統一王朝であっ
た**宋**との貿易を独占して自らの財源とします。平家が開い
た福岡や福原（現在の神戸）は今でも港湾都市として栄え
ています。ただ、以前のように日本が積極的に東アジアの
外交に関わることは最早ありませんでした。

　「平家にあらずんば、人にあらず」とまでに栄華を極め
た平清盛とその一族ですが、それは朝廷の権威の枠の中
での栄華でした。武家が本当の権力を手中に収めるのは、
その平家が滅亡したときだったのです。

🔍 ひとくちメモ
宋
国の王朝。960-1279

25 The Overthrow of the Heike

The Heian period saw continual power struggles between the imperial family, whose authority harked back to the golden days of the Ritsuryō Code, and influential families clinging to power at court, including the Fujiwara and later the Heike.

Retired Emperor Go-Shirakawa disliked the Heike's monopoly on power. Of course, many people sympathized with him, and his son, Prince Mochihito was particularly hostile to the Heike. In 1179, the Heike pre-empted any threatening move by Go-Shirakawa by imprisoning him and punishing Prince Mochihito. Subsequently, in 1180 Taira no Kiyomori ensured the succession of Emperor Antoku, the son of Emperor Takakura and Kiyomori's own daughter. At the same time, Prince Mochihito secretly put out a call throughout the country for the subjugation of the Heike.

Whenever there was trouble, the imperial family and nobility could only rely on either the armed warriors, or on the religious authority of temples such as the Mount Hiei complex. Conversely, the warriors needed the authority of the imperial family and the nobility at court. The temples were between these two poles and used their religious authority to put pressure on both the court and the warrior class. Nevertheless, the court typically occupied a pivotal point in the power balance and their authority was rarely challenged. This was perhaps due to the sense of "awe" for the gods and Buddha and for those in authority since olden times. For Japanese people, the imperial family had a divine existence.

平家はどのように打倒された？

　平安時代は、昔の律令体制に憧れる皇族と、藤原氏や平安末期の平家のように、朝廷での権力に固執する実力者との綱引きの時代です。

　後白河法皇は、平家が権力を独占する様子を疎んでいました。もちろん、彼に同情する人も多く、後白河法皇の王子、以仁王は特に平家に強い敵意をいだきます。1179年に後白河法皇の不穏な動きを察知した平家は、法皇を**幽閉し**、以仁王も処罰します。清盛はその後、1180年には高倉天皇と平清盛の娘との間に産まれた子供を安徳天皇として擁立します。そして同じ頃、以仁王がついに平家**討伐**の密命を全国に出したのです。

　当時、皇族も貴族も、事を起こすには武力を持つ武士か、宗教的威光をもつ比叡山のような寺社に頼るしかありません。逆に、武士は皇族や貴族の持つ朝廷という権威を必要としています。寺院はそのちょうど中間にあって、仏教の権威の元に、朝廷や時には武士に圧力をかけます。力のある者が衰えた者を倒し政権を握るという合理的な考え方がうまれず、**常に朝廷がパワーバランスの支点に存在したことが、日本の歴史の特徴ともいえるのです**。それは、神仏や太古からの権威者への「**畏れ**」という感覚によって支えられた価値観といえましょう。日本人にとって、皇族は神がかった存在だったのです。

On the other hand, after the Heiji Rebellion the Genji had scattered around various provinces, but now linked up with local armies and regrouped. Especially in Kanto, Minamoto no Yoritomo, who had been exiled in Izu, was gaining support. Yoritomo was the third son of Minamoto no Yoshitomo, the Genji leader killed in the Heiji Rebellion. He married Hōjō Masako, the daughter of the powerful Hōjō clan leader of Izu, and when Prince Mochihito's call to arms arrived, they joined forces with Genji-affiliated armies in their Kanto stronghold, including the Takeda Clan active in the later Sengoku period, and the Edo Clan that owned the land in Edo where the shogunate was based in the Edo period.

All over the country, people were rising up against the Heike. In the midst of this disorder, in 1181 Taira no Kiyomori passed away.

However, Minamoto no Yoritomo did not move right away, due to the threat of the Fujiwara clan in Ōshū and the need to strengthen his own territory, and Minamoto no Yoshinaka who had been in Kiso (present-day Nagano) invaded Kyoto and drove out the Heike. Subsequently, when Yoshinaka and Retired Emperor Go-Shirakawa fell out, Yoritomo sent an army and defeated Yoshinaka, and advanced his troops even further west. The Genji hero of this time was Minamoto no Yoshitsune, who defeated the Heike in battle at Ichi-no-Tani and again at Yashima, before routing them at the Battle of Dan-no-Ura in 1186. The story of the eight-year-old Emperor Antoku drowning in the sea with the rest of the Heike is famous.

　一方、平治の乱のあと、地方に拡散していた源氏も、地方の武士団と連携をとり、体制を立て直します。特に関東では、伊豆に流罪になっていた源頼朝が成長します。頼朝は平治の乱で死亡した源氏の頭領、源義朝の三男です。頼朝はやがて伊豆の有力者である北条氏の娘政子と結婚、以仁王の密命が届くと、彼らは、後の戦国時代に活躍する武田氏や江戸時代に幕府の置かれる江戸を領有していた江戸氏など、源氏ゆかりの武士団を従え、関東に拠点を造ります。

　その頃は各地で平家に叛旗を翻す者がでてきます。そうした混乱の中で平清盛が他界してしまいます。1181年のことです。

　しかし、源頼朝は奥州藤原氏の脅威と、自らの地盤固めのために、すぐには動けず、木曽にいた源義仲が京都になだれ込み、平家を都から追い払います。その後、後白河法皇と義仲が不和になると、体制を立て直した頼朝は軍を送り、義仲を討ち、さらに兵を西に進めます。この時の源氏側の英雄が源義経です。平家は一ノ谷、屋島と戦い、ついに**壇ノ浦の合戦**で滅亡。1186年のことでした。まだ8歳だった安徳天皇も平家と共に海に沈んだことは有名な話です。

赤間神宮にある平家一門の墓（山口県）

壇ノ浦古戦場址（山口県）

Part **2**

Medieval Japan
中世日本のあらまし

中世日本のあらまし

　中世は、日本に二つの政権が生まれ、その制度が紆余曲折を踏まえながら固定化していった時代です。いうまでもなく、古代から続いた天皇を頂点とした朝廷と、台頭してきた武士による幕府政権がそれにあたります。

　ヨーロッパの歴史で考えるなら、ローマ帝国が崩壊し、ローマ帝国が国教として指定したキリスト教の最高権威であるローマ法王と、その権威の下で分断され、現在の国家の原点となった各地の王国の存在という2重性と比較してみると、海外の人にもわかりやすいのかもしれません。

　ただ、武士の経営する諸国を統率した幕府のようなものは、ヨーロッパには存在せず、天皇と似た役割を演じるローマ法王の下にさまざまな国家が競合していたことが、ヨーロッパが日本に比べはるかに不安定であった原因なのかもしれません。

　いずれにせよ、日本の歴史の中で武家政権、すなわち幕府の果たした役割を説明することは、とても重要なことといえましょう。

　中世は仏教文化が多様化していった時代でもあります。ヨーロッパにも中世末期とされる16世紀にプロテスタントの各派が生まれたように、日本でも旧来の仏教権威とは分離した、現代に直接つながる仏教各派が成長してゆきます。京都などの寺社の起源とも密にかかわるそうした背景は、ぜひおさえておく必要があるでしょう。

　また、戦国時代に日本人ははじめて西欧社会からのコンタクトを受けます。この背景もヨーロッパでの宗教改革と大きく関わっています。それは、新教による影響力の拡大を怖れ、カトリック教会が海外への展開を推し進めたことと、そうした西欧の国々がトルコでのイスラム教徒の台頭により、陸路での東西交流が困難になったため、新たな交易ルートを求めた結果のできごとでした。日本が正に世界史と直結した瞬間だったのです。

　中世の日本を世界の中の日本として語ることは、外国の人の日本への理解を深める上でとても大切なことなのです。

　実際、欧米の人々が西欧の歴史により通じているのも事実です。したがって世界的視野で日本の歴史を観ることと、海外の人々と歴史的な情報をお互いに交換することとで、相互理解を深めてゆければと思うのです。

26 The Kamakura Shogunate

Yoritomo ventured to put as much distance as possible between himself and the politics of the capital, knowing that the retired emperor and imperial family, not to mention the nobility and even the temples, all had hidden agendas. As he was well aware, the court would use both the Heike and the Genji as pawns to their own ends, and when necessary would immediately switch allegiance without looking back.

It appears that Emperor Go-Shirakawa attempted to win over Minamoto no Yoshitsune after he defeated the Heike. However, even though Yoshitsune was his younger brother, Yoritomo could not forgive his connection to the imperial family and considered him a traitor. As a child Yoshitsune had been under the protection of the Ōshū Fujiwara clan, and Yoritomo must have planned to defeat the Fujiwara and subjugate Ōshū along with Yoshitsune.

In fact, when Yoshitsune later fled to the Fujiwara clan, Yoritomo demanded that the Fujiwara hand him over. Fujiwara no Yasuhira, the third generation after Fujiwara no Kiyohira who had led the Genji in the Later Three Years War, feared Yoritomo and killed Yoshitsune, but Yoritomo anyway dispatched an army and defeated the Fujiwara in 1189.

At the end of the Heian period, the imperial court was financially and militarily much weaker than it had been under the Ritsuryō system. Ultimately this was because provincial leaders had expanded their private armies, which gradually joined forces with either the Heike or the Genji. A serious conflict of interest arose between the regional authorities, including the provincial governors and private estates, and the warrior

鎌倉幕府はどのようにして成立した？

源頼朝

　頼朝は法皇や皇族、そして貴族のみならず寺社までが様々な思惑をもって政治に関わってくる京都とあえて距離をおきます。平家にしろ、源氏にしろ、必要なときには駒のようにそれを動かし、体制が悪くなるとすぐに昨日までの忠誠をも顧みず相手側についてしまう朝廷の様子を頼朝は知悉していたのです。

　後白河法皇は、平家を倒した源義経を取り込もうとしたようです。しかし、頼朝は義経が実の弟とはいえ、皇室と絡んだ人物を容赦せず、**謀反人**として処断します。源義経は幼い頃に、奥州の藤原氏の保護を受けていて、頼朝としては義経と共に藤原氏を倒し、奥州を**平定**しようとも思っていたのでしょう。

　実際、その後藤原氏の元に義経が逃れると、頼朝は藤原氏に彼の引き渡しを要求します。後３年の役で奥州藤原氏を興した藤原清衡から３代目にあたる藤原泰衡は、頼朝を畏れ義経を殺害しますが、頼朝はそのまま軍を差し向け、藤原氏を滅ぼしてしまいます。1189年のことでした。

　平安時代の末期、朝廷は既に資金力の上でも、軍事力の上でも律令体制の頃とは比較できないほどに衰えていました。それはなんといっても、地方の権力者が武士として成長し、その武士の集団が次第に源氏や平家によって統合されていったからです。**荘園**や**国司**の権限と、武士の豪族としての権益が深刻な対立を産みましたが、その分朝廷

clans, and as a result the court's tax revenues dropped.

A contributing factor to the Heike's subsequent defeat by Yoritomo's army was clearly the fact that they cultivated connections with the court only, neglecting to cooperate with the provincial armies. It is also said that Yoritomo's supporters, the Hōjō clan, originally belonged to the Heike line, which suggests that Yoritomo was more concerned with securing the warriors throughout Kanto than focusing on the imperial court.

When Yoritomo subjugated Ōshū, instead of going himself to the imperial court, he dispatched the Hōjō clan leader Hōjō Tokimasa to Kyoto and instead made his stronghold in distant Kamakura. At the command of an army of warriors from Kamakura, he succeeded in making a powerbase away from the court's influence. The court saved face by giving him the title of shogun, and generally treating him as a subject of the emperor. The shogun subsequently became the highest rank in the military government.

Yoritomo established the shogunate in Kamakura in 1192. This was the start of the military government that lasted for 776 years until the Tokugawa was defeated in 1868.

の税収が落ち込んでいったことは事実でしょう。

　頼朝の挙兵とその後の平家の打倒の経緯をみてもわかるように、平家は朝廷とだけ結びつこうとし、**地方の武士団**との連携を怠ったことがその敗因であったといえましょう。頼朝を支持した北条氏も、元はといえば平家の系統に属していたといわれています。このことからも、いかに頼朝が朝廷という「点」ではなく、関東一円の武士の集団という「面」を掌握していたかが伺えます。

　頼朝は奥州を平定すると、自らが朝廷に乗り込むかわりに、北条氏の頭領である北条時政を京都に派遣して朝廷を牽制します。そして、朝廷から離れた鎌倉に、拠点をおきます。鎌倉から武士を束ね、軍事を統率することによって、朝廷の影響なく、勢力基盤を盤石なものとしたのです。朝廷もそんな頼朝に**征夷大将軍**の称号を与え、一応皇室の臣下として処遇し、面子を保ちます。この征夷大将軍こそが、以降の武家政権の最高位となるのです。

　頼朝は 1192 年に鎌倉に**幕府**を開きます。それ以降、1868 年に徳川幕府が滅びるまで、776 年間にわたる**武家政権**がここにスタートしたことになります。

27 The Rise of the Hōjō Clan and the Jōkyū War

The establishment of the shogunate in Kamakura meant Japan's government was split between the military and the court. In effect, the imperial palace left the administration of government to the military while the emperor reigned as a symbol of authority, but this had not yet been established at the start of the Kamakura period, and Japan was ruled by two powers.

In order to suppress Yoshitsune, Yoritomo had set up a nominal police force with military governors (*shugo*) and land stewards (*jitō*) placed at strategic points throughout the country. The governors were regional administrators, while the stewards handled the taxation and administration of estates and national land holdings in the provinces.

Thus, when the Kamakura shogunate was formally founded, Yoritomo could link it to an established national network of government. The land stewards collected taxes on behalf of the provincial governors (*kokushi*) dispatched by the palace and the private estates of the nobility and temples, thus avoiding the confusion of a double-tiered government. Sometimes the imperial governors became land stewards. The land stewards eventually subjugated the estates, in effect taking over all their military and political power, and administration, from the mid-Kamakura period into the Muromachi period.

Following Yoritomo's death in 1199, Hōjō Tokimasa culled his political rivals and assumed the leadership. He assassinated the second shogun, Minamoto no Yoriie in Izu. The next shogun, Yoritomo's second son Sanetomo, was subsequently assassinated in 1219 by Yoriie's son Kugyō.

北条氏の台頭と承久の乱の あらましは？

　鎌倉幕府の成立は、そのまま日本に朝廷と武家との二つの政権が産まれたことを意味します。実質は、朝廷が武家に政権の運営をまかせ、朝廷は権威の象徴として君臨するのですが、鎌倉時代初期には、まだそうした体制が確立しておらず、日本は二つの権力に治められる形になります。

　源頼朝は義経を討伐するにあたって、警察組織を置くことを名目に、全国の要所に**守護**と**地頭**を設置します。守護は地方の行政長官で、地頭は地方の荘園や国の直轄地での徴税などを管理する職制です。

　これによって、正式に鎌倉に幕府が開府したとき、頼朝は全国ネットでの統治組織に幕府をリンクさせることができました。地頭は朝廷の派遣した**国司**や貴族や寺社の**荘園**の徴税を代行し、**2重政権**から産まれる混乱を回避します。時には国司がそのまま地頭になることもありました。やがて、地頭が荘園を圧迫し、実質上武家政権が行政の全てを担うようになるのは、鎌倉時代の中期以降、室町時代にかけてのことでした。

　中央では頼朝が1199年に没すると、北条時政が政敵を淘汰し、覇をとなえます。彼は2代将軍となった源頼家を伊豆で殺害します。しかも、後を継いで将軍となった頼朝の次男である源実朝は源頼家の子である公暁に1219

🔍 ひとくちメモ

守護
鎌倉幕府・室町幕府が置いた武家の職制で、国単位で設置された軍事指揮官・行政官

地頭
鎌倉幕府・室町幕府が荘園・公領を管理支配するために設置した職

With Sanetomo's death, the Genji clan's main family bloodline came to an end, and the Hōjō clan took power as regent. Finally, the shogun was a figurehead appointed by the court from the imperial lineage.

Not all private armies throughout the country served the Genji, however, and there were also quite a few powerful people who shunned the rise of the Hōjō. Although the imperial court was weakened it still had the strength to mobilize warriors, and in terms of the power structure, it still occupied a higher rank than the Kamakura shogunate. At the time, the court was ruled by the retired Emperor Go-Toba, who had succeeded Emperor Antoku after he drowned at sea along with the Heike, before subsequently abdicating and reigning as retired Emperor. Go-Toba sought to restore the leadership of the Imperial House, and carried out a reshuffle of personnel at the court. Taking advantage of the confusion following the assassination of Minamoto no Sanetomo, he roused the military to challenge the Kamakura shogunate and in 1221, the Jōkyū War broke out.

However, the court's army was defeated by the shogun's army, which was led by Yoshitoki, brother of Hōjō Masako, who was a widow of Yoritomo. Go-Toba was then exiled to the Oki islands. Thus the Kamakura shogunate came to rule in name and substance over the warriors.

年に暗殺されます。公暁は親の敵と思い実朝を討ったとされています。実朝の死で、源氏**本家の血筋**は途絶え、以降北条氏が**執権**となって政務をみます。やがて征夷大将軍は形式上、朝廷から皇族が送られてくることになりました。

　こうした一連の事件からみても、全国の武士団が全て源氏に服したわけではなく、また北条氏の台頭を疎む有力者もかなりいました。一方、朝廷は衰えたとはいえ、まだ武士を動員する力をもち、権力構造上は鎌倉の将軍の上に位置します。当時、朝廷を統治していたのは、平家と共に海に消えた安徳天皇の後を継ぎ天皇となり、その後譲位して上皇となった後鳥羽上皇でした。後鳥羽上皇は、皇室の指導力の回復を願い、朝廷内の**人事の刷新**などを実践します。そして、源実朝の暗殺後の混乱を好機として、兵を興し鎌倉幕府に挑戦します。1221 年、**承久の乱**の勃発です。

　しかし、頼朝の未亡人である北条政子とその弟の義時による幕府軍は朝廷の軍を破り、後鳥羽上皇は隠岐の島に流罪になります。これによって鎌倉幕府は名実ともに武家の上に君臨するようになるのです。

28 The Arts in the Kamakura Period

The Kamakura period was the age of the warrior.

The Tōdai-ji and Kōfuku-ji temples in Nara were burned down in the fighting between the Heike and the court and others who opposed them in the Genji-Heike war. In the Kamakura period there were endeavors to restore them, and at the same time new temples were built in Kamakura that contain works by the most representative sculptors of Buddhist images of the time, Unkei and Kaikei. Their works reveal a strength and vigor hitherto unseen in the culture of the nobility.

However, the social unrest since the end of the Heian period appears to have fuelled people's belief in the afterlife, and sentimentalism for this fleeting world. Looking at works of art from this period, we can infer the extent to which people felt a sense of loss for the demise of the charming culture of the nobility, their view of life as transient and empty, and their unease for the new times.

The clearest expression of the mood of the time can be seen in the *Heike monogatari* (Tale of the Heike), which opens "The sound of the Gion Shōja bells echoes the impermanence of all things". The *Tale of the Heike* is an epic account of the rise and fall of the Genji and Heike clans that originated in the Kamakura period and was subsequently passed down in the oral tradition by itinerant blind *biwa* musicians. The Buddhist view of impermanence, in which all things are in a constant state of flux, is connected to the Amidist faith that urges people not to flee death but to ponder the afterlife and humbly offer up prayers to Buddha.

Kamo no Chōmei's *Hōjōki* (An Account of My Hut), which espouses

鎌倉時代の芸術活動は？

　鎌倉時代は、武家の時代です。

　源氏と平家の争いの中で、反平家の立場をとる皇族など
との争いから、当時奈良の東大寺や興福寺が戦火によっ
て破壊されました。鎌倉時代に、その復興のために活動し、
同時に鎌倉にも新たに建立された寺社などに、運慶や快
慶という当時を代表する仏師の作品が残されています。彼
らの作品には、それまでの貴族文化にはない力強さやは
つらつさが見受けられます。

　しかし、この時代は、平安時代末期以降の社会不安が、
人々を来世信仰、はかないこの世へのセンチメンタリズム
に駆り立ててもいたようです。当時の文芸作品をみれば、
逆にいかに人々が、あでやかな貴族文化が滅んだあとの
喪失感や、無常観、そして新たな時代への不安にとらわれ
ていたか察知できます。

　「**祇園精舎の鐘の音、諸行無常の響きあり**」という文で
始まる『平家物語』は、当時の考え方を最も端的にあらわ
しています。平家物語は、源氏と平家との栄枯盛衰を語っ
たもので、鎌倉時代に創作され、**琵琶法師**が唄い継いだ
叙事詩です。物事に永遠はなく、常に空しく変化するとい
う仏教観は、人が死から逃れられず、来世を想い、仏に
祈りを捧げようという阿弥陀信仰へと繋がっています。

　同様の思いを美しい散文として世に残した鴨長明の『**方**

🔍 ひとくちメモ
奈良の東大寺や興福寺は勧
進上人重源によって復興さ
れた。東大寺南大門の運慶・
快慶合作による金剛力士像
に、その事業の大成功が象徴
される

赤間神宮にある琵琶法師像 (山口県)

this concept in beautiful prose, was written in 1212, while Urabe Kaneyoshi's *Tsurezuregusa* (Essays in Idleness) was written in 1331 at the end of the Kamakura period. Together with Sei Shōnagon's Heian-era *Makura no sōshi* (The Pillow Book), these are considered the three outstanding works of the *zuihitsu* essay genre. Both Kamo no Chōmei and Urabe Kaneyoshi were born into families with a long Shinto tradition, but later became Buddhist monks, demonstrating the close co-existence of Buddhism and Shinto.

An Account of My Hut, as the title suggests, was the work of a hermit written by a monk secluded in a small hut. Similarly, the *Sankashū* (Mountain House Collection) is a famous collection of poetry written by Saigyō Hōshi, a warrior who quit worldly life to become an itinerant monk in the late Heian and early Kamakura period. Both *An Account of My Hut* and *Essays in Idleness* were written in a simple style mingling Japanese and Chinese, showing that artistic endeavors were enjoyed by ordinary readers.

丈記』は 1212 年頃に記されました。また、鎌倉時代末期の 1331 年頃に吉田兼好によって著された『徒然草』は、平安時代の清少納言による『枕草子』、そして『方丈記』と並んで日本の三大随筆と呼ばれています。鴨長明にせよ、吉田兼好にせよ、共通しているのは、どちらも神道に深く関わった家系に生まれ、後に出家して僧として活動したことです。仏教と神道とがいかに近い存在になっていたかを物語ります。特に、『方丈記』はその名の通り、小さな庵に隠遁した僧が記した、いわゆる隠者の書です。

　同様の作品としては、平安時代末期から鎌倉時代初期にかけて、武家を捨て、出家して諸国を歩いた西行法師の歌集『山家集』なども有名です。『方丈記』も『徒然草』も当時としては平易な和漢混交文で記され、より文芸活動が一般に受け入れられていたことを物語っています。

ひとくちメモ
『枕草子』平安中期
『方丈記』1212 年
『徒然草』1331 年

Medieval Japan
中世日本のあらまし

ひとくちメモ
鎌倉時代も多くの和歌が作られた。後鳥羽上皇は、藤原定家に命じて『新古今和歌集をまとめさせた

29 Buddhism at the Start of the Kamakura Period

As with artistic activity, two main aspects can be seen in the Buddhism of the Kamakura period.

One was the stoical Buddhism of the warrior culture, while the other reflected the school of Buddhism that sought salvation in the afterlife.

Zen Buddhism was first taken up by the bushi, and later spread throughout the country with the expansion of the military government. Zen was a sect started in India in the fifth century and transmitted to China by the Bodhidharma, in which the Buddha-nature is sought within oneself by means of contemplation through *zazen* meditation. This approach had been transmitted to Japan earlier, but it was in the Kamakura period that it started putting down roots with the foundation of the Rinzai and Sōtō sects.

The core teaching of Rinzai, founded in the early Kamakura period by Eisai, who had studied in Song China, was the transmission of enlightenment from master to pupil, and this spread through the upper echelons of the warrior society with many powerful people having their own teacher. Dōgen, on the other hand, who had traveled to Song China due to Eisai's influence, established the Sōtō sect that emphasized meditation and which was adopted and practiced by common warriors. His thirteenth-century work titled *Shōbōgenzō* (Treasury of the True Dharma Eye) is fundamental to understanding Zen thought.

Originally both Eisai and Dōgen studied in the esoteric Tendai sect, but once it expanded to the point becoming a powerful political force,

鎌倉時代前期の仏教は？

　鎌倉時代の仏教にも、当時の芸術活動と同様二つの側面が見受けられます。

　ひとつは、武家文化を支えるストイックな仏教。そしてもうひとつがより一般的に**来世への救済**を願う仏教の一派の活動です。

　武士を中心に受け入れられ、その後武家政権が発展してゆくにつれ、全国に普及してゆくのが**禅宗**です。禅宗は5世紀はじめにインドから中国に帰化した**達磨**が開いた宗派で、座禅をして瞑想する中で自己の中に仏の真理を求めるものです。この考え方は以前から日本にも伝えられていましたが、鎌倉時代になって臨済宗と曹洞宗がもたらされたことによって、日本に根付いてゆきます。

　中国の宋に学び、鎌倉初期に栄西が開いた臨済宗は、師から弟子への悟りの伝達を核とする教えをもとに、上層部の武家に広がり、多くの権力者が自らの師を持つことになります。一方、栄西の影響を受けた後、宋に渡り、座禅そのものに重きをおく曹洞宗を開いた道元の教えは、一般の武士の修行にも取り入れられます。彼の13世紀に著した『**正法眼蔵**』は、禅の考えを知る基本図書です。

　もともと、栄西も道元も天台宗に学んでいます。彼らは、日本の密教が肥大化し、政治勢力とまでなった状況を疎

ひとくちメモ
達磨（ボーディダルマ）
禅宗の開祖とされている。
378?–528?

they apparently shunned it and instead turned to Zen. From mid-to late Heian, due to the pessimism of the Age of Buddhist Decline, the popular Jōdo sect was also swelled by monks from Tendai.

The Jōdo sect was established at a time of ongoing wars when people sought salvation in the afterlife, and the teaching spread that Amida Buddha would save those who recited his name. Hōnen, who studied in the Tendai sect in the late Heian through the early Kamakura period, went on to spread this philosophy as a teaching of Jōdo. Hōnen was persecuted by Mount Hiei and Kōfuku-ji, and forced to flee to Shikoku.

Shinran studied under Hōnen and further spread the teaching in the thirteenth century, taking a wife and reciting the Nenbutsu together with the common people. He founded Jōdo Shinshū (True Pure Land School, or Shin Buddhism), which subsequently developed in to the largest sect in Japan.

Other well-known monks from this time include Ippen from the Ji sect, who proselytized with the *nenbutsu odori*, or "dancing Nenbutsu" and later associated with the Ikkō sect, which also grew to be a political force.

The Kamakura period saw the beginnings of the biggest religions in Japan today. Seeing their subsequent growth and the power of Japanese Buddhism now, we can appreciate that their foundation was akin to a religious revolution seeking Buddha's salvation.

み、禅へと入っていったといわれています。平安後期から末期に、**末法**思想の元、一般に広く受け入れられた浄土教も、元々天台宗に学んだ僧によって広められています。

　戦乱が続き、人々が来世での救済を求める中、浄土教の考え方は、巷に出て、人々の様々な悩みや煩悩に苦しむ中、念仏を唱えることで阿弥陀仏によって救済されようという考え方を広めます。平安末期から鎌倉初期に天台宗に学んだ法然は、その教えを浄土宗としてさらに広げます。法然は比叡山や興福寺から迫害を受け、四国に流されたこともありました。

　そんな法然に学び、13世紀に自らも妻帯し庶民とともに**念仏を唱え**、教えを広めたのが親鸞です。彼の開いた宗派が浄土真宗で、後に日本で最も多くの信徒を有する教団に発展します。

　当時、念仏を踊りながら普及させる時宗という宗派の一遍上人なども現れ、後に一向宗として統合され、これも大きな宗教勢力として成長します。

　鎌倉時代は、現在の日本に最も受け入れられている宗教観が萌芽した時代なのです。それは、権力と共に成長し、権威となった日本の仏教が、その本来の姿に戻ろうと仏の救済を求めた**宗教改革**のようなものだったのです。

 ひとくちメモ

末法
仏教で、仏の教のみが存在して悟りに入る人がいない時期のこと。日本では最澄著の『末法燈明記』により、1052年（永承7年）が末法元年とされている

30 The Kamakura Period and World History

The Kamakura period was a major turning point in Japanese history in terms of both politics and culture.

Historians often question whether there was a medieval period in Japan. By medieval period, I mean the definition by Western scholars of a period of a feudal regime with a monarch and feudal lords (knights). The king's authority is not all that strong and is reliant on the cooperation of the feudal lords, who maintain their own land keeping the peasants as their serfs. Above the king is the Pope in Rome, the religious authority of the Holy Roman Empire.

A similar relationship can be seen in that of the shogun and the feudal lords in the Kamakura period. In the Ritsuryō system prior to the Heian period, the bushi were merely soldiers to protect the imperial court, and were under the control of the nobility (that is, members of the imperial family other than the emperor). In the Kamakura period, however, the emperor was reduced to a symbol of political and religious authority. Furthermore, until the shogunate and domain system was established in the Edo period, the shogun did not have absolute authority, but relied on the loyalty of his retainers (the *gokenin*).

Meanwhile, the major world religions were all formed around one religious character in a particular civilization by his followers, as with Christianity, Islam, and Buddhism. In Japan, however, as well as the ancient Shinto faith, Buddhist sects were formed by scholar monks who had studied Buddhism in China, with typical examples being the Tendai

鎌倉時代を世界史でどう位置づける？

　鎌倉時代は、政治と文化の双方から日本史の大きな転換点です。

　よく歴史家が、日本に**中世**はあるのかと問います。ここでの中世とは、西欧の歴史学でいう、王と諸候（騎士）の関係によって成り立つ**封建制度**の時代を指します。王の権力は後ほど強くなく、あくまでも諸候との連携の上にあり、諸候は自らの領地に農民を農奴として抱えていました。王の上には権威としての神聖ローマ皇帝などがあり、宗教的権威としてローマ法王が君臨していました。

　これと似た関係は、鎌倉時代の将軍と諸候との関係に当てはめられます。平安時代以前の律令体制では、天皇と貴族との連携の中で、武士はあくまでも朝廷を守る兵士に過ぎず、貴族（あるいは天皇以外の皇族）が武士への支配権力でした。しかし、鎌倉時代には、天皇は政治的、宗教的権威としての最高位にいる象徴的存在へ変化します。しかも、江戸時代に幕藩体制が確立するまでは、王としての将軍の権力は、御家人と呼ばれた家来の忠誠の上に成り立つもので、将軍が決して絶対的な権力をもっていたわけではありません。

　一方、世界宗教は、その発祥においては一人の宗教的人格と、その人格への信者によって形成されます。キリスト教でも、回教でも、仏教でもそれは同じで、日本の場合は、古代信仰である神道は別として、仏教を中国で学んだ学僧などが日本という島国に帰国した段階で、国内での

and Shingon sects founded by Saichō and Kūkai respectively.

Just as the Catholic Church grew in Europe as a result of the union of Christianity and political power, these Buddhist sects in Japan swelled under the protection of the state's authority. During the medieval period in Europe, the power of the Catholic Church was inviolate. During the Kamakura period in Japan, however, new sects such as Zen, Jōdo, Jōdo Shinshū, and Nichiren were formed to combat such power.

The religious revolution in the Christian world occurred in the late Middle Ages in the sixteenth century, another point of difference with Japan.

Applying the framework of Western European historians to the history of an Eastern island nation, it is impossible to define a specific medieval period. However, it is true that from the perspective of the progress and collapse of people and systems, the Kamakura period does have aspects in common with the flow of history elsewhere in the world. The Kamakura period ranks as a major turning point that occasioned major changes in Japan's systems and culture.

開祖として活動します。最澄や空海が開いた天台宗、真言宗はその典型的な例といえそうです。

　ちょうど、ヨーロッパにおけるキリスト教と権力との合体による、カトリック教会の伸長のように、これら日本の仏教も国家権力に保護されながら肥大化します。西欧における中世では、強大なカトリックの権威が不可侵に存在していました。しかし日本では、鎌倉時代にそうした宗教権威に対して新たな宗教運動がおき、禅宗や、浄土宗、浄土真宗、そして日蓮宗などが生まれます。

　キリスト教世界で宗教改革がおきるのは、16世紀という中世末期であり、その点が日本との相違点です。

　西欧歴史学の枠を東洋の一島国の歴史に当てはめ、中世がいつかを定義するのには無理があります。しかし、鎌倉時代が、人と制度の進化と崩壊という観点からみるならば、世界に共通した歴史の動きに通じるものがあることは事実です。鎌倉時代は、日本の国の制度と文化が大きく変化する重要な転換点に位置する時代だったのです。

31 The Mongol Invasions of Japan

After a period of disorder following the fall of the Tang dynasty, China was again unified by the Song dynasty in 960. However, the Song was not a world empire and did not expand China's balloon. Much of their rule was marked by oppression by the Jurchens of the northern Jin dynasty that had destroyed the Liao.

Japan was not connected by formal diplomatic relations with the Song, but maintained a trading relationship with them. Having been defeated by the Jin, in 1127 the Song established the Southern Song capital and continued its cultural exchange with Japan, although Japan maintained its isolationist policy.

However, the northern tribes were creating ever bigger waves on the continent. After a bitter power struggle, Genghis Khan led the Mongols into the Steppe of northern Asia, and in 1234 his son Ogedei Khan destroyed the Jin and gained possession of the rich culture and economy of China. At the same time the Mongols were expanding westwards, and established an empire that reached from the Middle East across southern Russia. The area covering Mongolia, China, and the Korean peninsula was under the rule of Kublai Khan, who established the Yuan dynasty, while the western part of the large empire was ruled by his clan. Then, turning his sights eastwards, he planned to invade Japan.

Other than the occupation following World War II, the Mongol invasions are the closest Japan has come to being invaded by an external enemy. The large fleets of the Yuan descended on the Fukuoka area of

元寇とは？

唐の滅亡のあとの混乱を経て、中国は 960 年に宋によって再び統一されます。しかし、宋は世界帝国ではありませんでした。宋は中国という風船を膨らますことなく、高句麗と同じ言語系の **遼**、それを滅ぼした**女真族**による**金**といった北方民族に圧迫されながら政権を維持します。

日本は、宋と正式な国交は結ばず、**商業活動**だけの**関係**を維持します。宋は 1127 年に金に滅ぼされ、その遺臣によって華南に**南宋**が建国されますが、日本は多少の文化交流はあったものの、国としては孤立政策を維持します。

しかし、大陸では、北方民族の活動がさらに大きな津波となります。北アジアの草原地帯で、熾烈な権力闘争のあと、**チンギス・カン**率いるモンゴル族が伸長し、その子の**オゴデイ・カーン**の時に金を滅ぼし、豊かな中国の文化と経済を手中に収めたのです。1234 年のことでした。モンゴル帝国は、同時に西へ拡大し、中近東から南ロシア一帯に至る大帝国を築きます。この大帝国のうち、モンゴル、中国から朝鮮半島一帯の統治を、元という国名で引き継いだのが**クビライ・カーン**でした。元の西は彼の一族が治めています。そこで彼は、東へと目を向けたのでした。元の日本への侵攻です。

それは、第二次世界大戦での日本の降伏による占領を除けば、日本史上唯一の本格的な外敵の侵攻となります。1274 年の文永の役、そして 1281 年の弘安の役の 2 度に

ひとくちメモ
女真族
満洲から朝鮮半島北部にかけて居住していたツングース系民族

金
中国北半分を支配した女真族の王朝。1115–1234

遼
内モンゴルを中心に中国の北辺を支配した契丹人（キタイ人）耶律氏（ヤリュート氏）の王朝。916-1125

南宋
中国の王 1127–1279

ひとくちメモ
チンギス・カン
モンゴル帝国の初代皇帝。在位1206–1227

オゴデイ・カーン
モンゴル帝国の第2代モンゴル皇帝、チンギス・カンの息子。在位1229–1241

クビライ・カーン
チンギス・カンの孫、モンゴル帝国の第5代皇帝。在位 1260–1294

蒙古塚（福岡県）

Kyushu first in 1274 (Battle of Bun'ei) and again in 1281 (Battle of Kōan). The first invasion was made up of an attacking force of 40,000, while the second force included 140,000 Mongols, Chinese, and also Goryeo, the leader of Goguryeo under Mongol rule. Not long before the second invasion, the Yuan had destroyed the Southern Song and unified China in 1279.

The fighting was fierce. However, on both occasions Japan was saved by typhoons that destroyed the Mongol fleets. The people called these typhoons *kamikaze* or "divine winds."

The awareness of the peril posed by these external attacks, rare in Japan's history, added to the sense of anxiety people already felt from so many natural disasters. It was at such a time that Nichiren expounded on the divine protection of the Lotus Sutra, continuing his religious activities despite being persecuted by other sects and the government. The sect he founded, also named Nichiren, became one of the foremost of the new Buddhist sects in Japan.

The Mongol expansion on the Eurasian continent is of utmost importance in world history. Japan was one of a very few countries that managed to avoid being brought under the control of their empire.

わたり元の大船団が九州の福岡周辺に押し寄せます。**文永
の役**では約 4 万人、**弘安の役**では約 14 万人のモンゴル人、
中国人、そして当時の朝鮮半島の王朝で、元に支配され
た高麗の軍人が日本を攻撃します。ちなみに弘安の役の
前、元は南宋を滅ぼし、1279 年に中国を統一しています。
戦いは熾烈でした。

　しかし、いずれの戦いでも、元の船団が台風によって壊
滅し、日本は救われました。この台風を人々は**神風**と呼ん
だのです。

　この日本史上希有な外敵の襲来は、文字通り国難として
意識され、当時多発した天変地異とあいまって、人心を不
安に陥れます。そうしたときに、法華経の加護を説き、他
宗派や時の政府の迫害を受けながらも宗教活動を繰り広
げた人が日蓮です。彼の開いた宗派を日蓮宗といい、他
の新たな宗派と共に、日本の主要な仏教教団の一つとなり
ます。

　モンゴルのユーラシア大陸での拡大は、世界史でも特
筆すべきものです。日本は、その大帝国に支配されずにす
んだ、ほんの一握りの国の一つだったのです。

志賀島にある日蓮上人像（福岡県）

32 The Downfall of the Kamakura Shogunate

The Kamakura shogunate was kept in power by the samurai, especially in the Kanto area.

The samurai pledged their allegiance to the shogunate in return for being granted the upkeep of a domain. In European terms, you could call it the relationship between the king and his knights, with the warriors corresponding to knights being called *gokenin*, retainers of the shogun. The relationship between these gokenin and the shogunate became law under the Goseibai Shikimoku, or the Formulary of adjudications of 1232.

However, with successive generations these domains were progressively subdivided and many of the gokenin found themselves economically destitute. Furthermore, the economic fallout from the Mongol invasions in Kyushu was serious, and it was not possible to reward many of the gokenin who participated in the war with new land as was the usual practice, and accordingly there was increasing dissatisfaction with the shogunate. The spread of the monetary economy was seen to be at odds with the old custom of remunerating gokenin through the granting of lands.

On the other hand, there was political infighting even within the shogunate following the two Mongol invasions. The Hōjō clan strengthened its grip on power, yet the mismanagement of government continued and discontent spread amongst the gokenin. Some of them began to build up their own power, giving the shogunate various causes for concern.

The shogunate's powerbase was founded on the original relationship

鎌倉幕府はどのように滅亡した？

　鎌倉幕府を支えていたのは、関東を中心とした武士団でした。

　彼らは幕府によって所領の維持を保証される代わりに、幕府への**忠誠**を誓います。ヨーロッパでいうならば、国王と騎士との関係を維持していたのです。この騎士にあたる人々のことを御家人と呼んでいます。1232年に制定された**御成敗式目**は、そうした御家人と幕府との関係を法制化したものでした。

　しかし、所領は相続が続くにつれ、子孫によって**細分化され**、中には経済的に困窮する御家人も多くなります。さらに、九州では**元の侵攻**によって受けた経済的ダメージも深刻で、戦争に参加した御家人の多くは、新たな土地を恩賞としてもらうという従来の慣例が実施しにくい戦争であったため、疲弊し、幕府への不満を募らせます。**貨幣経済**の浸透と、昔ながらの土地の給付による御家人への報酬のあり方との間の矛盾が顕在化したことになります。

　一方、文永、弘安の役の後、幕府の中でも政争がおき、その後北条氏は独裁体制の強化を画策しますが、かえって失政が続き、それに不満を持つ御家人も多くなります。御家人の中には、幕府の統治の外で、独自に勢力を蓄える者もうまれ、幕府は様々な不安要因を抱えることになります。

　もともと、御家人との信頼関係を基軸に、それを権力

of trust with the gokenin, and structurally it was not all that strong. Emperor Go-Daigo sought to take advantage of the social unrest to regain the reins of government as per the Heian times and earlier.

Gokenin dissatisfied with the Hōjō clan responded to this call, and thereby hastened the collapse of the Kamakura shogunate. Raising the banner of revolt, Ashikaga Takauji headed from Kamakura to Kyoto in order to bring the court under his control. In Kanto, Nitta Yoshisada attacked Kamakura with other gokenin and eventually destroyed the Hōjō clan in 1333. Both Ashikaga Takauji and Nitta Yoshisada were powerful gokenin and blood relations of the Genji clan.

After Ashikaga Takauji had brought the capital under control, while Kamakura was under siege, Emperor Go-Daigo returned from exile in the Oki isands announced the restoration of political power. The administration of Emperor Go-Daigo following the overthrow of the Kamakura shogunate is known as the Kenmu Restoration.

The Kamakura shogunate was the government started in 1192 by Minamoto no Yoritomo that lasted for 141 years until its overthrow in 1333. However, following the total collapse of the Kenmu Restoration, the shogunate was revived upon the succession of Ashikaga Takauji. The Kamakura shogunate had laid the foundations for an expanded military government.

基盤にしていた幕府は、構造的にはさほど強固なものでは
ありませんでした。こうした社会不安に対して、時の後醍
醐天皇は、平安時代以前の天皇親政を画策します。

　北条氏へ不満を持つ御家人がこれに呼応したことが、
鎌倉幕府の急速な瓦解へとつながります。朝廷への鎮圧
に鎌倉から向かった足利尊氏が幕府に**反旗を翻**し、京都
を制圧。関東では新田義貞が他の御家人と共に鎌倉を攻
め、ついに北条氏を滅ぼします。1333年のことでした。
足利尊氏も新田義貞も共に、源氏と血縁のある有力御家
人でした。

　足利尊氏が京都を抑えると、一時は幕府に攻められ、
隠岐の島に流されていた後醍醐天皇が京都に戻り、朝廷
による政権の復活を宣言します。鎌倉幕府の滅亡と共に始
まった、後醍醐天皇による朝政のことを**建武の新政**と呼ん
でいます。

　鎌倉幕府は源頼朝によって1192年に開かれ、1333年
に滅びるまでの141年間にわたる政権でした。しかし、そ
の政治形態は、建武の新政が程なく瓦解した後、足利尊
氏によって新たに継承されます。鎌倉幕府は武家政権が
伸張してゆくための土台作りの時期だったのです。

後醍醐天皇

足利尊氏

33 The Nanbokuchō Period

The autocratic regime installed at court by the Kenmu Restoration collapsed after about three years.

Emperor Go-Daigo conceived the imperial court as the apex of power, but ultimately it was not possible to bring the whole country under control without the cooperation of the samurai. However, the emperor enforced measures aimed at restoring the Ritsuryō system, directly countering the power structure and systems fostered by the Kamakura shogunate. Such extreme reactionism and discrimination against the samurai caused more social disorder, and led to the disaffection of the samurai with the new regime.

Eventually Ashikaga Takauji, who had led the Kenmu Restoration, was estranged from Emperor Go-Daigo, and took Kyoto after defeating Kusunoki Masashige and Nitta Yoshisada, the powerful samurai loyal to Go-Daigo, at the Battle of Minatogawa. Go-Daigo fled first to Mount Hiei, and then to Yoshino, in present-day Nara prefecture, where he established his own capital.

Backed by Emperor Kōmyō from the imperial family faction originally opposed to Emperor Go-Daigo, Ashikaga Takauji established a new regime in Kyoto in 1336. In 1338 he was appointed shogun, and formally established the new Muromachi shogunate. The court was split by the factional infighting at court, with Emperor Go-Daigo's new Southern Court, and Emperor Kōmyō's Northern Court. It was the start of the Nanbokuchō period, or Southern and Northern Courts period, that lasted until the court was again unified in 1392.

南北朝時代とはどんな時代？

建武の新政による朝廷独裁政権は約3年で崩壊します。

後醍醐天皇は、朝廷を頂点とした政権を構想しますが、なんといっても武士の協力なしには全国を平定することは不可能です。しかし、天皇は強引に律令時代への復古を求めた政策を断行し、鎌倉幕府によって培われた制度や権威、そして政策を否定します。こうした極端な**復古主義**と武士への差別行為が、新たな**社会混乱**を生み、朝廷政権からの武士の離反へとつながるのです。

楠木正成像（東京都）

建武の新政の立役者であった足利尊氏が、ついに後醍醐天皇から離反し、後醍醐天皇派の有力武将であった楠木正成、新田義貞を**湊川の戦い**で打ち破り、京都にはいります。後醍醐天皇は、最初は比叡山に、そして最終的には現在の奈良県にある吉野へと逃れ、そこに自らの朝廷を打ち立てます。

足利尊氏は、元々後醍醐天皇と対立していた皇族グループから光明天皇を擁立し、1336年に京都に政権を樹立します。そして1338年には征夷大将軍となり、正式に幕府が開かれます。室町幕府の成立です。後醍醐天皇が開いた朝廷を南朝、光明天皇による朝廷を北朝と呼びます。1392年に改めて二つの朝廷が一つにまとまるまでの南北朝時代の始まりです。

🔍 **ひとくちメモ**
湊川の戦い
建武新政の立役者、足利尊氏が後醍醐天皇派の楠木正成、新田義貞を破った戦い

In the Nanbokuchō period, not only was the Muromachi shogunate's sphere of influence weak and the two courts at war, but there were also much infighting within the shogunate itself. This was recorded for future generations in the historical epic the *Taiheiki* (Record of Great Peace). The actual author of the *Taiheiki* is unknown, but it is one of Japan's best-known epic war tales along with the *Heike Monogatari* (Tale of the Heike) about the Genji-Heike war.

Military rule developed with the political system of the shogunate and was perfected in the seventeenth century with the establishment of the Tokugawa shogunate. At the time of the Muromachi shogunate, various conflicts in the process of that growth were settled in the form of wars. First there was the discord between the Northern and Southern Courts, which arose from the tug of war between the authority of the court and the samurai. Subsequently, in the Sengoku (Warring States) period, there was a period of division and strife as the power regime became increasingly centralized and gave the samurai more power than ever. These two periods of conflict are included in the Muromachi period, under the government of the Ashikaga family that lasted for 237 years.

The Muromachi shogunate was temporarily stable under the third Ashikaga shogun, Ashikaga Yoshimitsu. The government took its name from his shogunal palace built in the Muromachi district of Kyoto in 1381.

南北朝時代は、室町幕府の地盤が軟弱で、二つの朝廷が争っていたのみならず、幕府内部の抗争も多かった時代でした。その様子は『太平記』としてまとめられ後世まで語り伝えらます。太平記は正確な著者は不明ですが、源氏と平家の抗争を綴った平家物語と共に、日本を代表する**軍記物語**として知られています。

🔍 ひとくちメモ
『太平記』
南北朝時代の2つの朝廷の争い・内部抗争をまとめた軍記物語（40巻）

　武家政権は、幕府という政治制度と共に成長し、17世紀に徳川幕府が設立した時に完成します。室町幕府の時代は、その成長の過程における様々な矛盾が戦乱という形で調整される時代です。まずは、朝廷と武家との権力を巡った綱引きが生み出した南北朝二つの政権の確執、そして次が、後年の戦国時代で、それは武士がより強力な中央集権体制へと進む過程で起きた**分裂と抗争**の時代でした。室町時代は、237年に及ぶ足利家による統治の中に、この二つの混乱の時期を含んでいます。

　室町幕府は、3代将軍足利義満の時代になってとりあえず安定します。それは室町幕府の名前となった、花の御所が、将軍家の居所として1381年に京都の室町に建てられた頃のことでした。

34 Kitayama Culture

Japanese culture can be likened to a tree.

This tree sprouted from indigenous Japanese soil. However, from the Yayoi period it was nourished by rich fertilizer brought in from the continent, and with the Buddhism imported from far off India and Middle East it benefitted not just from the new compost but also a new branch that was grafted onto it.

The tree grew rapidly and sprouted luxuriant new foliage. However, it had the fertilizer brought in from abroad running through its veins, and the grafted part had a different hue and fragrance. The Hakuhō and Tenpyō eras were the period of its beautiful young foliage.

As the tree went through the Heian period, the grafted branch was gradually assimilated by the original trunk, the nutrition from abroad was digested, and it grew into a single large tree. As its cells continued to divide, it changed and evolved. Then it was again fertilized by continental culture from the Song and Yuan Dynasties, and further flourished growing into a great tree.

This great tree symbolizes the culture of the Muromachi period.

The Muromachi shogunate brought the earlier period of confusion under control and stabilized the country, and succeeded in reconciling the Southern and Northern courts so that in 1392 the imperial court was once more unified into a single court.

While Japan was liberated from a long period of war, on the continent the Mongol rule under the Yuan Dynasty was ousted and the Han came to power under the Ming Dynasty. In order to create a solid financial base for

北山文化とは？

　日本文化を一本の木に例えます。

　それは、日本の土着の土壌から芽吹いた木です。しかし、弥生時代にはじまって大陸から滋養豊かな堆肥が持ち込まれ、仏教の伝来と共に遠くインドや中近東から肥料のみならず、新たな幹まで持ち込まれ、接ぎ木もされました。

　木はすくすくと育ち、若葉が茂ります。しかし、それは日本の外から持ち込まれた滋養が、葉脈の隅々に行き渡った木で、接ぎ木の部分は未だに違った色合いの薫る木でした。**白鳳・天平時代**はそんな美しい若葉の時代です。

　木は、平安時代を経て、次第に接ぎ木の部分が元々の幹に取り込まれ、海外からの栄養も消化され、一つの大木として伸びてゆきます。細胞分裂を繰り返す中で、変化し、進化もしてゆきます。そこに、さらに宋や元からの大陸文化が土壌に加えられ、華やぎが添えられ、大木となったのです。

　この大木の姿が室町時代の文化の特徴です。

　室町幕府が初期の混乱期を克服し安定すると、南朝と北朝の和解も進み、1392 年に朝廷は再び一つになります。

　この時代、日本は長い戦乱の時代から解放されますが、大陸ではモンゴル民族の政権である元が駆逐され、漢民族による**明**がうまれます。3代将軍の足利義満は、幕府の

ひとくちメモ

明
漢民族による国家。17世紀前半には中国全土を支配していたが、満州から勢力を伸ばしていた清によって滅ぼされた。1368–1644

the government, the third of the Ashikaga shoguns, Ashikaga Yoshimitsu, established formal diplomatic relations and started trading with the Ming. He also curbed the power of the temples that had long been a domestic problem, and gave his support to the Rinzai Zen sect.

After Yoshimitsu's death, the villa he built in the Kitayama district of Kyoto became Rokuon-ji temple, whose Golden Pavilion is one of the most representative buildings of its time. Other temples built at that time are still extant today, many of them in Kyoto, including the Zen temples known as the Gozan (Five Mountain system), which were under state protection. In addition to this Buddhist culture, it is worth mentioning the original folk dances Sarugaku and Dengaku that started to develop into the traditional arts known as Noh and Kyōgen around this time. Japanese poetry also developed further, and under Sōgi and others the *waka* form began to be read in succession, developing into the linked form known as *renga*.

Kyoto is said to have a refined culture. This can be thought to indicate a court culture unique to Japan, but in fact it represents the beautiful world of the Ashikaga culture at the height of its prosperity, the result of a global culture imported into Japan, digested, and brought to perfection in the Muromachi period. The Kitayama culture, and the Higashiyama culture that followed it, are directly connected to the aesthetic sense and sensibility of contemporary Japanese.

財政基盤を堅固なものにするために、明と正式に**国交**を開き、貿易をはじめます。また、国内では長年の課題であった寺社勢力を抑え、禅宗の一派である臨済宗を保護します。

　義満が京都の北山にたてた別荘は、彼の死後、鹿苑寺となりますが、そこにある金閣寺は当時を代表する建築物です。その他にも当時保護された**五山**と呼ばれる禅寺を中心に、現在日本、特に京都に残る多くの寺院が建設されたのも当時のことです。特筆すべきことは、こうした仏教文化に加え、元々民間の舞踊であった猿楽や田楽が、**能**や**狂言**と行った伝統芸能に進化をはじめたのもこの頃でした。和歌がさらに進化し、宗祇などによって、和歌を続けて詠み合うなかで、連歌という詩の形式が大成されたのもその頃です。

　京都の文化を雅の文化といいます。それは日本固有の宮廷文化を指すかに思えますが、実際は室町時代に完成された、グローバルな文化を日本流に消化し、足利氏の最盛期に繁栄に謳歌された美の世界を指します。北山文化とその後の東山文化は、現在の日本人の美意識や感性に直結する文化なのです。

ひとくちメモ
足利尊氏が夢窓疎石（臨済宗の禅僧。「苔寺」で知られる京都の西芳寺など、庭園の設計でも有名）に帰依して以来、臨済宗は将軍に保護された

ひとくちメモ
義満が京都の北山に建てた別荘にちなんで北山文化という

ひとくちメモ
五山・十刹
南禅寺を五山の上におき、五山に次ぐ禅寺を十刹とした。
京都五山＝天竜、相国、建仁、東福、万寿
鎌倉五山＝建長、円覚、寿福、浄智、浄沙

35 The Ōnin War

Under Ashikaga Yoshimitsu, the Muromachi shogunate took measures to secure the support of the powerful provincial military governors. While Shogun Yoshimitsu himself was the unifying force, those measures were secure. However, the fragility of the measures was exposed once the problem of the shogunal succession and the power struggles between the governors came to light.

The governors were becoming more powerful in their own domains, and were no longer mere public servants dispatched by the shogunate but powerful rulers with sovereignty over their entire area. Since the Heian period the estates and territories under the court's supervision had been assimilated, and it was becoming an established fact that the whole country was under the control of the powerful military. The governors who had thus been amassing power were called *shugo daimyo*, or military governor-turned-daimyo. The regime was supported by the delicate balance in the relationship between these shugo daimyo and the shogun at the head of the government.

Among these powerful shugo daimyo were two men called Hosokawa Katsumoto and his father-in-law, Yamana Sōzen. Both were highly influential in the shogunate, with Hosokawa holding the most important governmental position of *kanrei*, or deputy to the shogun, while Yamana was one of the powerful people in charge of military affairs. Since both had influence in the matter of the succession of the shogun and of the family heads of the powerful shugo daimyo, gradually their interests were polarized.

応仁の乱とは？

　足利義満の頃の室町幕府は、有力な守護によって将軍である義満の施政を支える体制をとっていました。将軍に求心力がある間は、その体制は安泰でした。しかし、いったん将軍の後継問題や守護間の権力闘争が顕在化したとき、室町幕府はその**体制の脆弱さ**を露呈してしまいます。

　当時、守護は自らの領国での統治権を拡大し、単に幕府の派遣した官吏というよりも、その地域全体を統治する実力者へと成長していました。平安時代以来の荘園や朝廷の直轄領もその中に吸収され、有力武士による全国支配が既成事実化してゆきました。このように力を蓄えた守護のことを、**守護大名**と呼びます。室町時代には、そうした守護大名と幕府の頂点にある征夷大将軍との微妙な均衡関係によって政権が維持されていたのです。そんな有力守護大名に細川勝元と山名宗全という人物がいました。

　彼らは特に幕府に影響力をもった存在で、細川勝元は、幕府の最も重要なポストである管領を務め、一方の山名宗全は幕府の軍務を担当した有力者の一人でした。彼らは、将軍の後継問題や他の有力守護大名の家督相続などにも影響力を持つ中で、次第に利害が対立するようになります。

The shogun at the time was Ashikaga Yoshimasa, the eighth of the Ashikaga shoguns. Yoshimasa had acceded to shogun at a young age, and he relied on powerful shugo daimyo like Hosokawa and Yamana for the actual running of the administration. These two went to war in 1467 over the issue of the succession of a certain powerful shugo daimyo. Both Hosokawa Katsumoto and Yamana Sōzen had large amounts of land in the provinces, and since they each also had the support of samurai the war spread throughout the country. Especially in Kyoto the fighting lasted for ten years in which time the whole city was almost completely burned out.

Many historical buildings were lost, and people were forced to flee by the fighting. The shogun himself escaped from Kyoto to the outskirts, and holed up in his mountain retreat at Higashiyama to the east of the city. This villa, called Ginkakuji, or Silver Pavilion, in contrast to the Golden Pavilion built by Ashikaga Yoshimitsu, is still an important building in Kyoto today.

The Ōnin War continued until 1477, even after the deaths of Hosokawa Katsumoto and Yamana Sōzen. As a result the Muromachi shogunate was weakened, and the Sengoku period of Warring States started in which rival houses vied for power. The samurai had already been at the center of history for 285 years since the times of the court and nobility. The Warring States period swept aside the conflict and opposition between the Ritsyryō (imperial) system and the military government, and was the last period of civil war before the state system centered around the samurai would be perfected.

　時の将軍は8代将軍足利義政です。義政は幼くして将軍職を継いだこともあり、政治の実態は細川や山名のような有力守護大名がつとめていました。そんな二人がある有力守護大名の家督相続への介入を巡ってついに戦をおこしてしまいます。1467年のことでした。細川勝元も山名宗全も地方に多くの領国をもっており、またそれぞれを支持する武士もいたため、戦火は全国に拡大してしまったのです。特に京都では市内が焼き尽くされるほどの戦いが10年も続きます。

　多くの歴史的にも貴重な建造物が失われ、人々は戦火に追われ逃げ惑います。将軍自身、京都から郊外に逃れ、京都の東（東山）にある山荘にこもります。この山荘は、足利義満のたてた金閣寺と対比し、銀閣寺と呼ばれ、今では京都を代表する建造物となっています。

　応仁の乱は細川勝元と山名宗全の死後、1477年まで続きます。この乱の結果、室町幕府は衰弱し、日本全国に群雄が割拠する**戦国時代**へと推移します。すでに、朝廷や貴族の世の中から、武士が歴史の中心に登場して285年。戦国時代は、律令体制と武家政権との矛盾や対立を一掃し、武士を中心とする国家体制が完成するための最後の混乱期だったのです。

銀閣寺（京都府）

36 The Higashiyama Culture

The Kitayama culture came to maturity during the Higashiyama period, when a desire for Buddhist salvation amidst the devastation of the Ōnin War led to an artistic aesthetic removed from reality.

Due to the prosperity of the Ashikaga shoguns, the Kitayama culture was a lively culture in which the Japanese arts were beginning to achieve a measure of perfection. It can be said that the Kitayama culture was digested and further refined during the Higashiyama period.

The Noh theater, started under Kan'ami and formulated by Zeami in works such as the *Kadensho* (Treatise on the Transmission of the Flower), had been highly praised by the shogun before the Ōnin War. However, it was in the flowering of the Higashiyama period that the world of *yūgen* (quiet and elegant beauty) described therein merged with the Japanese aesthetic of *wabi* (simple taste) and *sabi* (subdued refinement) to produce a new artistry.

In Noh, yūgen was the concept of the uncertain spirit world beyond human life and death. The world of wabi and sabi sought an artistry within a simple minimalism with an austere rustic aesthetic unaffected by the vicissitudes of fortune. Together with the Zen concept stressing the cultivation of the mind through meditation, it was also adopted in landscape gardening and temple construction. The fact that Zen thrived under the patronage of powerful samurai also is due to the support afforded artistic activities stressing this kind of mental world. The dry landscape gardens made of stone and sand called *karesansui* are representative of this, with the garden at Ryōanji being a world famous example.

東山文化とは

　北山文化が円熟し、応仁の乱の戦火の中で、仏教による救済への願望とも関連し、**東山文化**では現世から乖離した耽美的な芸術活動が育まれます。

　北山文化は征夷大将軍を継承する足利家の栄華のもと、日本文化の完成をも示唆できるはつらつとした文化でした。その北山文化が消化され、より洗練されたものが東山文化であるともいえます。

　観阿弥によって興され、世阿弥によって『**花伝書**』などで体系づけられた能が、時の将軍などにもてはやされたのは、応仁の乱の前のことです。しかし、そこで語られた**幽玄**の世界が「**侘び**」や「**寂び**」といった日本人の美意識と融合して、新たな芸術的境地を醸成したのが、東山文化が花開いた時代でした。

　能を通して語られた人の生死の向こうにある不確かな霊の世界を表現する「幽玄」という概念。そして、栄枯盛衰の向こうに見える枯れた世界、ひなびたものへの美意識を表現し、簡素なミニマリズムの中での芸術性を追求した「侘び」、「寂び」の世界などは、瞑想による精神修養を重んずる禅の概念と相まって、当時の造園や寺院建築の中にも取り入れられました。禅宗が有力武家によって保護され繁栄していたことも、こうした精神世界を重んずる芸術活動が支持を受けた背景にあります。枯山水と呼ばれる砂と石で表現される庭園はその代表で、京都の龍安寺の石庭な

中尊寺・白山神社能舞台（岩手県）

This philosophy of beauty was cultivated in the refined arts of the tea ceremony and flower arrangement, and through architecture was assimilated into the Japanese way of life.

The Higashiyama culture is named after the cultural activities enjoyed at the mountain villa in Kyoto's Higashiyama district to which the eighth Ashikaga shogun, Ashikaga Yoshimasa, retreated during the Ōnin War. However there were many other artists and intellectuals who fled to the provinces to escape the fighting between the prominent shugo daimyo in the capital, and they spread the Higashiyama culture throughout the country. One example is ink painting, which the artist Sesshū, under the patronage of the Ōuchi family of Yamaguchi, had studied in Ming China. As a result the traders patronized by the powerful shugo daimyo, and even some of the townspeople, also absorbed cultural pursuits such as tea, as well as the styles of homes and gardens fostered in the Higashiyama culture.

In the Sengoku period, these cultural activities spread even further throughout Japan, and as the Muromachi shogunate became weaker and less centralized, wealth also continued to spread. The Higashiyama culture, too, was part of that trend as it developed into a national culture that had a major influence on the aesthetic of Japanese people all over the country.

どは、世界的に有名です。

こうした美に対する哲学から、その後**茶道**や**華道**などといった洗練された芸道が育まれ、和建築の中での生活様式にとけ込んでゆきます。

東山文化は応仁の乱を逃れた8代将軍足利義政が京都の東山の山荘で楽しんだ文化活動にちなんで名付けられました。しかし、その後守護大名が台頭し、戦乱の京都を逃れ、多くの文化人が地方で活動したこともあり、東山文化は日本全国に伝搬してゆきます。山口の大内氏が保護した雪舟が明で学んできた**水墨画**などはその一つです。その結果、有力守護大名などに保護された商人や、さらに庶民の間でも、茶道をはじめとした文化的なたしなみや、住宅やそこの庭園などに東山文化で育まれた様式が取り入れられます。

戦国時代になるとこうした文化活動はさらに日本の隅々に浸透し、室町幕府が弱体化し、そのことによる分権が進むにつれ、富の分散がさらに進むと、東山文化はその流れに乗って、各地の日本人の美意識に大きな影響を与え、国民文化として成長するのです。

龍安寺石庭（京都府）

37 Japan's Expansion

After the Ōnin War, as war spread throughout the country, some major changes took place. Firstly, the shugo daimyo began to rule their provinces as independent states, and the shogun was reduced to a mere titular head of the samurai.

Then, during the century following the Ōnin War, the powerful regional clans gradually ousted the shugo daimyo and redrew the map of power in Japan. Furthermore, rebellions broke out here and there under leaders who fought hard and amassed power. This phenomenon was called *gekokujō*, or "the lower rules the higher." By means of this process, the ancient court system was completely eradicated.

On the other hand, the Sengoku period also represented a time when individuals were given hopes and the chance to gain power irrespective of their status. Moreover, it was a period in which the powerful samurai broke free of the fetters of state control and were able to govern their own province according to their own principles. This free atmosphere was the driving force for Japan to once again face the world and expand.

At the time, the pirates known as the Wokou were extremely active around Japan. The name Wokou was given by China to the bands of armed traders from Japan and the Korean peninsula, as well as the actual pirates who raided China. They caused a surprising amount of damage, and the Muromachi shogunate received requests from the Ming rulers in China and Korean ruler Goryeo to clamp down on them.

日本の膨張

　応仁の乱の後に日本全国に広がった戦火は、国のあり方に大きな変化をもたらしました。まず、有力守護大名が、それぞれの国を実質上は独立国として統治し、将軍は単なる武家の長としての役職のみの存在となります。

　また、応仁の乱から1世紀以内に、守護大名の統治する領国の中の有力豪族が、次第に守護大名そのものを駆逐し、日本の勢力地図が塗り替えられてゆきます。まさに、実際に汗を流して戦い、力を蓄えてきた者による革命があちこちで起きたのです。こうした現象を**下克上**と呼んでいます。この下克上の過程を通して、古代からの朝廷による秩序も完全に払拭されるのです。

　一方、戦国時代は、それまでの身分にとらわれず、一人一人にのし上がるチャンスと希望を与えた時代でもありました。さらに、国家統制という束縛を壊し、それぞれの有力な武士が、自らの国を自らの方針で統治できる時代でもありました。こうした自由な雰囲気は、日本そのものを再び世界に向けて膨張させる原動力となったのです。

　当時、日本の周辺では**倭冦**という海賊が横行していました。倭冦は、中国側の呼称ですが、それは日本人の他に朝鮮半島などにいた武装した商人の集団や、実際に海賊行為を働いていた者たちによる中国への侵攻を意味する言葉です。被害は思いの他甚大で、時の中国の王朝である明や、朝鮮半島を統治していた高麗から、倭冦を取り締まってほしいという要請が室町幕府に届いています。

The Wokou were in the vanguard of Japan's latest expansion overseas. As state control weakened, a new form of expansion began.

At the time, the Europeans were seeking a new trade route and Columbus and others went after a sea route instead of the existing continental route. One of the reasons for this was the fact that Europe was emerging from the Middle Ages and gaining independence with newly emergent empires. Politicians supported this overseas challenge as a new source of revenue.

In Japan, too, there were politicians in favor of new economic activity. In the fifteenth century, when these moves in Europe and Japan were destined to bring them in contact, for the first time in about six hundred years, Japan was embarking upon a period of overseas trade.

From an economic point of view, the Sengoku period allowed for a more liberal and broadminded activity than had been possible until now.

倭寇は日本が再び海外に向けて膨張するさきがけでした。日本が国家としての統制を解いたとき、新しい形での日本の膨張が始まったのです。

　当時、ヨーロッパでは、新たな交易ルートを求めて、**コロンブス**などが従来の陸のルートの代わりに海のルートへ挑んでいます。これも、ヨーロッパが中世を脱し、新興の王国によって分立したことが背景にあります。時の為政者が新たな収入源として、こうした海洋への挑戦を支持したのです。

　日本でも、為政者たちがそれぞれの判断で、新たな経済活動を承認します。15世紀になって、ヨーロッパと日本の二つの動きが、二つの文明の出会いへと導かれたとき、日本は約600年ぶりに、自らが望んで海外と交流する時代へと向かうのです。

　戦国時代は、経済活動でみるならば、このように今までにはない自由で闊達な活動が可能だった時代だったのです。

🔍 ひとくちメモ
コロンブス
1492年イタリア生まれ。スペイン女王の援助で、インドへの航海に出る

The Sengoku Period

For most people, the Sengoku period conjures up the image of a brutal war-torn period of suffering for the Japanese.

However, that is not the whole picture. The Sengoku period saw the decentralization of government and an increase in the power of the daimyo, who developed the provinces and allowed people to thrive through trade and cultural activities.

After the Ōnin War, the position of shogun was compromised by the 1493 Meiō Political Incident over the shogunal succession, and in the provinces some of the shugo daimyo were overthrown by their own clans and retainers. Originally, those in power in the Muromachi period maintained their position by the support of their followers — the shogun by the shugo daimyo, and the shugo daimyo by their own powerful followers — so if one's lord was foolish or there were internal disputes, it was relatively easy for those below to oust them.

At the same time, the simple teachings of the Jōdo Shinshū sect started by Shinran were spreading throughout the provinces. They were called the Ikkō (single-minded) sect by other sects. The followers often confronted the shugo daimyo, especially in the fifteenth century when Rennyo organized believers at Hongan-ji. In Kaga, the Ikkō followers drove out the shugo daimyo and self-governed the domain themselves. These rebellions by Ikkō followers are known as the Ikkō-ikki Revolts.

In the sixteenth century, the new feudal lords that rose to power under *gekokujō* (lower rules the higher) ruled their domains as Sengoku daimyo.

戦国時代はどのように推移した？

　戦国時代というと、日本中が戦乱に苦しみ、血で血を洗う乱世であったような印象を持つ人も多いでしょう。

　しかし、実態は必ずしもそうではありません。戦国時代は強大化した戦国大名による分権の時代であり、彼らによって、地方が開発され、商業や文化活動を通して人々が活発に活動できた時代だったのです。

　応仁の乱のあと、将軍の後継争いによって 1493 年の**明応の政変**がおきると、以後将軍の権威は完全に失墜し、地方では多くの守護大名がその一族や家臣によって滅ぼされるという事件がおこります。元々、室町時代には将軍は守護大名に、守護大名は自らの有力配下に支えられその地位を維持していたため、主君が暗愚であったり、内部抗争がおきたりすれば、下の地位の者が上の地位の者にとって代わることは、比較的容易だったのです。

　また、地方では、親鸞の興した浄土真宗がそのわかりやすい教えをもって、全国に広がります。彼らのことを他の宗派は一向宗とよびます。特に 15 世紀に蓮如によって、本願寺を中心に門徒の組織化がすすむと、信徒がしばしば、地方の守護大名とも対立しました。加賀では、そんな対立によって、守護大名が追い出され、**一向宗門徒**による自治が行われたこともありました。こうした一向宗門徒による反乱を**一向一揆**と呼んでいます。

　16 世紀には、下克上によってのし上がってきた新たな領主が戦国大名として領国を支配します。彼らの勢力の伸

As they gained power, skirmishes and wars flared up around the country. Many stories of the fighting around the country have been handed down, such as the battles between Takeda Shingen, whose extensive power was centered in (Yamanashi prefecture) and Uesugi Kenshin, ruler of Echigo (Niigata prefecture), as well as the overthrow of the Ōuchi family of Suō (Yamaguchi prefecture) by their retainers, after which the Mōri clan came to power.

On the other hand, in order to increase the wealth of their domains, the Sengoku daimyo encouraged economic activity, brought in artists from Kyoto and elsewhere, and invested in their domains. With the promotion of commerce and industry, towns grew up around the castles of the Sengoku daimyo. A major feature of the period was the promotion of commerce, as the privileges conferred upon the merchants who enjoyed the patronage of the former shugo daimyo and nobility were abolished in favor of establishing free markets and open guilds to guarantee free trade and commerce. Having extended their power with the overthrow of neighboring domains and ensured the success of the economy, the Sengoku daimyo eventually started openly expressing an ambition to reunify the country.

長とともに、日本各地で小競り合いや、戦争が勃発するのです。甲斐（現在の山梨県）を中心に勢力を拡大した武田信玄と、越後（現在の新潟県）の覇者となった上杉謙信との争いや、周防（現在の山口県）に君臨していた守護大名大内氏が家臣に滅ぼされ、さらに毛利氏にとって代わられるなど、長く語り伝えられる攻防と興亡の物語が日本各地で見受けられます。

上杉謙信

　一方、戦国大名は、自らの領国を豊かにするために、進んで経済活動を促進させ、京都などから文化人を呼んで領国に投資します。そして、戦国大名の居城は、城下町として商工業が振興し、人口も増えてゆきます。また、旧来の守護大名や貴族の保護によって特権化していた御用商人などを排除し、自由な交易や商業活動を保証した**楽市楽座**が設けられるなど、商業が振興したのも当時の特徴です。領国の経営に成功し、他国を圧倒し勢力を伸長させた戦国大名は、やがて国の再統一に向けた野望をあらわにしてゆくのです。

39 The Arrival of Guns and Christianity

It was precisely because the Sengoku period was an era of civil war that two things introduced into Japan at this time were necessary. One was the tool of massacre, the gun, while the other was the religion counselling love and the salvation of the soul. The guns arrived with the Portuguese who drifted ashore the island of Tanegashima in 1543, while Christianity arrived six years later with the missionary Francis Xavier.

Needless to say, the introduction of guns greatly changed the concept of warfare in the Sengoku period. Also, Christianity arrived with the trading ships and was patronized by many of the Sengoku daimyo, with some of them even converting to Christianity. Ōtomo Sōrin, the Lord of Bungo (Oita prefecture), was one of these so-called Christian daimyo.

This was the result of the Age of Discovery in Europe. In the sixteenth century, both Spain and Portugal established bases in Manila and actively pursued trade in East Asia. Since Marco Polo, who had visited Yuan China, had introduced Japan as the "country of gold" in his *Books of the Marvels of the World* (or, *The Travels of Marco Polo*), they gathered further information in China and then headed their ships for Japan. Europe was not the only part of the world to engage in trade overseas; China and South East Asia contributed to propagating their products in Japan, and also in informing Western Europe about Japan's civilization. In 1582, at the end of the Sengoku period, the Christian daimyo dispatched an envoy called the Tenshō Embassy to Rome.

The arrival of trading ships from far-off lands also inspired the

鉄砲とキリスト教の伝来が
日本にもたらしたものは？

　戦国時代には、戦いの時代だからこそ必要な二つのものが日本に伝来します。一つが殺戮の道具である**鉄砲**、そしてもう一つが愛と魂の救済を諭す**宗教**です。鉄砲が種子島に漂着したポルトガル人によってもたらされたのは1543年。そしてその6年後には**フランシスコ・ザビエル**によってキリスト教が伝導されます。

　いうまでもなく、鉄砲の伝来は、戦国時代の戦いの概念を大きく変えました。そしてキリスト教は交易船と共にもたらされたこともあって、多くの戦国大名から保護され、中にはキリスト教に改宗する大名まであらわれました。現在の大分県にあたる豊後の大名、大友宗麟はそのひとりで、こうした大名はキリシタン大名と呼ばれました。

　これは、ヨーロッパでの大航海時代の賜物です。16世紀、ポルトガルはマカオに、スペインはマニラに拠点を設けて、東アジアでの交易に積極的でした。彼らは、中国の元を訪れた**マルコ・ポーロ**が、著書『**東方見聞録**』で、日本を黄金の国と紹介したことから、中国でさらに情報を収集し、日本へ船出したのです。航海による交易は、単にヨーロッパのものだけではなく、中国や東南アジアの商品の日本への伝搬にも一層貢献し、同時に日本の文物が西欧に伝わりもしました。戦国時代の終末期である1582年には、キリシタン大名が、**天正少年使節**と呼ばれる使節をローマ法皇庁に派遣しています。

　遥か海の向こうからの交易船の到来は、日本人にも新

🔍 ひとくちメモ
フランシスコ・ザビエル
カトリック教会の司祭、宣教師でイエズス会の創設メンバーの1人。1549年に日本に初めてキリスト教を伝えた。1506–1552

フランシスコ・ザビエル

🔍 ひとくちメモ
マルコ・ポーロ
ヴェネツィア共和国の商人、旅行家。『東方見聞録』を口述したとされる。1254–1324

Japanese to again dream of overseas. Traders were making enormous profits, especially from the importation and sale of firearms to the Sengoku daimyo, and Sakai prospered as a city-state created by those merchants. They were also active in South East Asia, setting up Japanese settlements in various countries. The Japanese Age of Discovery had arrived — the latest instance of Japanese people actively seeking international exchange. The vestiges of those Japanese settlements remain even now in places like Hoi An in central Vietnam. With the economic stimulus measures of the Sengoku daimyo business was brisk, and the spread of the monetary economy stimulated trade with Europe and Asia.

In 1575, one Sengoku daimyo who had risen quickly to power, and also patronized Christianity, acquired guns through trade and created a new army with which he famously defeated the cavalry of the powerful Sengoku daimyo Takeda at the Battle of Nagashino. This was Oda Nobunaga who, as the winner of this battle and the last victor of the Sengoku period, set the stage for the reunification of Japan.

たな海外への夢を育みます。特に鉄砲の輸入と戦国大名
への販売は、商人に莫大な利益をもたらし、堺はそんな商
人たちによって造られた都市国家として繁栄します。彼ら
は逆に東南アジアに積極的に進出し、各地に日本人町を
建設します。日本人にとっての大航海時代の到来であり、
それは、日本人が自ら積極的に海外に交易を求めた珍し
い事例となりました。ベトナム中部の**ホイアン**などには、
そうした日本人町の名残が今も残っています。戦国大名の
経済振興策で、商業活動が活発になり、貨幣経済が浸透
したことが、西欧やアジアとの交易を刺激したのです。

1575 年、急速に台頭してきた 1 人の戦国大名が、キリ
スト教を保護し、交易によって入手した鉄砲で新手の軍団
を造り、有力な戦国大名であった武田の騎馬軍団を打ち
破るという事件がおきました。有名な**長篠の合戦**です。こ
の戦いに勝利した織田信長こそが、戦国時代の最後の勝
者として、日本の**再統一**へ王手をかけるのです。

🔍 ひとくちメモ
ホイアン
ベトナム中部の港町。鎖国に
入るまで日本人街が栄えた

🔍 ひとくちメモ
種子島の島主、種子島時尭(ときたか)がポ
ルトガル人から鉄砲を購入し、
家臣にその製法を学ばせた。鉄
砲が、「種子島」という名で国
内に広まり、生産されるように
なった背景には、日本の刀鍛冶
の技術力があった

40 Oda Nobunaga

All turning points in history require someone to break with the past.

This person emerge from the old system, but dares to start a wave of opposition to the conservative ways of that system, and is sometimes destroyed along with it. Alternatively, an outsider might carry out revolutionary subversive activities.

The Oda clan served as vice-governor of Owari (Aichi prefecture) and rose to be the Sengoku daimyo for Owari; they had come from the old system and rose to power through *gekokujō* to take center stage in history. Oda Nobunaga, however, was probably someone who intended to destroy the system from outside. Born to the position of lord of a small province as head of the Oda family, he killed the powerful *shugo daimyo* Imagawa Yoshimoto of the neighboring province in a surprise attack, and subsequently subjugated everywhere from Owari through Mino. In 1568 he entered Kyoto, installed Ashikaga Yoshiaki as the fifteenth shogun, and assumed the leadership.

In 1571 he attacked Mount Hiei, which had wielded such strong influence over politicians since the Heian period, murdering many monks. Then in 1573 he drove out Ashikaga Yoshiaki, who had started opposing him, and effectively ousted the Muromachi shogunate. Subsequently, thinking that Ikkō-ikki had been wiped out, he supported Christianity and actively imported western European culture and institutions. In order to do this, he imposed restrictions on Sakai, the thriving trading town, and purchased large numbers of firearms with which to arm his troops to overpower the Takeda clan of Kai. News of his actions reached as far afield

織田信長とはどんな人物？

　歴史の転換点には、**過去を壊す人**が必要になります。

　その人は、旧体制側にいて、あえてその保守的な行動によって旧体制そのものへの反発の波をおこし、体制とともに滅びてゆくこともあります。また、ある人は外からやってきて革命的な破壊活動を行います。

　尾張（現愛知県）の守護の代官を務め、そのまま尾張の戦国大名にのし上がった織田家は、旧来の制度の中から下克上によって歴史の表舞台に出てきた一族です。しかし、小国の主であった織田家の当主として生まれ、隣国の有力守護大名である今川義元を奇襲によって殺害し、その後尾張から美濃一帯を平定した後に 1568 年に京都に入り、15 代将軍足利義昭を担ぎ出して天下に覇を唱えようとした織田信長は、外から体制を破壊しようと試みた人物かも知れません。

　1571 年には、平安時代以来、為政者への強い影響力を維持してきた比叡山を攻撃し、多くの僧侶を殺害します。次に、織田信長と対立しはじめた足利義昭を 1573 年に京都から追放し、室町幕府を実質上滅ばします。その後、一向一揆を壊滅させたかと思えば、キリスト教を保護し、西欧の文物の輸入を積極的に行います。そのために、商業都市として繁栄していた堺を抑えて鉄砲を大量に購入し、その鉄砲隊の威力で甲斐の武田氏を圧倒します。こうした彼の活動は、ポルトガルの宣教師などによってヨーロッ

as Europe through the Portuguese missionaries and others.

Nobunaga was also innovative in terms of employing his own followers. He is famous for the unusual move of singling out Kinoshita Tōkichirō, who had been born into a family of the lowest samurai rank, and promoting him as his own powerful retainer. This Tōkichirō was none other than the man who reunified the land after Nobunaga's death, Toyotomi Hideyoshi.

Nobunaga built Azuchi Castle overlooking Lake Biwa to the northeast of Kyoto, where he established free markets and open guilds. At the same time he abolished checkpoints and aimed to establish a powerful centralized state with himself as the supreme political sovereign.

With these creative measures and military talents, Nobunaga unified central Japan in 1582 and advanced his soldiers further west and to the north.

However, in June that year, his retainer Akechi Mitsuhide betrayed him and he was killed in a surprise attack in Kyoto known as the Incident at Honnōji.

Oda Nobunaga was despot who brought the Sengoku period to a close and opened the door to a new era.

パにも伝えられました。

　信長は自らの配下への人事でも革新的でした。彼が武士の身分の中で最も低い足軽の家に生まれた木下藤吉郎を抜擢し、最終的には自らの有力家臣へと昇進させた異例の人事を行ったのは有名です。この藤吉郎こそが、信長の死後天下を統一する豊臣秀吉に他なりません。

　信長は京都の北東、琵琶湖に面した安土に安土城を建設し、そこに自由な商業活動を保証した**楽市楽座**を設けます。同時に**関所**を撤廃し、政治の上では絶対君主のように、自らを頂点とした強力な中央集権国家の創立を目指します。

　この独創的な政策と天才的な軍事能力によって、信長は 1582 年には中部日本を統一し、さらに兵を西、そして北へと進めます。

　しかし、その年の 6 月に、彼の有力な家臣、明智光秀の裏切りにあい、京都で奇襲を受けて死亡します。このクーデターを**本能寺の変**といいます。

　織田信長は、戦国時代を終焉に導き、新しい時代への扉を開いた独裁者だったのです。

41 Toyotomi Hideyoshi and the Reunification of Japan

Toyotomi Hideyoshi is an extraordinary figure in Japanese history, having risen from the lowliest samurai rank through repeated promotions by Oda Nobunaga.

When Oda Nobunaga was killed by Akechi Mitsuhide, Hideyoshi was on the front line of battle with the Mōri clan in western Honshu.

When the news of the Incident at Honnōji reached him, he kept it secret and reached a compromise with the powerful general of the Mōri, before returning in haste to Kyoto with his soldiers to defeat Akechi Mitsuhide. Then, having put a system in place with himself firmly in the leadership, he set out to conquer his rivals. The year after Nobunaga's death, he built Osaka Castle and made it his base in place of Azuchi Castle, which had burned down when Nobunaga was killed.

Not long after this, he went to war with Nobunaga's close friend and biggest rival Tokugawa Ieyasu, eventually reaching a truce and making Ieyasu his subject. Many other powerful daimyo were also likewise brought under Hideyoshi's wing by means of his talent for skillful coercion and diplomacy. And in 1590 he destroyed the Hōjō clan of Odawara who had resisted until the last, finally putting an end to the Sengoku period that had lasted for a hundred years since the Ōnin Wars.

With the destruction of the Hōjō clan, Toyotomi Hideyoshi installed Tokugawa Ieyasu in Edo (present-day Tokyo), thus bringing Kanto under his possession. The imperial court promoted Hideyoshi to their highest ranks of *kanpaku* (regent) and *dajō daijin* (grand minister), and the people called Hideyoshi by the honorific title of Taikō Hideyoshi.

豊臣秀吉はどのようにして日本を統一した？

　最下層の武士から身を起こし、織田信長に見いだされて昇進を重ね、信長の死後に天下を統一した豊臣秀吉は、日本史上希有な存在といえましょう。

　織田信長が明智光秀に殺されたとき、秀吉は本州の西部を領有していた毛利氏との戦いの最前線にいました。

　本能寺の変のニュースが伝わると、それを秘密にしたままに毛利側の有力武将と和解をし、自らの兵と共に瞬く間に京都に戻り、明智光秀を打ち破ります。そして、自身が主導して織田信長亡き後の体制を固め、さらに彼と敵対するライバルを攻め滅ぼします。信長の死の翌年には、大阪に大阪城を建設し、信長の死と共に焼失した安土城に代って、そこを自らの拠点にしたのです。

　それから間もなく、信長の盟友で、最大のライバルでもあった徳川家康との戦いの後、家康と**和睦**し、臣従させます。同様に多くの有力大名が秀吉の巧みな威圧と外交の才によって次々と傘下となります。そして 1590 年に最後まで抵抗を続けた小田原の北条氏を滅ぼし、遂に応仁の乱以来 100 年以上続いた戦国時代を終焉させたのでした。

　豊臣秀吉は、北条氏が滅びると、江戸（現東京）に徳川家康をおき、関東を領有させます。朝廷は、秀吉に**関白**、そして**太政大臣**という、朝廷での最高位を与え、人々は秀吉のことを太閤秀吉と呼びました。

Hideyoshi made a nationwide survey of the rice crop yield and used this data to forcibly transfer land between daimyo. He also collected weapons from farming villages, established a system of distinguishing warriors from farmers by making samurai professional soldiers, and instituted the four distinct classes of warriors, farmers, artisans, and tradesmen under a large-scale family register census. This disarmament of farmers was known as the *katanagari*, or "sword hunt." He was also vigilant of Portuguese territorial ambitions in Japan, and in 1587 issued a decree banning proselytizing by Christian missionaries.

The period from Oda Nobunaga to Toyotomi Hideyoshi is called the Azuchi-Momoyama period. Oda Nobunaga laid the groundwork for the unification of Japan, and Toyotomi Hideyoshi succeeded in bringing it about, not merely in terms of the land itself but by directing national surveys to bring the people and land under a state system.

Controling the samurai was not just a matter of force, but in order to eclipse the past system of private estates and Ritsuryō system there was a need to gain control of the land and its productivity, and to perfect a class system with the samurai at the top. Hideyoshi subjugated the entire country, and initiated an era of centralized samurai rule that, unlike the previous Kamakura and Muromachi shogunates, did not include the nobility and the temples.

秀吉は、全国を米の収穫高に基づき検地し、その資料を元に有力大名の国替えなどを実施します。また、農村から武器を徴収し、武士が職業軍人として農民から区別されるよう制度化し、大規模な**戸籍調査**を行い**士農工商という身分制度**を固定化します。この農村での武器徴収のことを刀狩りと呼んでいます。また、ポルトガルなどの日本への領土的な野心を警戒し、宣教師のキリスト教の**布教を禁止する**禁教令を 1587 年に発布しています。

　織田信長から豊臣秀吉に至る時代を、安土桃山時代と呼びます。織田信長が全国統一の礎を築き、それを引き継いだ豊臣秀吉が、単に領土の上だけではなく、検地などを通して人と土地を国家制度の中に組み込んで統率していったのです。

　武士の支配が力の支配だけでなく、過去の荘園制度や律令制度を凌駕してゆくためには、土地と生産力を把握し、**武士を頂点とした身分制度**を完成させる必要がありました。秀吉が全国を平定したとき、以前の鎌倉幕府や室町幕府とは異なった、貴族や寺社を排除した武士による日本の一元支配が完成したのです。

🔍 ひとくちメモ
秀吉の施策として有名なのが検地と刀狩り。全国を米の収穫高に基づき検地し、全国の国替えに利用する、また農村から武器を徴収することで、一揆を抑え、兵農分離を進めた

Part 3

Feudal Japan
幕末体制下の日本

幕藩体制下の日本

　江戸時代というと、わたしたちは即座に鎖国し、厳しい禁教令が布かれ、日本独自の文化が花開いた時代であるとイメージします。

　それは、一面事実です。実は、この時代、お隣りの中国でも清朝が勃興し日本と同じように鎖国に近い政策を実施していました。その影響は朝鮮半島にもおよんでいたため、極東諸地域は、ヨーロッパが近世へと時代を進め、産業革命を経験しようとしていたときに、丸ごと世界から閉ざされていたことになります。

　しかし、面白いことに、今世界でもてはやされている日本文化の多くが、江戸時代が起源なのです。浮世絵もそうであれば、世界語となった Sushi（寿司）の起源も江戸時代です。さらにアニメや漫画の原点を浮世絵にみるとするならば、世界中で愛好されている日本文化のかなりのものが、江戸時代に芽吹いたことになります。

　徳川幕府による鎖国の決定には、旧教国であるスペインやポルトガルと新教国であるオランダとの確執も影響しました。そして、日本ではオランダに軍配があがり、オランダは以後長崎の出島で交易を続けます。そして、出島から西欧に輸出された商品の多くは、ヨーロッパの王室や貴族社会の調度品にも使用され、後年の西欧での日本趣味の原点となりました。

このように、日本が世界との交流を閉ざしている間も、世界はさまざまな角度から日本を見つめていたことになります。

江戸時代を英語で説明するとき、その文化活動にふれることがきわめて大切な理由はこうしたことにあるのです。

一方、海外の人にわかりにくいのが、大名と将軍との関係でしょう。地方の政権を担った大名は、いわば独立国の王でした。従って、英語ではlordと表現し、その上に君臨していた将軍と区別します。しかし、将軍をkingとすれば、その上の権威である天皇 (emperor) との説明が難しくなります。ですから、多くの場合将軍は軍事独裁者 (military dictator) として、Shogunのままで表記されます。実際、今ではShogunはベストセラー小説のタイトルにもなったため、英語としても定着しており、その言葉を知る欧米の人も増えているのです。

42 Tokugawa Ieyasu

After the confusion of the Sengoku period, and indeed ever since Minamoto no Yoritomo had established the Kamakura shogunate, Japan had experienced the inconsistencies of the growing military regime and it would take three talented statesmen to stabilize the nation once more.

Oda Nobunaga laid the foundations, Toyotomi Hideyoshi unified the country, and their successor Tokugawa Ieyasu established a new shogunate in Edo.

Tokugawa Ieyasu was born in 1542 in Mikawa, the son of a minor daimyo. Though he experienced many difficulties, he expanded his own power by forming an alliance with the increasingly powerful Oda Nobunaga. Although he proved a match for Toyotomi Hideoyoshi in battle, he ultimately went over to Hideyoshi's side and made a strong base in Edo as one of the "five *Tairō*" (the council of five elders appointed by Hideyoshi to rule until his son Hideyori came of age).

Toyotomi Hideyoshi made an error at the end of his life by appointing his infant son Toyotomi Hideyori as his successor instead of his heir apparent, his nephew Toyotomi Hidetsugu. Also, when diplomatic relations with Ming China and the Yi Dynasty, then in control of the Korean peninsula, grew tense he assembled an army in Kyushu and twice invaded Korea, in 1592 and again in 1597, inflicting enormous damage. This dispatch of troops also incurred great losses on the part of the daimyo he had mobilized, and accelerated the backlash against Ishida Mitsunari, Toyotomi Hideyoshi's favorite retainer who was then head of the government.

徳川家康は、どのようにして幕府を開いた？

　戦国時代の混乱を経て、また源頼朝が鎌倉幕府を開いて以来成長してきた武士の長による統治体制の様々な矛盾を経て、日本が、国家として安定するには、3人の天才的な為政者の存在が必要でした。

　織田信長が土台をつくり、豊臣秀吉が日本を統一し、それを引き継ぎ新たな幕府をつくったのが、江戸を拠点として成長した徳川家康でした。

　徳川家康は、三河地方の**小さな大名**の子供として1542年に生まれ、様々な苦労を重ねながらも、織田信長の伸長とともに信長と同盟して勢力を拡大した人物です。豊臣秀吉とは互角に戦いながらも、最終的にはその政権に参加し、**五大老**の1人として江戸に盤石な地盤を築きました。

　豊臣秀吉は、晩年にその政策にほころびができます。跡継ぎに指定した甥の豊臣秀次を廃し、遅くに生まれた我が子秀頼を後継者にします。また、中国の明や当時朝鮮半島を支配していた**李氏朝鮮**との外交関係が緊張すると、九州に兵を集結させ、朝鮮に1592年と97年2度に渡り侵入し、朝鮮に甚大な被害を与えます。この出兵は動員された大名にも大きな負担を与え、当時の政権を指導していた豊臣秀吉の**寵臣**石田三成への反発も加速します。

🔍 **ひとくちメモ**
文禄・慶長の役
中国明や李氏朝鮮との外交関係が緊張すると、秀吉は2度にわたって朝鮮に出兵。朝鮮に甚大な被害を与える

李氏朝鮮
朝鮮半島最後の王朝。李朝とも。1392-1910

When Toyotomi Hideyoshi passed away in 1598, the dispatch of troops to Korea was halted. Then when Maeda Toshiie, who had been a close ally and supporter of Hideyoshi, died a year later the schism between government factions intensified and the powerful daimyo separated into two camps. The anti-Ishida faction was led by Tokyogawa Ieyasu and in the end these two men clashed at Sekigahara, midway between Kyoto and Nagoya, in 1600. The Battle of Sekigahara, said to be the decisive confrontation, was concluded in just one day, with Tokugawa Ieyasu the victor. Ishida Mitsunari was executed in Kyoto not long afterwards.

Tokugawa Ieyasu consolidated his powerbase of daimyo friendly to him, and in 1603 was appointed shogun and established his shogunate in Edo.

With Oda Nobudaga as destroyer, Toyotomi Hideyoshi as creator, and Tokugawa Ieyasu as ruler, these three strong-minded men unwittingly took over the baton of change in history and led Japan towards unification and the modern era.

At the Tōshōgū Shrine in Nikko, built for Tokugawa Ieyasu, there are three portable mikoshi shrines that understandably deify these three men. Their great efforts were only possible due to the collapse of the old ways in favor of the meritocracy and *gekokujō* (lower ruling the higher) during the Sengoku period.

1598年に豊臣秀吉が死去し、朝鮮への出兵は中止されます。そして、その翌年に盟友として秀吉を支えていた前田利家が秀吉の後を追うように亡くなると、内部分裂が激化し、有力大名が2分されます。反石田の勢力を束ねていたのが徳川家康で、ついにこの2者は1600年に京都と名古屋の中間にある関ヶ原で衝突します。天下分け目の合戦といわれた**関ヶ原の戦い**は、一日で決着がつき、徳川家康側が勝利。石田三成は間もなく京都で処刑されます。

　徳川家康は、自らに味方した大名を中心にその地盤を固め、1603年に征夷大将軍に任命され江戸に幕府を開いたのです。

　織田信長は破壊者、豊臣秀吉は創造者、そして徳川家康は統治者として、この3人が、強烈な個性をもって、自らの意志ではないにせよ、歴史の転換のバトンを引き継ぎながら、日本を近代へとまとめてゆきました。

　徳川家康を祀る神社として知られる日光東照宮には、3体の神輿があります。それがこの3人を祀る神輿であることを考えれば、そのことがよく理解できます。3人が活躍できた土壌、それは旧習が壊され、下克上と実力主義に支えられた戦国時代だったのです。

日光東照宮にある徳川家康の墓（栃木県）

43 The Azuchi-Momoyama Culture

Toyotomi Hideyoshi's dispatch of troops to the Korean peninsula was a mistake in terms of both foreign relations and domestic politics.

However, the reason he turned his sights to the mainland was due to the need for expansion of the island nation at the end of the Sengoku period. Historically, the first wave of expansion since Yamato and Hakuhō eras was prompted by contact with western European culture.

Let's take the example of ceramics. With the dispatch of troops to Korea, many Korean potters were forced to move to Japan, with the result that continental ceramics took root in Japan with Kyushu at the center of pottery manufacture. Many pieces produced here were in turn taken home to western European countries such as Holland and had a major influence on European ceramics, especially in Germany with Meissen being a prime example.

A sophisticated globalism can be seen in the two-way cultural exchange between east and west.

In Japan, the culture from western Europe is known as the Nanban (southern barbarian) culture. Their manners and customs are depicted in paintings on folding screens of the time. A glimpse of European painting techniques can also be seen in these *byōbu*, and they are more colorful and picturesque than traditional Japanese paintings. As with ceramics, many of these were taken back to Europe where they also influenced decoration of palace architecture. The ancient Silk Road was blocked by the Islamic

安土桃山文化とは

豊臣秀吉が**朝鮮半島に出兵**したことは外交上からも、内政的にも失政でした。

しかし、彼が大陸へと目を向けた背景は、戦国時代以降の日本にあった"島国からの膨張志向"に深く関わっています。歴史上、大和、白鳳時代に継ぐ、第二の波を海外に向けた日本は、当時西欧からの文化融合にも影響されました。

陶器を例にとってみます。朝鮮出兵で朝鮮の陶工の多くは日本に移住させられ、大陸の陶器が日本に根付き、九州で陶芸が盛んに行われます。こうして生まれた作品の多くは、逆にオランダをはじめとした日本に接触した西欧の国々によって本国に持ち帰られ、ドイツをはじめとした各地の陶芸活動に大きな影響を与えます。マイセンなどはその典型です。

文化活動が西から東へ、そして東から西へと行き来する中で洗練されていったグローバリズムをここにみることができるのです。

日本では、西欧からの文化を**南蛮**文化と呼んでいました。彼らの風俗が当時の屏風絵等に描かれます。こうした屏風絵には西欧の絵画技術の片鱗もみられ、伝統的な日本画がより華やかにかつ豪快に変化し彩られます。多くは、陶器と同様に西欧にも伝えられ、西欧の宮殿建築などの装飾にも影響を与えるのです。古代のシルクロードは、当時イスラム勢力によって分断され、その代替として開かれた

empire at the time, and the alternative sea routes connected the furthest extreme of Europe with Japan at the edge of the Far East. As mentioned earlier, the Japanese also participated in the exchange, sailing as far as the midway point where they established colonies.

The Azuchi-Momoyama period was a time when the country was headed for stability. Castles were built for defensive and military purposes, and as the homes of the politicians were also beginning to function as the seat of government. Therefore, they began to require stylish decoration. Artists such as Kanō Eitoku, the leader of the Kanō school, was actively involved in painting the walls and doors of Osaka Castle, the Jurakudai mansion, and Fushimi Castle in Kyoto, all built by Toyotomi Hideyoshi. Also, the tea ceremony started in the Muromachi period became a popular pastime of the samurai, and Sen no Rikyu, the Sakai tradesman known for his mastery of the tea ceremony, was highly valued by Toyotomi Hideyoshi. Tearooms were a place for the samurai to reflect, as well as for social gatherings.

In the Azuchi-Momoyama period the merchant culture thrived under the patronage of the samurai class. It was at this time that the *kosode* kimono, originally the underwear worn by court nobles, became a fashionable garment for the samurai and later for the merchant class.

海のルートが、西の端のヨーロッパと東の端の日本とをつないだのです。日本人もその中間点まで船を出し、植民地を造り、この交流に貢献をしたことはすでに説明した通りです。

　安土桃山時代は、国が安定に向かった時代です。城郭は防衛的、軍事的な建築物から、為政者の居城であり、行政府として機能しはじめます。従って、自ずと、城郭建築の中にも瀟洒な装飾が求められるようになってゆきます。豊臣秀吉が立てた大阪城、京都の聚楽第や伏見城には、その建築物を彩る障壁画などが描かれ、狩野永徳などに代表される狩野派の画家が活躍します。また、室町時代に始まった**茶の湯**も武士のたしなみとしてもてはやされ、堺の商人で茶人としても知られた千利休などが豊臣秀吉に重用されます。茶の湯の場は有力武士にとっての思考の場であり、会合の場ともなったのです。

千利休

　安土桃山時代は、このように、有力武士階級によって庇護された町人文化が栄えます。元々公家（貴族）の下着であった小袖が洗練され、武士によって実用的なファッションとして流行し、町人階級へと広がったのも当時のことでした。

The Tokugawa Shogunate

Tokugawa Ieyasu was appointed shogun in 1603 and established the Tokugawa shogunate. Two years later he announced he was abdicating in favor of his son Hidetada and the Tokugawa clan there after ruled officially the head of the samurai. In 1614 and 1615 he twice attacked Toyotomi Hideyori at Osaka Castle, destroying the Toyotomi clan and finally completing the unification of the country. These two stages in the Siege of Osaka are known as the Winter Campaigns and Summer Campaigns.

Succession in the Tokugawa shogunate was restricted to the branches of the family known as "three houses of the Tokugawa" in Mito, Owari (Nagoya), and Kii (Wakayama). Daimyo of long-standing support, known as *fudai* daimyo (hereditary vassals), were placed in strategic positions for governing the country such as around Edo, and given the opportunity to participate in the shogunate. The rest of the daimyo were called *tozama* daimyo (outsiders) and were assigned to distant provinces.

Retainers of the Tokugawa in Edo were divided into the high status *hatamoto* (direct retainers to the shogun) and the lower ranking *gokenin* (low-level retainers) and employed as administrators or soldiers. They were known as *jikisan* (immediate vassals), and in effect became an army guarding Edo. All in all there were some fifty thousand jikisan. The shogunate gave them a *han* (domain) under their direct control as daimyo and allowed them autonomy. However, each han was allowed only one castle, and even repairs required the permission of the shogunate. Also, many daimyo were obliged to take up residence in Edo on alternate years,

徳川幕府はどのようにして日本を支配した？

　徳川家康は 1603 年に征夷大将軍となって、徳川幕府を開きますが、その 2 年後には将軍職を子の秀忠に譲り、以後徳川家が武士の長として君臨することを公にします。1614 年から 15 年にかけて、大阪城の豊臣秀頼を 2 度にわたって攻めて、豊臣氏を滅ぼし、名実共に全国を統一します。この 2 度の戦いを大阪**冬の陣**、そして**夏の陣**と呼んでいます。

　徳川幕府は、自らの親戚を御三家とし、水戸、尾張 (名古屋)、紀伊 (和歌山) に配置し、昔からの恩顧の大名を、江戸周辺をはじめ、国内を治める要所におき、幕政への参加の機会を与えます。こうした大名を**譜代大名**といいます。それ以外の大名は**外様大名**と呼ばれ、遠隔地に配置されます。

　江戸には徳川家の直接の家臣で身分の高い者を**旗本**、それ以下を**御家人**として居住させ、役人、軍人として勤務させます。彼らは**直参**と呼ばれ、実質上江戸を守る常備軍となりました。直参は、家来までいれると 5 万人以上に及びます。幕府は大名には彼らの直轄地として**藩**を与え、**自治**を許します。ただし、一つの藩に城郭は一つに制限され、改修なども幕府の許可を必要としました。また、多くの大名は一年毎の江戸での居住が義務づけられ、妻子は江戸に留め置かれます。この制度を参勤交代と呼び、大名の

and to leave their wife and children in Edo. This system, called *sankin kōtai*, was a strain on the daimyo's finances, further compounded by the shogunate's frequent orders for daimyo to undertake public works or restoration of Edo castle. Meanwhile, all around the country territories other than the han were placed under the direct control of the shogunate and called *tenryō*.

The imperial court existed, but the Tokugawa shogunate had shored up the weak points of the Kamakura and Muromachi shogunates to become the enormously powerful rulers of the country. The Kamakura period had had a legal system in the Goseibai Shikimoku, but in the Edo period the *Buke Shohatto* (Laws Governing Military Households) laid out the duties of the samurai in even finer detail.

In emergencies, the *tairō* (chief minister to the shogun) advised the government, while in peacetime the *rōjū* (senior councilor), a powerful *fudai* daimyo, took care of affairs of state. Various public offices called *bugyōsho* (magistrate's office) were established in Edo to govern affairs of state, temple management, the police force and so forth, and were run by the hatamoto and gokenin. The system of government by the Tokugawa shogunate and the regional han, with the shogun as ruler, was called the *bakuhan taisei* (shogunate-han system).

Thereafter, for 263 years, this foundation for ruling the entire country was perfected by the Tokugawa regime.

財政を圧迫します。また、幕府はしばしば江戸城の修復や公共事業も大名に命じています。一方、藩以外の土地は幕府の直轄地として**天領**と呼ばれ、全国に広がっています。

🔍 ひとくちメモ
天領で生産される米の量（石高）は、全国の石高の25%にもおよび、それが幕府の財政を支えていた

このように、朝廷は存在するものの、徳川幕府は、鎌倉、室町幕府の弱点を補強し、強大な権力をもって全国を統治します。鎌倉時代に御成敗式目という武士を統制する法律がありましたが、江戸時代には、**武家諸法度**によって、さらに武士の義務が細かく記されます。

🔍 ひとくちメモ
江戸幕府が大名を統制するために発布した武家諸法度。文武両道、築城、婚姻、参勤交代、関所などについて規定した

幕府には非常時に**大老**という将軍の補佐をおき、平時は、有力譜代大名が**老中**として、政務をみていました。江戸には財務や寺社の管理、そして警察機能などを司る様々な役所をおき、旗本や御家人がその役務を担います。こうした役所を**奉行所**と呼んでいます。この将軍を頂点とする徳川幕府と全国の藩によって国を治めてゆく体制を**幕藩体制**と呼びました。

その後263年に渡り、徳川政権が全国に君臨する基礎がこのようにして完成したのです。

45 Tokugawa Shogunate and Foreign Affairs

During the early Edo period there were major upheavals elsewhere in the world.

Englalnd and Holland had risen to prominence in Europe during the sixteen century. England had undergone a religious revolution and declared independence from the Vatican and Pope in Rome, and in 1588 the English navy defeated the invincible Spanish Armada, the symbol of the Old World. In 1609 the largely Protestant nation state of Holland achieved independence from Spain, guardians of the Roman Catholic church, and started developing as a seafaring nation active in trade.

Both England and Holland actively sought to have a part in the management of the New World, and in 1626 Holland established a colony called New Amsterdam in what is now New York.

Both sought trade with Asia. Both established East India trading companies and vied with rivals Spain and Portugal for dominance in trade. In 1619 Holland established a trading house in Batavia, present day Jakarta, in Indonesia, sending their ships ever further east.

The Engish and the Dutch first had dealings with Japan in 1600. A Dutch ship with the Englishman William Adams and the Dutchman Jan Joosten on board drifted ashore at Bungo (Oita prefecture), and both were given a warm welcome by Tokugawa Ieyasu. Incidentally, the name of the Tokyo district of Yaesu where Jan Joosten's mansion was located derives from the Japanese pronunciation of his name. Meanwhile William Adams naturalized and took the name Miura Anjin, and both men subsequently

徳川幕府はどのような外交政策を展開した？

江戸時代の初期は世界史的にも大きな変動がありました。

ヨーロッパでは、16世紀の**宗教革命**を経て、**ローマ教皇**によるカトリック支配から自立した、イギリスやオランダという民族国家が台頭し、1588年にはイギリス海軍が、**旧世界**を代表する**スペインの無敵艦隊**を打ち破るという事件がおき、1609年には、新教徒の多いオランダが旧教の守護神でもあるスペインからの自治を獲得し、交易を生業とする海洋国家として発展をはじめます。

イギリスもオランダも、**新大陸**の経営にも積極的に参画し、1626年にはオランダは現在のニューヨークにニューアムステルダムという植民地を拓いています。

彼らは同時にアジアへも交易を求めます。両国とも東インド会社を設立し、ライバルであるスペインやポルトガルと商業上の覇権を競います。オランダは、1619年に現在のインドネシアのバタビア（現ジャカルタ）にオランダ商館を拓き、さらに東へと船を進めます。

イギリス人とオランダ人が最初に日本と交流したのは1600年のことでした。オランダ船に搭乗したイギリス人の**ウイリアム・アダムス**とオランダ人**ヤン・ヨーステン**の二人

🔍 **ひとくちメモ**
ローマ教皇
カトリック教会のローマ司教にして全世界のカトリック教徒の精神的指導者

スペインの無敵艦隊
（スパニッシュ・アーマーダ）1588年にスペイン国王フェリペ2世がイングランド遠征に派遣した艦隊

旧世界
コロンブスのアメリカ大陸発見以前にヨーロッパに知られていた世界のこと。対して新世界とは、大航海時代に新たに発見した土地に対する呼称。新大陸ともいう

🔍 **ひとくちメモ**
ウイリアム・アダムス
（三浦按針）
江戸時代初期に徳川家康に外交顧問として仕えたイギリス人航海士・貿易家。1564–1620

ヤン・ヨーステン
オランダの航海士、朱印船貿易家。「八重洲」の地名は彼の名に由来する。1556?–1623

左：ウイリアム・アダムス像（長崎県）写真提供 木村直哉
右：ヤン・ヨーステン記念碑（東京都）

became central figures in establishing trade between Japan and England and Holland.

To begin with, the Tokugawa shogunate and particularly Tokugawa Ieyasu sought to strengthen their own financial base by actively pursuing trade with other countries, and *shuinsen* (red seal ships) authorized to trade outside Japanese waters sailed throughout South East Asia exporting Japanese silver and camphor and bringing raw silk and sugar back to Japan.

The powerful daimyo also invested in trade, and Date Masamune, daimyo of Sendai, famously dispatched Hasekura Tsunenaga across the Pacific Ocean to Europe, where he was granted an audience with the Pope in Rome.

However, the disputes between Spain and Portugal on one side and England and Holland on the other also led to disagreements over trade with Japan. In 1623 England withdrew voluntarily from Japan, but Holland kept a trading house in Hirado, and the Tokugawa regime warned Portugal and Spain over using their catholic missionary work to further their territorial ambitions. This was exacerbated by disputes over the rights of importation of raw silk from China monopolized by Portugal. Ultimately this friction greatly influenced the regime's later foreign policy.

が豊後（現大分県）に漂着し、二人とも徳川家康に厚遇
されたのです。ちなみに、ヤン・ヨーステンの屋敷のあっ
た場所であることが、現在の東京の八重洲の語源となって
います。一方、ウイリアム・アダムスは、日本に帰化し三浦
按針と名乗りますが、二人ともその後のイギリス、そしてオ
ランダと日本との交易を拓いた立役者となります。

　江戸幕府、特に徳川家康は、自らの財政基盤の強化の
ためにも、当初海外との交易に積極的で、**朱印船**という幕
府が公認した交易船が東南アジア各地へ出向いて日本の
銀や**樟脳**などを輸出し、生糸や砂糖などを日本にもって帰
りました。

　貿易には、有力大名も投資し、仙台の大
名である伊達政宗が支倉常長を太平洋経由
でヨーロッパに派遣し、ローマ法王と謁見し
たのは有名な話です。

伊達政宗公騎馬像（宮城県）

　しかし、スペインやポルトガルとイギリスやオランダとの
争いは、日本での商業圏を巡る争いにもつながります。イ
ギリスは 1623 年に自発的に日本から撤退しますが、オラ
ンダは平戸に**商館**を維持し、徳川政権にポルトガルやスペ
インのカトリックの**布教**を通した**領土的野心**を警告します。
ポルトガルなどが独占していた中国からの生糸の輸入への
利権争いもそれに拍車をかけました。こうした駆け引きが、
その後の幕府の外交政策に大きな影響を与えてゆくので
す。

46 The Suppression of Christianity and the Seclusion Policy

At the time of Toyotomi Hidiyoshi's invasion of Korea and the foundation of the Tokugawa shogunate, the relationship with Joseon Korea and Ming China had been worsening. Trade with western European countries was not just about the importation of European goods, but also indirectly accelerated the fall in trade with China. However, diplomatic relations with Korea were resumed in 1609, and subsequently Korea dispatched a diplomatic mission to each new shogun.

Meanwhile the Satsuma domain in the south annexed the Ryūkyū islands (Okinawa) and even traded indirectly with China. Also, while it did not have formal diplomatic relations with China, private commerce was gradually restored. The Portuguese had held the monopoly of the raw silk trade, the most important import from China at the time, but now silk traders authorized by the shogunate established a pricing cartel and dealt a major blow to the Portuguese. At the same time, trade with newly emergent nations such as Holland gradually increased.

In these conditions, the merits of trading with the zealous Christian missionaries from Portugal and Spain gradually lessened, and conversely the shogunate began to be wary of the territorial ambitions of these Catholic countries.

Eventually, Tokugawa Ieyasu issued the Ban on Christianity in 1612 and embarked on a crackdown on Christian believers. The subsequent repression was at times excessively cruel, with Christians who refused to to step on an image of Christ to prove their apostasy being mercilessly persecuted. Especially in Kyushu where there were many believers, they

徳川幕府はどのようにキリスト教を弾圧し、鎖国した？

　徳川幕府が成立した頃は、豊臣秀吉が朝鮮に侵攻し、李氏朝鮮や明との関係が悪化していたときでした。西欧諸国との交易は、単にヨーロッパの商品の輸入のみならず、交流の途絶えていた中国との交流も間接的に促進する効果がありました。しかし、1609 年には朝鮮との国交が回復し、その後朝鮮は将軍の代替わり毎に**通信使**を派遣してくるようになります。

　一方、南国の大大名薩摩は琉球を傘下にいれ、中国とも間接的に交易します。また、明との正式な国交は開かれませんでしたが、私的な貿易は次第に復活してきました。特に当時の中国からの重要な輸入品であった生糸は、ポルトガルの独占状態から、幕府の保護する糸割符商人による**価格カルテル**が成功し、ポルトガル人に大きな打撃を与えます。同時にオランダなどの新興国との交易もだんだん多くなってきます。

　こうした状況の中で、キリスト教の布教に熱心なポルトガルやスペインとあえて交易をするメリットも幕府には少なくなり、逆に時の為政者は、旧教国が抱く、宗教の背後にある**領土的野心**に警戒感を持つようになります。

　ついに徳川家康は 1612 年に**禁教令**を発布し、キリスト教徒の弾圧に乗り出します。その後の弾圧は時には過酷を極め、宗教画を模したものを踏ませ、躊躇した者は容赦なく弾劾されるという踏み絵などが行われ、特に信者の多かった九州では、訴追された者は火刑など、残酷な方

🔍 **ひとくちメモ**
キリスト教徒への弾圧は過酷を極め、宗教画を踏むこと（踏み絵）を躊躇すると火刑などに処せられた

踏み絵

were executed by brutal methods such as burning at the stake.

The shogunate viewed the rapid expansion of religion as a threat, much like the Ikkō-Ikki movement of the Sengoku period.

At the same time, the shogunate was also wary of the fact that the powerful daimyo in Kyushu were trading independently overseas and growing ever wealthier. Therefore, having banned Spanish ships from landing in Japan in 1624, in 1635 a complete ban on overseas travel was imposed on the Japanese and the country was all of a sudden closed to the outside.

Then, in Shimabara on Kyushu, there was an uprising of the peasant Christians suffering under persecution in which the shogunate's army suffered heavy losses.

As a result of the Shimabara Rebellion, the shogunate intensified its persecution of Christianity. It also also constructed the artificial island of Dejima in Nagasaki, from which after 1641 only the Dutch were permitted to trade after the Portuguese were expelled and the national seclusion policy imposed. From then on, until 1854, Japan closed its doors to the outside world and permitted only limited exchange with Korea and China as well as Holland. Japan had suddenly retracted into its island nation.

法で処刑されました。

　幕府にとっては、戦国時代の一向一揆のように、体制のあり方と矛盾する宗教が急速に拡大することは脅威だったのです。

　同時に、九州の有力大名が独自に海外と交易をして財力をつけることも幕府は警戒しました。そのため、1624年のスペイン船の来航の禁止を皮切りに、1635年には日本人の海外渡航と帰国を一切禁止し、国を一気に閉ざしてゆきます。

　折悪しく、九州の島原で、圧政に苦しむキリスト教を信奉する農民が一斉に放棄するという事件がおきます。この**島原の乱**での幕府軍の損害は甚大でした。

　その結果、幕府はキリスト教の弾圧を強化し、同時に長崎に人工の島である出島を築き、ポルトガルと断交、1641年以降、オランダ人のみ、そこでの交易を許可するという**鎖国政策**を打ち出したのです。以後、1854年まで日本は世界から門戸を閉ざし、オランダ以外は、朝鮮、中国との限定的な交流のみが認められることになったのです。日本は急速に島国の中に収縮していったのでした。

天草四郎像（熊本県）

ひとくちメモ
島原の乱
天草四郎を筆頭にした農民とキリスト教徒が、1637年11月から翌年の2月にかけて島原の原城に立てこもった。幕府により城を落とされ、参加者は皆殺しにされた

Tokugawa Society

Japan's seclusion occured in the reign of Tokugawa Iemitsu, the third Tokugawa shogun.

By Iemitsu's time, all traces of the Sengoku period had disappeared, and the shogunate-han system was stabilized. Many daimyo considered a danger to the shogunate were dismissed, and the imperial court's activities were restricted by the *Kinchū Gohatto* law.

The retainers of the deposed daimyo were left masterless and unemployed. The increase of these so-called *rōnin* during the Edo period became a social problem.

Also, temples and shrines were placed under the jurisdiction of magistrates, and in order to expose Christian believers everyone was forced to have an affiliation with either Buddhism or Shintoism.

The Tokugawa regime enforced the four feudal classes, with the samurai at the top followed by, in order, the farmers, artisans, and merchants, and added a further strata below them consisting of the *eta* and *hinin* outcasts. With this rigid class system the shogunate restricted contact between the classes and gave the samurai absolute authority. Meanwhile farmers had their produce strictly supervised, and were regulated by means of the Five Household System of collective responsibility. A system of primogeniture was imposed on all households, including the samurai, and the *ie* (home) became the cornerstone of the concept of family in which women were discriminated against.

This system shackled people to the land and social standing of their family, not just in the territories under the direct control of the shogunate

徳川幕府は、どんな社会を創造した？

　鎖国が完成したのは、三代将軍徳川家光の治世でした。

　家光の頃になると、戦国時代の名残も消え、幕藩体制も安定します。安定の過程で、徳川家にとって危険と見なされる多くの大名が改易され、朝廷に対しても禁中御法度という法律を定めて、その活動を制限します。

　改易された大名の臣下は主君を失い、失業します。この武士の失業者のことを**浪人**と呼び、その増加は江戸時代を通しての社会問題になってゆきます。

　また、寺社は**寺社奉行**の管轄の元に統率され、キリスト教徒の摘発の必要性からも、全ての人を仏教、神道のいずれかの宗派に結びつけて管理してゆきます。

　徳川政権は、武士を頂点として、農民、職人、そして商人の順に**士農工商**という身分を設け、さらにその下に穢多、非人という最下層の身分を造りました。幕府は身分を固定し、身分間の交流を制限し、武士に絶対的な権威を与えたのです。一方、農民は生産者として厳しく管理され、**5人組制度**という連帯責任制度の元に統制しました。武士を含め、全ての家は長子相続を義務づけ、人々は「家(氏)」を家族の概念の基本におき、女性は差別されます。

　こうした制度は、幕府の直轄領のみならず、各藩にも及び、以後人々はそれぞれの土地と家柄に結びつけられ、

but in all the domains.

Isolated from exchange with the outside world, and restricted by the rigid class system within the country, we can say the Edo period had a major effect on the Japanese character. It was during this period, in which the authority of the politicians called *O-kami* (Big Brother, the powers that be) and absolute submission to them, and the fact that the home and organizations were considered more of a priority than the individual, people began to care more about the group they belonged to, and to cultivate the art of living without standing out in any way.

While the shogunate governed the nation as a whole, the country was divided into domains ruled by daimyo. Since travel was restricted, people therefore became more aware of the domain they belonged to as their "country" than the nation as a whole.

On the other hand, under the seclusion policy and stability of the shogunate system, Japan enjoyed over two hundred years of peace. In the Heian period the country had looked inward and the culture of the earlier Nara period was digested and matured. Likewise, in the Edo period, one can see the process of the culture assimilated during the period of expansion and exchange with Europe being digested and converted into Japan's own unique culture.

This cultural activity flourished as the Genroku culture in the time of the fifth Tokugawa shogun, Tokugawa Tsunayoshi.

拘束されることになります。

　海外との交易が遮断され、国内では厳しい身分制度によって様々な制限を課せられた江戸時代は、その後の日本人の国民性に大きな影響を与えた時代といえましょう。「お上」と呼ばれた為政者の権威と、彼らへの絶対的な服従の意識、家や組織を個人よりも優先する考え方、さらに常に自らの属するグループのあり方を気にしながら、自己を突出させずに生きてゆく処世術などが培われたのはこの時期でした。

　日本としての国の政治は幕府が行い、国は大名の統治する藩に分かれ、移動も制限されていたことから、人々は、国家ではなく、自らの属する藩や天領が、「国」として意識されるようになります。

　一方、国を閉ざし、幕藩体制の元で安定した日本は、以後 200 年以上平和を謳歌します。ちょうど奈良時代以降、平安時代に内に向けて文化を消化し円熟させたように、江戸時代にも一時西欧とも交流し世界に拡大しながら吸収した文化が消化されながら、日本独自の文化へと変化してゆく過程が見受けられます。

　そんな文化活動が5代将軍徳川綱吉の頃に、元禄文化として花開くのです。

48 The Genroku Era

We are already approaching the modern era of Japan's long history.

The Edo period was feudal, with a rigid class system. On the other hand, it was marked by a developing monetary economy and merchants thrived in the prosperity of Edo. Taxation and remuneration were both calculated in rice, but the hatamoto could obtain cash from authorized moneylenders called *fudasashi* on the security of their rice stipend.

The shogunate also established a bureaucracy and judiciary, and although the shogunate-han system at first glance appeared feudal, the shogun ruled as an absolute monarch with enormous authority. There was also a highway system with post stations, and people had to obtain a transit permit from the government office in order to travel. Post towns thrived along the five principle highways, including the Tōkaidō connecting Edo to Kyoto.

The extended period of peace under the Tokugawa shogunate led to the development of various artistic activities in Edo and Kamigata, as the area around Osaka is known, towards the end of the seventeenth century.

Kabuki is said to have originated in the dance by the former Izumo shrine maiden Okuni that was held to offend public morals and banned by the shogunate in the early Edo period. When it later came to be performed by an all-male cast, it developed as popular entertainment. Also the lively puppet theater called Bunraku thrived in Kamigata with its performances of plays written by Chikamatsu Monzaemon and Takemoto Gidayū's

元禄時代はどんな時代？

　我々は長い日本の歴史を見る中で、すでに近代にはいっています。

　江戸時代は身分制度が固定された封建的な時代でした。しかし、一方で経済活動には貨幣経済が浸透し、江戸の繁栄と共に、町人が活発に活動した時代でもありました。税金や報酬の基本は米でしたが、例えば旗本などに支給された米は札差と呼ばれた金融業者によって換金されていました。

　幕府による**官僚制度**や**司法制度**も整い、その強大な権力が一見封建制度のように見える**幕藩体制**の中で、絶対君主のように君臨した時代でもありました。街道や駅制度も整い、人々は役所から通行手形を発行してもらい移動します。江戸と京都を結ぶ東海道を始め主要5街道などでは**宿場町**が栄えます。

　こうした徳川幕府の元での平和な時代によって、17世紀も末頃になると江戸と上方とよばれる大阪を中心とした関西で、様々な文化活動が展開されます。

　もともと、江戸初期に出雲の巫女であった阿国の踊りが起源とされる**歌舞伎**は、風紀を乱すとのことで幕府に規制されました。後に男が演じる演目で興行されるようになると、それが大衆演劇に発展します。また**文楽**という人形劇のために上方で独特の義太夫節を作曲した竹本義太夫や、そのために作品を書いた近松門左衛門などが活躍し

幕末体制下の日本

scores for its unique chanted narration. This was entertainment along the lines of contemporary musicals. Hishikawa Moronobu and others started putting out printed copies of genre paintings, which later developed as entertainment prints and came to be known as ukiyo-e woodblock prints. Such activites flourished in the Genroku era in the time of the fifth shogun Tokugawa Tsunayoshi and lent brilliance to Edo culture.

Art had traditionally been nurtured under the patronage of the nobility and the powerful daimyo. The ink paintings by Sesshū and others in the Muromachi period, the murals of the Kanō school, early Edo Arita ceramics by potters like Sakaida Kakiemon and the refined Kutani wares of Kaga, all developed into industries with the backing of powerful domains.

However, the art of the Genroku period started amongst the merchants, and is characterized by its development as cheerful entertainment that sometimes challenged the moral code espoused by the shogunate and authorities. Instead of being patronized by the samurai, performances were held as a business and the visual arts were used as publicity material to promote these. Contemporary Japanese commercial art has its origins in the performance art of the Genroku period.

ます。これらは現在のミュージカルのように興行されます。菱川師宣などが従来の風俗画を刷り物として世に出し、それが将来、興行のための印刷物へと発展します。**浮世絵**の登場です。こうした活動は5代将軍の徳川綱吉の時代、元禄と呼ばれた頃に広がり江戸文化の彩りとなりました。

浮世絵

　もともと、芸術は貴族や有力武士などの庇護の元に育成されました。室町時代の雪舟等の水墨画にはじまり、狩野派の障壁画、陶磁器でいえば、江戸初期の酒井田柿右衛門などによる有田焼やそれを発展させた加賀の九谷焼などの背景には、それを産業として育成しようとした有力藩の後押しが欠かせません。

　しかし、元禄時代の芸術は町人の間に生まれ、ともすれば幕府や権力者の道徳律にも挑戦するような快活な芸能として発展したことがその特徴です。それは、武士の保護を受ける代わりに、商業として興行を行い、そのためのプロモーションを目的とした芸術として発展します。元禄時代にみられたこれらのパフォーミングアートこそが、現代の日本の商業芸術の源流となるのです。

雪舟の水呑の龍 (岡山県)

🔍 ひとくちメモ
もともとは戦争のためであった城郭が、有力大名のための天守閣をもった豪華な居城として変化した中で、絵画や障壁画も装飾芸術として発展した

49 Samurai in the Edo Period

While Edo and Osaka enjoyed a thriving merchant culture, the samurai pursued Bushidō (the Way of the Warrior) as their own spiritual foundation.

The samurai were warriors. Samurai means "one who serves his lord" and they were required to swear loyalty to their master, train themselves in self-discipline, and be prepared for any emergency. They were constantly aware of death, and had to be spiritually prepared for it. Bushidō is the name given to the samurai's own aesthetic of life. However, the Edo period was an era of peace, and since the warriors were sent to work every day as administrators and high ranking samurai wallowed in luxury, Bushidō gradually went into decline.

The background to Bushidō lies in the Confucianism promoted by the shogunate, especially the observance of hierarchical relationships as propounded by Zhu Xi. It also included some scholarship that emphasized spiritual training, such as Zen and the unified knowledge and action taught by Wang Yangming. The fifth shogun Tokugawa Tsunayoshi established the Shōheizaka Gakumonsho, a school for neo-Confucianist based on the teachings of Zhu Xi for government-appointed samurai.

Meanwhile, the samurai culture gradually developed in the domain schools established for such studies. At the same time sword fighting masters opened schools where samurai studied not just letters but also the martial arts.

In the Genroku period, in 1702, forty-seven rōnin from the Akō domain, who had been left masterless after their lord was stripped of

江戸時代の武士の生活とは？

　町人文化が江戸や大阪を彩っていた頃、武士は自らの精神的な拠りどころとしての**武士道**を大切にします。

　武士は、侍と呼ばれます。侍は「主君に仕える者」を意味し、主君に忠誠を誓い、修養鍛錬して変事に備えなければなりません。死を常に意識し、それを乗り越える強い精神が求められます。この侍独自の人生への美学を武士道と呼ぶのです。しかし、江戸時代は平和な時代で、武士も役人として毎日を送り、上級武士は贅沢に溺れ、武士道が廃れていったともいわれています。

　武士道の背景には、幕府が奨励した**儒教**、特に上下関係の規律を説く**朱子学**があります。その他、禅や知行合一を説く**陽明学**のように、精神修養を重んずる学問が取り入れられ、五代将軍徳川綱吉は、朱子学の学問所として昌平坂学問所を開校し、武士の官製学問所とします。

 ひとくちメモ

朱子
朱子学の創始者。宋代の儒学者、1130–1200

王陽明
陽明学の創始者。明代の儒学者、1472–1529

昌平坂学問所があった湯島聖堂（東京都）

　一方、それぞれの藩は、藩校を開いて、こうした学問を教え、武士のたしなみとしてゆきました。同時に剣術の腕のある者が剣術道場を開き、文のみならず武を鍛えるために、侍がそこに集まりました。

　元禄時代、1702年に有力大名である吉良上野介に落し入れられて改易され、切腹した主君の敵をとろうと、浪

samurai status and forced to commit suicide for having attacked the court official Kira Kōzuke-no-suke, raided Kira's mansion and cut off his head.

From the perspective of Confucianism and Bushidō, their action was considered ideal as it demonstrated their loyalty by avenging the shameful death of their lord. Nevertheless, the shogunate had to make them bear responsibility for the crime of killing the powerful lord Kira Kōzuke-no-suke and agonized over the best way to do this. In the end, they ordered all forty-seven rōnin to commit *seppuku*. In other words, this was not an ordinary punitive death sentence, but an honorable death in which the samurai themselves chose death by cutting open their own bellies—a perfect example of the Way of the Warrior.

Ever since Toyotomi Hideyoshi deprived farmers of the right to carry swords in order to distinguish between samurai and peasantry, the samurai had a high position within the bureacracy. However, this also meant that the samurai's only job was as bureaucrats managing the government and domains, and they did not produce anything. If a samurai was punished by removal of his samurai status and benefits, his retainers were left unemployed and, being unproductive, faced a tough life. Eventually this paradox strained the finances of the shogunate.

人となった侍（**赤穂浪士**）47人が吉良家に討ち入り、見事に吉良上野介の首をとったという事件がおきました。

　主君への恩を思い、その無念の死を敵討ちという形式で家臣が償ったことは、儒教的観点からも武士道の上からも、理想的なこととされました。しかし、幕府は有力大名である吉良上野介を殺害したことへの罪をどのように負わせるかという点で、苦慮します。結果、47人全員に切腹を申し付けます。すなわち、単なる死罪とは異なり、切腹は武士が自らの腹を切って死を選ぶという刑罰とは異なる**名誉な行為**なのです。まさに、当時の武士道のあり方が伺えます。

　豊臣秀吉が農民から刀を奪い、武士と農民の区別をつけて以来、武士は為政者側につく地位の高い存在でした。しかし、それは武士が官吏として幕府や藩の運営にあたる以外の仕事を持たない、非生産者であったことも意味しています。また、改易を受けた大名の元家臣などは浪人となり、かつ非生産者として苦しい生活を強いられます。この矛盾が徳川幕府の経済的歪みとなってゆくのです。

🔍 ひとくちメモ
赤穂浪士の物語は、武士だけでなく庶民の間でも人気をはくし、以後さまざまに劇化され、今に伝わっている

Feudal Japan
幕末体制下の日本

50 Industry and Economy in the Edo Period

For practically the entire Edo period, there was no contact with the outside world.

These two hundred years were crucial to Japan. Europe and America at that time were going through the industrial revolution.

The combustion engine proved to be a major turning point in the history of humankind. With this invention the means of transporting people and objects dramatically improved, and industrial production rose substantially. Amidst the contradictions caused by the hitherto undreamed-of scale of productivity, by trial and error society began to modernize. The industrial revolution in Europe and America greatly changed their standing in the world.

Although like Europe, Japan had also been developing technical knowhow and society structure, it was completely left behind by these events.

Japan had established a monetary economy, manual industries were developing, and there had also been great advances in agricultural tecniques. Merchants trading in rice and other produce formed guilds and collaborated with the shogunate and domains to control prices. Cargo ships such as the *higaki-kaisen* and *taru-kaisen* plied regular sea routes in Japan's coastal waters, underpinning the distribution of goods. Also, highways and lodging facilities developed due to the daimyo's alternate-year residence in Edo, and the express messengers of the mail service delivered documents and money orders. In major cities like Edo, brokers dealing in gold and silver were thriving, and gradually took on the role of

江戸時代の産業、経済は？

江戸時代は、そのほとんどの時期、海外との交流を断絶していました。

その200年は、日本にとって決定的でした。欧米諸国は、その間に**産業革命**を迎えるのです。

飛脚

人類の歴史は、**内燃機関**の発明の前後で大きく変化します。この発明で人や物の移動の手段が飛躍的に向上し、工業生産力も大幅に上昇します。それによって、生産規模も生産性も以前と比較にならないほど変化し、社会もそれに応じて矛盾と試行錯誤の中で近代化します。欧米での産業革命は、それまでの世界での欧米の地位を大きく変化させていったのです。

日本は欧米と同じように、それなりに高い技術や社会構造を整えながらも、これらのイベントから完全に置き去りにされたのです。

日本国内では、すでに貨幣経済が浸透し、様々な**手工業**が発展し、農耕技術も以前に比べれば大きく進歩していました。米や産物を商う商人は**株仲間**を結成し、幕府や藩と連携して商品の価格をコントロールします。日本の近海の航路は、菱垣廻船や樽廻船などの**定期航路**が周回し、物流を支えていました。また、大名の参勤交代によって、**街道**や**宿場**が整備され、**飛脚**という郵便業者が書類や為替を運んでいました。江戸などの大都市には、金や銀の交換を商う**両替商**が活躍し、次第に現在の銀行のような役割を担っていたのです。

today's banks.

However, these changes were happening within Japan's closed borders. It was the same with China and Korea. In China, the Ming had been ousted in 1644 by the Manchus who established the Qing Dynasty, whose foreign policy was essentially seclusion. The fact that the leading territories in Asia were all negative about trading with Europe and America probably contributed to Japan's own extended seclusion.

Nevertheless, Japan was steadily progressing and the cornerstones of feudalism little by little loosened. In the farming villages, freehold landowner farmers were divided into winners and losers with the introduction of a monetary economy, and those who were successful became landlords, some of whom profited from getting advance payment for fertilizer and farming equipment from the tenant farmers who rented fields to cultivate. Life was tough for farmers living in abject poverty, and crop failures led to displaced people, with peasant uprisings from time to time. This affected tax revenue, and hit the finances of the shogunate.

Some of the unproductive samurai, too, found themselves impoverished by the monetary system, and the foundations of the shogunate-han system were shaken by the worsening economic circumstances of the samurai, including the government and the domains.

しかし、これらの変化は、日本という島国の中だけの進化でした。中国や朝鮮も同様です。中国では1644年に明が満州族に滅ぼされ、清が興きますが、その外交方針も基本的には鎖国でした。アジアの主要地域がこぞって欧米との交流に消極的であったことが、日本の鎖国をより長期化させたのかもしれません。

しかし、そうした中でも日本は着実に進化し、封建制度の土台が少しずつ緩んできます。農村では土地を持つ**本百姓**が貨幣経済の流入によって勝ち組と負け組に分化し、成功した者は**地主**化し、田畑を借りて耕作する**水呑百姓**への肥料や農具の前貸しなどで利益をあげる者も現れます。貧困に喘ぐ貧しい農民の生活は深刻で、飢饉などによって流民が生まれ、**百姓一揆**と呼ばれる蜂起も時々おこりました。これは税収に影響を与え、幕府の財政を直撃します。

生産手段を持たない武士の中にも、貨幣経済に巻き込まれ、困窮する者があらわれ、幕府や藩を含め、武士の経済状況が悪化してゆくことが、幕藩体制の土台を揺るがしてゆく原因となったのでした。

51 The Kyōhō Reforms

The fifth shogun Tokugawa Tsunayoshi had tended towards extravagance. Furthermore, the shogunate had to pay the high cost of reconstruction following the Great Fire of Meireki that had destroyed much of Edo. There was therefore an urgent need to restore public finances. The Confucian scholar and Tokugawa adviser Arai Hakuseki launched the reforms known as Shōtoku no Chi designed to control government spending.

In 1716, when Tokugawa Yoshimune became the eighth shogun, he dismissed Arai Hakuseki and enforced the Kyōhō Reforms. Yoshimune was from the Kii branch of the Tokugawa Gosanke, the three hereditary houses for the shogunal line. Because of this, he was relatively distant from the existing personnel, and could take the initiative in making appointments. He famously promoted the provincial magistrate Ōoka Tadasuke to the important post of magistrate for the city of Edo.

The reforms were wide-ranging, returning the legal system to the way it was at the time the shogunate was founded, and promoting simple frugality within the government. A complaints box was established through which the common people could make a direct appeal, and as a result carried out public works such as building a health center in Koishikawa in Edo.

Also, to encourage merchants to help develop new land for rice fields it adopted innovative measures regarding currency and the price of rice, although not with any great success.

The daimyo were already in straitened financial circumstances due to the expense of maintaining two households under the system of

享保の改革とその後の状況は？

　5代将軍徳川綱吉の時代は奢侈に傾いた時代でした。しかも、**明暦の大火**での江戸の救済など幕府の出費は多く、財政の立て直しが急務となりました。綱吉のあと登用された儒学者新井白石は、正徳の治と呼ばれる改革を進め、幕府の経費を節減しようとしましたが追いつきません。

　1716年に徳川吉宗が8代将軍に就任すると、新井白石を罷免し、**享保の改革**を断行します。吉宗は、**御三家**の一つである紀伊の徳川家から将軍になりました。そのため、以前からのしがらみが薄い分だけ、人材の登用なども積極的に行えます。地方の奉行であった大岡忠相を江戸町奉行に抜擢したことは有名です。

　改革は多岐に渡り、法制面では幕府創設期の幕藩体制の基本に戻り、**質素倹約**を奨励する中で、支配体制の整備を行います。**目安箱**を設置して庶民の直訴を可能にし、その意見をもとに、江戸の**小石川**に**養生所**を設立したりしました。

　また、新田開発に商人の参入を奨励し、斬新な通貨対策や米価対策をとりますが、大きな成果はあげられませんでした。
　すでに、参勤交代や、江戸と領国との2重生活での経費の負担等で、大名の財政も逼迫していました。彼らの多

ひとくちメモ
当時、江戸は焼失面積、死者ともに江戸時代最大といわれる明暦の大火に襲われ、その復興のため幕府の財政は困窮した

幕末体制下の日本 Feudal Japan

ひとくちメモ
目安箱
1721年（享保6年）に徳川吉宗が設置した

小石川養生所
1722（享保7年）開設。無料で庶民の病気治療にあたった

alternate residence between Edo and their own domains. Many of them were managing their domain finances with loans secured on their income from the land tax, borrowing from the merchants called *kuramoto* who handled things like the land tax in their domain. The samurai were unable to sustain their government without these merchants. Yoshimune investigated abuse of the monetary economy under the shogunate's management of trade. However, the shogunate-han system was already aboard the ship of the monetary economy.

One person who must have been acutely aware of this was Tanuma Okitsugu, a hatamoto from Kii province who had come to Edo together with Yoshimune. He carried out reclamation work on Lake Inba and the development of new rice fields, while also promoting trade guilds, awarding patents on copper and steel products to designated merchants, and collecting fees from these merchants in much the same way as today's corporate tax, as well as proposing a new tax on various trading activities. He also expanded the trade with Holland in Nagasaki, and endeavored to control customs tariffs.

Tanuma's measures were revolutionary, but have also been censured for the collusive relationships with traders and rampant bribery. At the same time there were many outbreaks of famine in the provinces, with peasant revolts throughout the country, and infighting amongst factions within the shogunate, all of which led to his downfall in 1786.

くは藩の年貢収入等を取り扱う蔵元と呼ばれる商人から、年貢収入を担保に藩の運営資金を借り入れて財務を切盛りしていました。武士は商人なしには施政を維持できなかったのです。吉宗は、商業活動を幕府が管理することによって、貨幣経済の弊害を糺そうとしたのです。しかし、幕藩体制はすでに貨幣経済という船の上に乗っていたのでした。

　そのことをよく知っていたのが、吉宗と共に江戸に移動した紀伊出身の旗本、田沼意次でしょう。彼は、印旛沼の開墾など、新田開発に熱心な一方、**株仲間**を奨励し、銅や鉄などの製品について、特定の商人に専売特許を与え、これらの商人から**冥加金**を徴収する、現在でいう法人税を導入する他、様々な商業活動に対する新たな税金を企画します。また、長崎でのオランダとの貿易も拡大し、**関税**をコントロールしようとしました。

　田沼の政策は画期的でしたが、商人との**癒着**や**賄賂の横行**を非難されます。同時に地方で**飢饉**が多発し、**百姓一揆**が各地で起きたことなどから、幕府内部の政治抗争に破れ、1786 年に失脚します。

52 The Collapse of the Shogunate

Let's think back to the Heian period.

The imperial court clung to the Ritsuryō system it had instigated. However, in reality it could not govern without the cooperation of the newly risen samurai class. A major task of politicians is to perceive new forces in society, and to realign themselves to these in response.

During the Edo period, the samurai had a firm grip on power. However, the merchant activity that had been developing the country ever since the Sengoku period flourished as Japan was suppressed by the Tokugawa shogunate. However much the domains tried to instigate independent administration and finances, to raise funds they had to convert their own land tax into currency and distribute their produce.

The shogunate, too, depended on the economic activities of the merchants to collect taxes and rebuild finances. The samurai, who did not produce anything, could no long support their administration without commerce. Tanuma Okitsugu had not appreciated this change and was ousted, after which Matsudaira Sadanobu was appointed *rōjū shuza* (chief senior councilor) in 1787 and carried out further reforms. Sadanobu's Kansei Reforms consisted of eminently reasonable measures such as the promotion of simple frugality and storing emergency supplies of rice in villages in case of famine. However, the cultivation of surplus crops was prohibited, the merchants' inroads into farming villages were restricted, trade guilds disbanded, and the merchant fees system suspended. Also, in order to redress the finances of the hatamoto and other retainers, a decree

幕府はどのようにして衰弱した？

平安時代のことを思い出しましょう。

朝廷は、自らの築いた律令体制に執着します。しかし、実態は新興階級である武士の協力なしには政権を維持できません。世の中の変化による新たな力をいかに察知し、自らを変えて対応してゆくかは、為政者の大きな課題なのです。

江戸時代は、武士が権力を握った時代です。しかし、戦国時代以降各地で芽生えた商業活動は、日本が徳川幕府の元に平定されるといっそう活発になります。いかに藩が独立した行政や財政を行おうと、自らの年貢による収入を換金し、産物を流通させることが資金調達の上では欠かせません。

幕府も同様で、税金を徴収し、財政を再建するには商人による経済活動が必要不可欠でした。非生産人口である武士は、すでに商業活動なしには、政権を維持できなかったのです。その変化を知らずに、田沼意次の追放のあと、1787年に**老中首座**に就任して改革を行ったのが松平定信です。定信の政策は**寛政の改革**と呼ばれ、**質素倹約**を奨励し、農村での囲い米という飢饉に備えた米の備蓄の奨励など、一見理の通ったものでした。しかし一方で、余剰作物の栽培を禁止し、商人の農村進出を制限、株仲間を解散させ、**冥加金制度**を停止します。また、旗本などの財政難を救済するため、札差などからの借金を棒引きにする**棄捐令**を実行します。

🔊 **ひとくちメモ**
寛政の改革
1787年から始まる。倹約令、囲い米、商人の農村進出の禁止、株仲間の解散、冥加金制度の停止など、時代に逆行するもので、改革は2年で挫折した

棄捐令
寛政の改革の一環で発令された。1784年以前の借金は棒引きにし、それ以後のものは利子を下げるなどして武士の財政難を救済しようとした

was issued cancelling debts on loans secured on their rice stipend.

These measures were against the trend of the times and made it harder for the merchants to help the samurai, with the result that the samurai class was even further impoverished. Consequently, in just two years the reforms collapsed. Matsudaira Sadanobu had been appointed by the eleventh shogun, Tokugawa Ienari. After his downfall, Ienari instigated the personal rule of the shogun in order to exercise power even after retirement, effectively governing until 1841. Under his rule, the shogunate fell into luxury habits, worsening public finances even further. There were also occasions when the currency was revalued to generate extra income, plunging the markets into chaos.

Mizuno Tadakuni, the chief senior councilor upon the succession in 1841 of the twelfth shogun, Tokugawa Ieyoshi, tried to address this with his Tenpō Reforms.

These reforms were almost identical to the Kansei Reforms, prohibiting migrant workers and again disbanding trade guilds. They also envisaged expanding shogunal lands, but this met with fierce opposition from feudal lords and hatamoto retainers. The strict enforcement of extreme public morals and simple frugality stifled Edo's vitality, and these reforms too collapsed within two years. Without any drastic measures to tackle the monetary economy, the Tokugawa shogunate was headed for chaos in its final years.

こうした対策は、時代の流れに逆行し、逆に武士への商人からの援助を困難にし、武士階級の困窮を助長しました。これによって、改革は2年で挫折してしまいます。松平定信の時代は、11代将軍徳川家斉の時代です。家斉は松平定信失脚後、親政を実施し、将軍引退後も大御所として権勢をふるい、1841年まで幕政の実権を握りました。この親政の間、幕政は奢侈に流れ、財政はさらに逼迫します。臨時収入をもくろんだ**貨幣価値の変更**などで市場が混乱したこともありました。

これを立て直そうと、1841年に12代将軍徳川家慶が就任すると老中首座として改革に乗り出したのが水野忠邦でした。**天保の改革**です。

この改革は、寛政の改革のコピーに近く、農村から出稼ぎを禁止し、株仲間を再び解散させます。また、天領の拡大をもくろみますが、これが諸侯や旗本の大反対にあいます。極端な風紀の粛正と質素倹約の強制は、江戸の活気に水を差し、この改革も2年で挫折します。幕政は貨幣経済への根本的な対応なしに、そのまま幕末の混乱期にはいってゆくのです。

水野忠邦

🔍 ひとくちメモ
天保の改革
老中水野忠邦が行った風紀の粛正、質素倹約を強制する改革。その方法が過激で失敗に帰した

53 Scholarship in the Late Edo Period

Right from the start, the Tokugawa shogunate promoted the teachings of Zhu Xi in order to establish a class society with the samurai at the top. Nevertheless, these teachings emphasize respect for the sovereign and are also connected to the ideology of emperor worship.

During the Edo period as Confucianist studies progressed, there was a movement to eliminate the influence of Buddhism and the afterlife, and to return to the origins of the ideology to discern its essence. In the seventeenth century Yamaga Sokō and others criticized Zhu Xi's teachings from this perspective.

Tokugawa Mitsukuni, who in 1661 became daimyo of the Mito domain, one of the three Tokugawa houses, compiled the *Dai Nihonshi* (Great History of Japan). Fusing studies of the Japan classics with Confucianism, it aimed to provide later generations with a broad candid account of Japanese history undistorted by religious ideology. Along with Shinto studies, this developed into the Kokugaku (national learning) revival that was further developed by eighteenth century scholars such as Kamo no Mabuchi and Motoori Norinaga. Motoori Norinaga particularly, who wrote the *Kojiki-den* (Commentaries on the *Kojiki*) among other works, is notable for his insistence on an appreciation that eliminates any Confucian or Buddhist interpretation in the study of the Japanese classics, which was groundbreaking for its time.

In the Edo period, commoners attended the private educational institutions known as *terakoya* to learn how to read and write. Also, in addition to the Shōheizaka Gakumonsho in Yushima and the domain

江戸中期から後期の学問や思想は？

　徳川幕府はその創世記から、武士を頂点とした階級社会を確立させるために**朱子学**を奨励しましたが、そこに説かれている帝王を尊重する考え方をつきつめれば、それは天皇を崇拝する尊皇思想に結びつきます。

　江戸時代は儒教全般の研究が進む中で、後世の仏教などの影響を排除し、原点に立ち返って、その思想の本質を見極めようとする動きがありました。17世紀にその立場に立って朱子学を批判した山鹿素行などがそれにあたります。彼らの考え方は、日本史の研究にも影響を与えます。

　徳川御三家のひとつ水戸藩では、1661年に藩主となった徳川光圀が『大日本史』を編纂しますが、こうした歴史の研究と儒教研究とが融和して、日本史を後年の伝承や思想宗教による改竄から解放し、ありのままの姿で見極めようという考え方が広がります。これが神道の研究と重なって、**国学**へと進化するのです。18世紀の学者、賀茂真淵や**本居宣長**がそれを大成します。特に本居宣長は、『古事記伝』などの著書の中で、古典を研究する上での儒教的・仏教的解釈を排除したものの見方を強調しますが、それは当時としては画期的なものでした。

🔍 **ひとくちメモ**
本居宣長
江戸中期の国学者。『古事記伝』は古典の研究に仏教的・儒教的解釈を排除したもので、当時としては画期的なものであった

寺子屋

　江戸時代、一般の庶民は寺子屋という私塾に通い読み書きを覚えました。また昌平坂学問所や藩校の他に、各地には私塾があって、儒学や国学が

schools, there were private schools all over the country teaching Confucianism and Kokugaku. This led to a new appreciation for the fact that Japan was originally a country ruled by the imperial court and the emperor. The shogunate considered this idea to be subversive, and there were cases of them cracking down on it. It was of course directly related to the ideology of Sonnō jōi (revere the Emperor, expel the barbarians) towards the end of the shogunate.

On the other hand, despite the seclusionist policy, studies of the Western sciences thrived through books obtained from Dutch traders. This was called Rangaku (literally, Dutch studies), also actively pursued by the shogunate as a means to find out about foreign countries. The translation into Japanese of the Dutch medical book *Kaitai shinsho* (New Book of Anatomy) by Maeno Ryōtaku and Sugita Genpaku in 1774 is well known.

Later, in 1823 a physician at a Dutch trading house, Philipp von Siebold, obtained the shogunate's permission to open the Narutakijuku, a medical school in Nagasaki, which had many talented students such as Takano Chōei.

At first glance Kokugaku and Rangaku would appear completely different fields of studies, but they both came to exert an influence on various ideologies at the very end of the shogunate.

教えられました。その中で、日本は本来、天皇を中心とした朝廷の治める国であったことが再認識されます。この考え方は危険思想として、幕府の弾圧を受けることもありました。もちろん尊皇思想は、幕末の**尊王攘夷**論に直結するのです。

一方、鎖国の中で、オランダから西欧事情を読み取ろうという動きも盛んになります。これを**蘭学**と呼び、幕府も諸外国の事情を知る上で蘭学には積極的でした。1774年には、前野良沢と杉田玄白がオランダの医学書を翻訳し、『**解体新書**』という解剖書を出版したことはよく知られています。

その後、1823年には、オランダ商館の医務官であった**シーボルト**が、幕府の許可を得て鳴滝塾を長崎に開き、高野長英などの逸材がそこで学びます。

国学と蘭学という一見全く異なる学問が、後年の幕末期の様々な思想へ影響を与えるようになったことは、興味深い限りです。

解体新書

🔍 **ひとくちメモ**
蘭学
オランダ語による西洋の研究。始まりは青木昆陽の蘭書の翻訳、後に前野良沢、杉田玄白による『解体新書』は有名

🔍 **ひとくちメモ**
シーボルト
ドイツの医学者・博物者。鳴滝塾では高野長英らに医術を教授した。1859–62の間、幕府の外事顧問となり、『日本動物誌』『日本植物誌』を著す。またシーボルトは日本地図を持ち出そうとしたことが幕府に見つかり、高野長英などの門人が厳しく訴追されたという話も残っている

54 The Bunka-Bunsei Period

The merchant culture in the Edo period managed to slip through the gaps in governmental control and restrictions on the freedom of speech to spread its vigorous roots. During the Bunka-Bunsei period at the beginning of the nineteenth century, under the rule of the eleventh shogun Tokugawa Ienari, commerce was brisk and the merchant culture also flourished. Under the influence of Tanuma Okitsugu's policy of appeasing businesses, Edo developed into a city with a population of a million, one of the biggest cities in the world.

The merchants could read about goings on in society in the commercial newssheets called *kawaraban*, and enjoyed the scenes, customs, and political satires featured in illustrated storybooks and humorous novelettes set in the entertainment quarters. The *ukiyozōshi* books written in kana by writers such as Ihara Saikaku, author of *Kōshoku ichidai otoko* (The Life of An Amorous Man), had been all the rage in the Genroku period. In the Bunka-Bunsei period, this publishing activity developed further, with epics such as Takizawa Bakin's *Nansō Satomi hakkenden* (The Tale of Eight Dogs).

In the Genroku period, the short seventeen-syllable haiku developed from *renga* linked verse by Matsuo Bashō became widely read. Bashō's account of his travels in Tohoku and Hokuriku, *Oku no hosomichi* (The Narrow Road to the Interior), is still a favorite today. The Bunka-Bunsei period, however, saw a witty literary trend with the poets Kobayashi Issa and Yosa Buson developing new forms of haiku such as the satirical *senryū*.

文化文政時代とは

　江戸時代の町人文化は、幕府の規制や言論統制の合間をかいくぐって逞しく根を張ります。19世紀初頭の文化文政時代は、11代将軍徳川家斉の統治下、商業活動も活発で、町人の文化活動も盛んでした。もともと田沼意次の商業との宥和政策の影響で、江戸は100万都市に発展し、世界屈指の大都会となっていました。

　町人は、**瓦版**という新聞で世の中の話題を読み、黄草紙や洒落本などで、江戸の風物や風俗、政治への風刺を楽しみました。元禄時代には**浮世草子**と呼ばれる仮名書きの本が流行し、『**好色一代男**』を書いた井原西鶴などが世に出ました。文化文政時代にはそんな出版活動がさらに発展し、滝沢馬琴の『**南総里見八犬伝**』などスケールの大きな読み物が出版されました。

🔍 **ひとくちメモ**
浮世草子
江戸時代の小説の一種。井原西鶴の『好色一代男』、八文字屋から出された本などが有名

　元禄時代に、松尾芭蕉によって連歌から派生してきた17文字の短詩である俳句が体系づけられ、広く詠まれるようになります。芭蕉の東北北陸への紀行文『**奥の細道**』などが今も愛読されていますが、文化文政時代には、小林一茶や与謝蕪村という俳人がでて、さらに俳句の形式で世の中を風刺する川柳などが生まれ、洒脱な文芸活動が展開されます。

松尾芭蕉像（山形県）

Kabuki and Bunraku thrived amidst this literary activity, with dramatists such as Tsuruya Nanboku, and portraits of popular actors were produced in woodblock prints. In 1765, Suzuki Harunobu developed a technique for making full-color prints, called *nishiki-e*, and the genre exploded with the pictures of beautiful women by Kitagawa Utamaro, the actor prints of Tōshūsai Sharaku, and the landscapes of Katsushika Hokusai and Andō Hiroshige. Works by these artists reached Europe towards the end of the Edo period and early Meiji, and are well known for the major influence they had on artists such as the Impressionists.

Nihonga, the style of Japanese painting that had its origins in the early *yamato-e* painting developed out of the traditions of the Kanō and other schools, in the Genroku period gave rise to the vigorous paintings of artists like Ogata Kōrin. Maruyama Ōkyo and others broke new ground in Nihonga with the addition of influences from Rangaku and realism techniques from Holland and China. These included artists like Shiba Kōkan, who created works using techniques from Western painting.

The Bunka-Bunsei period was characterized by people trying to outmaneuver the authority of the shogunate, satirizing society and developing an active media at a time when there was no freedom of speech, either verbal or in print.

こうした文芸活動と呼応するように、歌舞伎や文楽が隆盛し、鶴屋南北などの脚本作家が活動し、人気役者の人物画が浮世絵として刷られます。1765年に鈴木春信が多色刷りの錦絵の技法を開発し、喜多川歌麿などの美人画、東洲斎写楽などの役者絵、葛飾北斎や安藤広重などの風景、風俗画が一世を風靡します。彼らの作品が幕末から

北斎

明治にかけて西欧に持ち込まれ、印象派などの芸術活動に大きな影響を与えたことはよく知られています。

もともと大和絵からはじまり、狩野派などに受け継がれ発展してきた日本画は、元禄時代に尾形光琳などの躍動感ある作品を生み出しました。そこに蘭学などの影響もあって、オランダや中国から伝わった写実的な技法が加わり、円山応挙たちが新しい日本画の境地を切り開きます。中には司馬江漢のように洋画の技法で創作をした人物もいたのです。

人々が幕府という権力と駆け引きをするように、世の中を風刺し、出版や言論の自由のない時期に、メディア活動を展開したのが当時の特徴といえるのです。

写楽

🔍 ひとくちメモ
文人画
当時、中国の南画の画風をもった文人画が、与謝蕪村、渡辺華山などの知識人の間で流行

55 Japan's Neighbors

There were major changes in the region around Japan during the eighteenth and nineteenth centuries.

Ever since ancient times, Japan's much larger neighbor China had been familiar both culturally and politically, and Japan had frequently felt the effect of its balloon expanding and contracting. The Spanish and Portuguese had come to Japan in the sixteenth century as missionaries, but they were also attracted to Japanese and Chinese culture. Prior to this Europe had been in thrall to Christianity, which had hampered scientific development, and absorbing Asia's advanced culture through the Islamic world became the driving force for the Renaissance — so much so that when Marco Polo and others wrote about China, some European thinkers were influenced by the political system of the Chinese emperors.

However, once the modern states were founded in Europe and the Industrial Revolution got underway, the situation changed. China particularly was threatened by Russia's advance eastward. Previously, China's politics had been largely influenced by the rivalry between the northern tribes and the Han. However, as a modern power Russia extended their border as far as China. China at the time had become a strong unified nation under the Qing dynasty of the Manchu. The Qing concluded an agreement with Russia over the border, under which they each respected the other's territory.

Subsequently, however, on the back of the success of the Industrial Revolution, Britain and France had rapidly gained power and had started

日本周辺の状況は？

　18世紀から19世紀にかけて、日本周辺の状況も大きく変化します。

　太古から近世まで、中国は文化的にも政治的にも日本の身近な超大国でした。その風船の拡大と縮小が日本に影響を与えてきたことは、何度か触れています。16世紀に来航したポルトガルやスペインは、布教という野心はあったものの、日本や中国の文化へのあこがれも抱いていました。それ以前、ヨーロッパはキリスト教の束縛の中で、科学技術の発展が遅れ、イスラム圏を通してアジアの進んだ文化を吸収し、ルネッサンスの原動力としました。**マルコポーロ**等によって中国の事情が詳しく紹介されると、ヨーロッパの思想家にはむしろ中国の皇帝による政治制度から影響を受ける者もいたほどだったのです。

　しかし、ヨーロッパに近代国家が生まれ、**産業革命**が起きると状況が変化します。特に、中国にとってはロシアの東進は脅威でした。以前は北方民族と漢民族との争いが中国の政治を大きく左右していました。しかし、ロシアは近代的な力で北方民族を飲み込んで、中国と国境を接するようになったのです。当時中国は、**満州族**の**清**が強力な統一王朝をつくっていました。清はロシアと国境についての協定を結び、お互いの領土を尊重する政策にでます。

　しかし、その後産業革命の成功で、急速に力をつけたイギリスやフランスが、東南アジアを傘下にいれつつ、中

🌀 ひとくちメモ
満州民族
満州に発祥したツングース系民族。古くは女真族といった

colonizing South East Asia and now began demanding trading rights with China. Especially after China's defeat by Britain in the First Opium War in 1840, which had been caused by the export of opium to China, the advance of the great world powers on the Qing gathered pace. From China's point of view, it had been continually exposed to conflicts with its neighbors throughout history, and this war with Britain was just another of these.

However East Asia was steadily being pressurized by the advancing threat of modern states with a global strategy, Russia from the north, and Britain and France from the south.

Towards the end of the eighteenth century, Russia was eyeing up Hokkaido and at the start of the nineteenth century the American merchant ship, the Morrison, tried to land in Japan but was turned away under the isolationist policy, and intellectuals who criticized this were severely repressed by the Tokugawa shogunate.

The shogunate was already aware of the Opium War, and knew from the Dutch what was happening in Europe. What the shogunate was afraid of was the domestic disorder that would arise from a U-turn in national policy. They were no doubt hoping that nothing would happen and they could get by simply by controlling public opinion.

国との交易を迫ってきます。特に、アヘンの中国への輸出が原因で1840年におこった**アヘン戦争**によって、中国がイギリスに敗れると、清への列強の進出が加速します。中国からみれば、歴史上常に周辺民族との抗争にさらされていたこともあり、イギリスとの戦争もそうしたものの一つ程にしか実感していなかったという話も残っています。

しかし、北からロシア、南アジアからイギリスやフランスというふうに、世界戦略をもって活動する**近代国家の脅威**は、着実に東アジアに迫っていました。

徳川幕府は、18世紀の終わり頃から北海道でロシアからの接触を受け、19世紀になると、**モリソン号**というアメリカ合衆国の商船も日本にやってきますが、頑に鎖国を維持し、それを批判する知識人を厳しく弾圧します。

幕府はすでにアヘン戦争の情報も入手しており、オランダを通して西欧の事情も把握していました。幕府が恐れていたのは、急速な国策の転換による国内の混乱でした。世論を統制し、できれば何も起きずに過ごしたいというのが、当時の幕閣の本音だったのでしょう。

ひとくちメモ
アヘン戦争
1840年から2年にわたって、アヘンの密輸が原因で清とイギリスの間で行われた。アヘンの清への密輸入が続き、国内にはアヘンを吸引し健康を害する人が増え、社会も堕落していった

ひとくちメモ
モリソン号事件
1837年、アメリカのモリソン号が浦賀にやってくるが、浦賀奉行からの砲撃を受けて退去した

The Arrival of the Black Ships

The economic hardships under the shogunate-han system were felt throughout the country, and some domains were on the verge of bankruptcy. The Satsuma domain was no exception. However, under the leadership of chief retainer Zusho Hirosato, the Satsuma domain promoted trade through its vassal state the Ryūkyū Kingdom. It monopolized the sugar trade, and through Nagasaki learned about Western technology enabling it to develop its industry and ultimately restore its finances. There were several other domains that managed to reform in this way. These domains, one of which was Chōshū, played a leading role in the downfall of the shogunate.

The Satsuma daimyo Shimazu Nariakira actively sought to reform his domain following Zusho Hirosato's lead. Nariakira busied himself with the country's defence, especially the coastal defences around the strategic position of Kagoshima at the southernmost tip of the Japanese mainland, and although he was a *tozama* daimyo not directly linked to the hereditary Tokugawa line, his influence within the shogunate grew in line with his achievements.

Within the shogunate, following the failure of the Tenpō Reforms, Mizuno Tadakuni was replaced by Abe Masahiro as Chief Senior Councilor, who analyzed the international situation and addressed the problem of coastal defense measures with Shimazu Nariakira and others.

Meanwhile, America's warships had reached the west coast and were seeking to extend their power across the Pacific. Behind this was the increased demand for candles made from whale fat obtained from whaling

黒船来航前後の日本は？

　幕藩体制の経済矛盾は全国の藩におよび、中には破産
寸前の藩もでてきます。薩摩藩も例外ではありませんでし
た。しかし薩摩藩は家老であった調所広郷の指導によっ
て、傘下の琉球との貿易を促進します。砂糖の専売制を手
がけ、長崎を通して西洋の技術を導入しながら産業を育成
して、財政再建に成功します。このように藩政改革に成功
した藩もいくつかありました。長州もその一つで、これら
の藩が幕末の混乱期を牽引してゆくことになります。

　調所広郷の政策を支持し、積極的に藩政改革に取り組
んだのが藩主の島津斉彬でした。斉彬は日本本土の最南
端にある鹿児島という戦略的な位置からも、国防、特に
海防に熱心で、元々外様大名であった斉彬ですが、こうし
た実績の中で、次第に幕府の中でも発言力を増してゆきま
す。

　幕府内部では、天保の改革が失敗し、水野忠邦に代っ
て阿部正弘が老中首座となり、国際情勢の分析から、島
津斉彬などと海防対策に取り組みます。

　一方、当時西海岸まで国土を伸長したアメリカ合衆国は、
太平洋への進出に熱心でした。背景には太平洋での**捕鯨
漁**によってクジラの脂から製造される蝋燭の需要が高まっ

in the Pacific Ocean, and the need for a safe port from which they could promote trade with China. They thus demanded that Japan open her borders to the outside world.

The shogunate had received the information that the commander of the East India squadron, Commodore Matthew C. Perry, was headed for Japan with four warships, but when they arrived in Uraga in 1853 it was nevertheless cowed by their military force and Perry's uncompromising stance.

Perry had brought a letter from U.S. President Millard Fillmore demanding relations with Japan, and negotiations were conducted against a threat of force. In order to counter Russia's advance on Japan, Perry returned in 1854 with seven warships to find Japan compliant and ready to conclude the Kanagawa Treaty. This ended two hundred years of national seclusion.

The problem for the shogunate was not just America, but Britain and France's colonization of Asia under their global trading strategy and pressure from Russia in the north to allow trade.

Just as the shogunate had feared, the end of the seclusion policy had an enormous impact within the country, and even within the leadership there was a backlash of antiforeign sentiment and opposition to opening the country. This was compounded by complications in the shogunal succession, and the political situation descended into chaos. The uprising at the end of the shogunate all started from the arrival in Japan of just four ships.

ていたことや、中国との交易の促進のために、安全な港を求めていたことなどがあげられます。彼らは日本に開国を求めようとします。

東インド艦隊の司令官であった**ペリー**が、4隻の軍艦を率いて日本に向かっているという情報は、幕府も得ていましたが、実際に1853年に浦賀に軍艦が現れたとき、その軍事力とペリーの**強硬な姿勢**に幕府は圧倒されてしまいます。

ペリーは、アメリカ合衆国の大統領、フィルモアの国書をもって開国を日本に求め、武力を背景に交渉します。ロシアの日本への接近に対抗するため、1854年に再度7隻の軍艦をもって来日したとき、日本はそれに屈し、**日米和親条約**を締結したのです。これによって、200年にわたった鎖国は終わります。

幕府の問題は、アメリカのみならず、世界戦略の中でアジアを**植民地化**し、商業活動を拡大するイギリスやフランス、そして北方から南下をもくろむロシアも日本に開国を要求し、通商を求めていたことです。

幕府が恐れていた通り、鎖国政策の放棄は、国内に大きな衝撃を与え、幕府の中枢でも開国と、外国を打ち払う**攘夷**との議論が沸騰し、それに将軍の後継者をめぐる紛糾が加わり、政局が混乱します。幕末の動乱は、たった4隻の軍艦が日本にやってきたことから始まるのです。

🔍 **ひとくちメモ**
産業が発達した欧米では、工場やオフィスの灯火に鯨油を使用していたため、太平洋での捕鯨が熱心に行われた。また中国との貿易拠点としても日本を寄港地とすることが望まれた

🔍 **ひとくちメモ**
マシュー・ペリー提督
鎖国をしていた日本へ艦隊を率いて来航し、日本を開国させた。1794–1858

日米和親条約
横浜近辺に応接所を設置したことから、神奈川条約とも呼ばれる

57 Revere the Emperor and Expel the Barbarians

There was a backlash throughout Japan over the perceived threat from abroad, and the shogunate was under pressure to maintain a hardline to protect the country.

However, the shogunate was well aware of the superior military strength and technology of the European and American powers, and despite harsh public opinion they entered into Trade Treaties with several countries. First in 1858 it signed the Japan-America Treaty of Amity and Commerce, and opened the ports at Kanagawa, Nagasaki, Niigata, and Hyogo to foreign residents. This was an unequal treaty in that it ceded the right to independently charge import-export duties and conferred the jurisdiction of foreigners onto their own consular representative. Japan subsequently signed similar treaties with Holland, Britain, Russia, and France. America established a consulate at Shimoda, in Izu, with Townsend Harris as the first consul.

In response, Tokugawa Nariaki, the daimyo of Mito domain, protested fiercely to the government. He accused them of signing the treaties without any regard for the imperial palace, thus belittling the emperor who was still Japan's primary ruler, and above all of submitting to Europe and America.

Influential clans of the time, including Satsuma, Tosa, and Echizen (present-day Fukui) were the most outspoken, and sympathized with Tokugawa Nariaki who was recommending his own son Tokugawa Yoshinobu as the next shogun. However, this was opposed by the fudai

尊王攘夷と安政の大獄とは

　外国の脅威をじかに感じた日本の世論は沸騰し、外国から日本を守るために強行姿勢を貫くように幕府に期待します。

　しかし、幕府は欧米列強との軍事力や技術の差をよく分かっており、厳しい世論をかわしながら、各国と**通商条約**を締結します。まず1858年にアメリカと**日米修好通商条約**を締結し、神奈川、長崎、新潟、そして兵庫の開港とそこでの外国人の居留を許可します。この条約は関税を自主的にかける権利や外国人への裁判権を領事に与えるとい

ハリス

う**不平等な条約**で、幕府は同様の条約をオランダ、イギリス、ロシア、フランスとも締結します。アメリカは伊豆の下田に領事館を設け、**タウンゼント・ハリス**が初代領事として着任します。

　これに対し、**水戸藩**主徳川斉昭は、幕府に厳しく抗議します。海外との条約を、朝廷を無視して締結したことは、日本本来の君主である天皇をないがしろにしたことになり、何よりも欧米に屈服した幕府の姿勢を彼は断崖します。

徳川慶喜

　当時、薩摩や土佐、越前 (現福井) などの雄藩が幕政への発言権を強めており、次期将軍に自らの子供である徳川慶喜を推薦する徳川斉昭の動き

daimyo, the hereditary vassals who held the real power in the shogunate, and the conflict between the fudai and the other influential clans deepened. The shogunate was shaken by this political standoff and the fervor of the Sonnō jōi movement.

In times of emergency, the shogunate would appoint a *tairō*, a "great elder" to preside over the *rōjū* senior councilors. When amidst the political confusion the physically frail shogun Tokugawa Iesada passed away, he was succeeded by Tokugawa Iemochi with the support of the fudai daimyo, while Ii Naosuke, the daimyo of Hikone, attended to government affairs as tairō.

In order to maintain the shogunate's foreign policy, Ii Naosuke restrained Tokugawa Nariaki and Tokugawa Yoshinobu, and cracked down on the Sonnō jōi movement by arresting its activists. This crackdown was called the Ansei Purge.

However, Ii Naosuke earned the enmity of the Sonnō jōi supporters, particularly the Mito domain, and in the winter of 1860 was assassinated outside the Sakuradamon Gate of Edo Castle. The perpetrators were rōnin who had seceded from the Mito Domain in order to carry out the act. The Sakuradamon Incident made it even more difficult for the shogunate to govern.

と呼応します。しかし、元々幕府の実権を握っていた譜代大名はそれに反対し、雄藩との確執が深まります。この政治的対立と、尊王攘夷運動の加熱に幕府は揺れたのです。

　幕府は国政の緊急時には、老中の上に**大老**をおきます。こうした政治的な混乱の中で、病弱であった将軍徳川家定が他界し、新将軍に譜代大名の推す徳川家茂が就任すると、彦根藩主であった**井伊直弼**が大老となり、政務をみます。

　井伊直弼は、幕府の外交方針を貫くために、徳川斉昭や徳川慶喜を謹慎させ、尊王攘夷の活動家を逮捕、弾圧します。この弾圧を**安政の大獄**と呼びます。

　しかし、井伊直弼は水戸藩をはじめとする尊王攘夷派の恨みを買い、1860年の冬に江戸城の桜田門にて暗殺されてしまいます。犯人は、水戸藩から犯行のために脱藩した浪士たちでした。この事件を桜田門外の変と呼び、これによって幕府はますます困難な舵取りを強いられるようになるのです

58 The Downfall of the Shogunate

Many people were disillusioned by the shogunate's negative stand on Sonnō jōi.

Influential clans such as Satsuma and Echizen took advantage of the fact that the fourteenth shogun Tokugawa Iemochi was still young, and took the lead in urging a coalition between the imperial court and shogunate to deflect criticism of the shogunate and attempt to achieve a breakthrough in the deadlock. This was called *kōbu gattai*, Union of the Imperial Court and the Shogunate, and as a symbolic act in 1861 the younger sister of Emperor Kōmei, Kazu-no-Miya, was betrothed to Tokugawa Iemochi.

Following Shimazu Nariakira's death, Shimazu Hisamitsu served as regent for his young son, and in order to strengthen the union of the imperial court and shogunate, headed for Edo with an imperial messenger to hasten government reform. As a result, Matsudaira Katamori, daimyo of Aizu, was made military commissioner of Kyoto, a hotbed of the Sonnō jōi faction.

Meanwhile in Chōshū, the students of Yoshida Shōin, a Sonnō jōi intellectual executed in the Ansei Purge, were exerting a major influence in the politics of the domain. They made contact with Sonnō jōi activists all around the country, and gained the support of nobles in the imperial court in Kyoto. The royalists of Chōshū led by Katsura Kogorō (who later took the name Kido Takayoshi) despaired of the shogunate's indecision with regard to the foreign threat and schemed to establish a new government based at the imperial court.

倒幕への流れは？

　幕府が尊王攘夷に消極的であることを知ると、多くの人が失望します。

　幕府は、14代将軍徳川家茂がまだ若年なため、薩摩、越前などの雄藩が将軍の代わりに朝廷と幕府との宥和をすすめ、共同して幕府への批判をかわし難局を打開しようと画策します。これを**公武合体**と呼び、その象徴として当時の孝明天皇の妹である和宮と徳川家茂の婚礼が1861年に行われました。

🔍ひとくちメモ
公武合体
孝明天皇の妹である和宮内親王を、将軍徳川家茂に嫁がせた

　島津斉彬の死後しばらくして若年であった藩主に代わって政務をみた島津久光は、公武合体をさらに盤石にするために勅使と共に江戸に向かい、幕政の改革を進めます。この結果、尊王攘夷派が活動する京都に、会津藩主松平容保が京都守護職として赴任します。

　一方、長州では、**安政の大獄**で処刑された尊王攘夷の思想家、**吉田松陰**の門下生が藩の政治に大きな影響を与えていました。彼らは全国の尊王攘夷の活動家と連絡をとり、京都では宮廷の中にも彼らの動きと同調する公家が増えてゆきます。桂小五郎（後に木戸孝允と名乗ります）を中心とした長州の志士は、攘夷に対して優柔不断な対応をする幕府を見限って、朝廷のもとに新しい政府を樹立しようと目論みます。

桂小五郎

This movement was quelled by the volunteer troops of Aizu and the Kyoto-based shogunal police force, the *shinsengumi*. The Chōshū domain protested outside the imperial palace, and were routed by the combined Aizu and Satsuma forces. This was the Hamaguri Rebellion of the summer of 1864.

The shogunate sent a punitive military expedition to Chōshū to subdue the domain.

Chōshū continued to pursue Sonnō jōi, and the same year opened fire on foreign ships sailing close to Shimonoseki. The combined fleet of Britain, America, Holland and France retaliated by attacking Chōshū, ultimately occupying Shimonoseki due to their superior military strength.

Meanwhile in Satsuma, in the summer of 1863 British warships attacked Kagoshima. Known as the Anglo-Satsuma War, this was in retaliation for the slaying of a British merchant who had obstructed the retinue of Satsuma daimyo Shimazu Hisamitsu at Namamugi in Kanagawa.

Following these two incidents, the two domains were forced to accept that the superior military strength of the Europeans and Americans meant that any reckless attempt to expel the foreigners was useless. Subsequently, both domains actively pursued the introduction of foreign technology.

Satsuma and Chōshū had been bitter rivals, but now colluded to bring about the downfall of the shogunate.

この動きに、会津が自らの義勇軍であった**新撰組**を使い、長州の活動家を粛正します。そして、それに抗議した長州藩を薩摩藩と共同して京都御所の前で撃破したのです。この戦いを**蛤 御門の変**といいます。1864年の夏のことでした。

幕府は長州征伐を決め、軍を長州との国境に進め、長州藩を屈服させます。

同じ年、独自に攘夷運動を進めていた長州は、下関の近くを航行する外国の艦船に砲撃を加えていました。イギリス、アメリカ、オランダ、フランスの連合艦隊がその報復に長州を攻撃、彼らの進んだ軍事力の前に下関が占領されます。

一方、薩摩は薩摩で、大名である島津久光の行列を遮ったとして、イギリス人の商人が神奈川県の生麦で殺害される事件がおこり、その報復でイギリス艦隊が1863年の夏に鹿児島を砲撃する**薩英戦争**がおこっています。

この二つの事件で、両藩は無謀な攘夷が不可能であり、いかに西欧諸国の軍事力が卓越しているか、身をもって実感することになります。

薩摩と長州という仇敵が、その後連携したとき、幕府はついに瓦解するのです。

🔍 **ひとくちメモ**
蛤御門の変は、禁門の変、元治の変とも呼ばれる

🔍 **ひとくちメモ**
欧米列強は薩長の2藩の実力と将来性を知り、とくにイギリスはこの2つの藩に接近することになる

Feudal Japan
幕末体制下の日本

59 The Restoration of the Emperor

Under the shogunate-han system, people considered their own domain their homeland. Therefore, although they felt the threat from the foreign countries and advocated Sonnō jōi, it did not mean that they had any sense of Japan as a nation. Satsuma acted for Satsuma, Chōshū for Chōshū, and beyond that there was the shogunate and the emperor.

Chōshū had been dealt devastating blows by the shogunate's punitive expedition against them and the Battle of Shimonoseki, but before long the power of the anti-shogunate movement led by Katsura Kogorō and Takasugi Shinsaku was restored. They were both from the lower class of samurai that came to the fore towards the end of the shogunate, a phenomenon that sealed the fate of many domains. Chōshū and Satsuma were two of the domains that successfully placed such people in high positions.

At the time, Tokugawa Yoshinobu of the Mito domain was in Kyoto as the shogun's guardian. Yoshinobu was averse to Shimazu Hisamitsu's involvement in government, and prevaricated over the demand from the imperial court for action against foreigners while seeing to government affairs.

Active in Satsuma were people like Saigō Takamori and Ōkubo Toshimichi, low-ranking samurai who had been promoted on merit. Amidst the conflict between Shimazu Hisamitsu and the shogunate, Saigō Takamori and Katsura Kogorō from Chōshū had secret talks in Kyoto in March 1866, in which both domains settled their differences and formed

大政奉還へのみちのりは？

　幕藩体制下では、藩に属する者にとっては自らの藩が国そのものでした。従って、諸外国の脅威を感じ、尊王攘夷を唱えても、多くの人は**日本という国家意識**を持っているわけではありません。薩摩は薩摩のために、長州は長州の利益を考え、その延長に幕府が、さらにその上に天皇が君臨していたのです。

　幕府による長州征伐と下関戦争で、長州は壊滅的な打撃を受けますが、間もなく桂小五郎や高杉晋作に率いられる**倒幕派**が、藩での実権を回復します。彼らは下級武士の出身でした。幕末には、身分の低い武士が頭角を現し、藩の命運を左右する現象があちこちでおこります。こうした人材登用に成功した代表的な藩が、長州であり薩摩だったのです。

高杉晋作

　当時、幕府は将軍の後見役として、御三家である水戸出身の徳川慶喜が京都に駐在していました。慶喜は薩摩の島津久光が、幕政に介入することを嫌い、朝廷からの攘夷の要求ものらりくらりとかわしながら幕政を運営します。

　薩摩には、**西郷隆盛**、**大久保利通**等、下級武士から抜擢された人材が活躍しています。島津久光と幕府との確執の中、西郷隆盛と長州の桂小五郎（以後木戸孝允と名乗ります）が1886年3月に京都で密談し、両藩が和解し、同盟が成立します。このお膳立てをした人物が、土佐の下

🔍 ひとくちメモ
1866年京都の薩摩藩邸で締結された薩長間の密約。蛤御門の変や長州征伐で対峙する関係にあった薩摩と長州の間を、土佐の坂本龍馬がとりもった

an alliance. The person who arranged this was Sakamoto Ryōma, a low-ranked samurai from Tosa who was under the protection of Satsuma. He is one of the most popular heroes of the period at the end of the shogunate.

Exasperated by the threatening moves in Chōshū, the shogunate again sent forces in the summer of 1866. This was the second Chōshū Expedition. However, Satsuma did not join this due to its secret pact with Chōshū, and even the domains that did cooperate were afflicted by a feeling of war weariness due to financial constraints and frequent peasant revolts by starving farmers. In the end, the shogun's forces failed to defeat the newly modernized Chōshū domain, and used the death of shogun Tokugawa Iemochi as an excuse to withdraw their army. Tokugawa Yoshinobu was appointed as the new shogun, but the fact remained that the shogunate had failed to defeat this one domain in battle.

Tokugawa Yoshinobu had thought to restore the authority of the shogunate, but he met with opposition from Satsuma and others. In the end it was the Tokugawa who were destined to lose power, while the influential domains such as Satsuma sought a coalition with the imperial palace. In November 1867 the shogunate formally returned the authority of government to the imperial court, which accepted it.

And so 264 years of rule by the Tokugawa shogunate came to an end.

級武士で、薩摩に保護されていた**坂本龍馬**です。彼は幕末の英雄として、最も人気のある人物の一人です。

坂本龍馬　　　　　　　西郷隆盛

　長州の不穏な動きに業を煮やした幕府は、1866年の夏に再び長州に向けて兵を進めます。**第二次長州征伐**です。しかし、長州と密約のある薩摩は参戦せず、藩の財政が逼迫し、困窮する農民による百姓一揆が頻発するなか、協力する藩にも厭戦気分が蔓延します。結局、幕府軍は急速に近代化した長州藩を打ち破れず、将軍徳川家茂が死去したことを理由に兵を引きます。将軍職は、徳川慶喜が継ぎますが、幕府が一つの藩を打ち破れなかったことは、決定的でした。

　徳川慶喜は幕府の権威の再興を考えますが、薩摩などの雄藩と対立し、最終的に徳川家だけでの政権維持をあきらめ、雄藩と朝廷を交えた連合政権を模索します。1867年11月に朝廷に行政統治の権限を返上するという**大政奉還**を行い、それが朝廷に認められます。

　これで264年にわたって日本をおさめてきた徳川幕府は滅亡したのでした。

ひとくちメモ
大政奉還
1867年11月、第15代将軍慶喜は行政統治の権限を朝廷に返上し、ここについに264年におよぶ徳川幕府は滅亡する

Part 4

Imperial Japan
大日本帝国の興亡

大日本帝国の興亡

　アメリカなどでの世界史の教科書で、日本が積極的に登場するのは、ペリーが鎖国を解いて、明治維新によって日本が近代化を進めていったころからです。

　実際、それ以前の日本にふれている欧米の教科書は希少です。

　文字通り日本は明治以降、積極的に世界に進出しました。

　戦前の日本は Empire Japan、つまり日本帝国と呼ばれ、日本は自らを大日本帝国と呼んでいました。この激動の時代を英語で説明することは、現代の日本を語る上でもきわめて大切です。日本の戦争責任、太平洋戦争へと向かう日本への評価などは、今も日本の外交のあり方に影響を与える重要なテーマだからです。

　実際、日清戦争から日露戦争を経て、その後の満州事変から太平洋戦争に至る対外戦争の数々は、その頻度と規模からみても、過去の日本が経験したことのないものでした。

　特に19世紀から20世紀初頭まで、日本は近代化と国際化を加速させなければなりませんでした。皮肉なことに、同じ時代に、欧米列強はすでに国家とし君臨し、世界へ積極的に進出していました。それは、産業資本のニーズに押されて世界へ市場を拡大した結果でもありました。日本

はその隙間をこじ開けて海外進出を試みたことになります。

　やがて、第一次世界大戦で列強の政治体制が変化し、世界が帝国主義から離脱したとき、日本は世界へ進出しようという強迫観念から踏んだアクセルに対して、ブレーキを踏み損なったのでした。

　ここでは、あえてそうした近代日本の皮肉と悲劇にスポットをあて、「大日本帝国の興亡」という章の名前をつけたのです。

　英語で、日本を取り巻く国際政治や、日本の世論、さらに日中関係や日韓関係を説明し、議論するときに欠かせないのが、この時代の政治であり国際関係の推移なのです。少なくとも事実はしっかりと英語で把握しておくことが、より論理的で冷静な会話を産み出すことになるはずです。

　明治から昭和前期までの日本の歴史は、過去のことではなく、現代の日本の影として、今もしっかりと理解しておくべき事柄なのです。

60 The Meiji Restoration

Although the shogunate had handed back power to the imperial court, to the court's consternation it appeared that Tokugawa Yoshinobu intended to retain the leadership.

However, Satsuma and Chōshū, joined forces with the court noble Iwakura Tomomi and others to bring about a coup d'état to restore imperial rule, forcing Tokugawa Yoshinobu to resign from government service and return all the shogunate's territories to the emperor. Yoshinobu fled Kyoto to Osaka Castle, but finally his followers and the allied armies of Satsuma and Chōshū clashed south of Kyoto in the Battle of Toba-Fushimi of January 1868. Tokugawa Yoshinobu lost and, now considered an enemy of the emperor, fled back to Edo where he lay low.

Satsuma and Chōshū appointed Saigō Takamori as commander in chief and made to attack Edo, but Katsu Kaishū who had been promoted from minor hatamoto to the shogunate and who had established the shogunate's navy, managed to persuade them not to attack and Edo Castle capitulated without a shot fired.

The European and American powers were steadily colonizing Asia at the time. France provided assistance to the Tokugawa side, while their rivals, the British, supported the Satsuma-Chōshū alliance. Katsu Kaishū believed that if Japan divided into pro-Tokugawa and pro-Emperor factions and continued fighting, they would provide the foreigners with the perfect opportunity to colonize Japan.

Above all, the negotiations between Saigō Takamori and Katsu Kaishū ended without any damage to Edo, which although the imperial court

明治維新とは？

徳川慶喜は、幕府の権限を朝廷に返上することで、逆に朝廷を戸惑わせ、自らの主導権を回復しようと考えたようでした。

しかし、薩摩と長州は、公家の岩倉具視などと組んで、**王政復古**の大号令を行い、徳川慶喜に官職を辞して幕府の領地を天皇に返上するよう迫ります。徳川慶喜は京都を離れ大阪城に逃れますが、ついに彼の配下と薩摩、長州の連合軍が 1868 年 1 月に京都の南で衝突します。**鳥羽伏見の戦い**です。この戦いに敗れた徳川慶喜は、朝敵の汚名を着せられたまま、江戸に逃げ帰り、謹慎します。

薩摩と長州は、西郷隆盛を総大将として、江戸を攻撃しようとしますが、小旗本から幕府に抜擢され、開明的な発想で幕府の海軍を創設した**勝海舟**の説得にあい、攻撃を中止し、江戸城を**無血開城**します。

当時、欧米列強はアジアをどんどん植民地化していました。徳川側にはフランスが、薩摩長州側にはフランスのライバルであるイギリスが援助を行っていました。こうした中で、日本が**徳川派**と**朝廷派**に割れて戦えば、欧米諸国に日本を植民地化する絶好の機会を与えてしまうと勝海舟は考えたのです。

そして何よりも、西郷隆盛と勝海舟との交渉で、京都に朝廷があるとはいえ、実質上の日本の行政上の首都であっ

ひとくちメモ
武家政治が終わり、元の君主制に復する。徳川慶喜が官職を辞し、幕府の領地を天皇に返上することになる

岩倉具視

勝海舟

ひとくちメモ
日本が徳川派と朝廷派に割れて戦えば、日本が欧米列強の植民地になってしまうと勝海舟は恐れた

was in Kyoto was still the political capital of Japan with a population of a million.

Yet for the next year or so, the fighting continued in the Aizu domain in Tohoku that had such close links with the Tokugawa shogunate, and after Aizu capitulated the former shogunate's army continued its resistance holed up in Hakodate, Hokkaido. This series of battles is called the Boshin War, literally the "War of the year of the Dragon" after the Chinese year name. It was only after the annihilation of the former shogunate's army in Hakodate in May 1869 that Japan was finally unified under its new government led by Emperor Meiji.

The fall of the Tokugawa shogunate and the formal rebirth of Japan as a modern state in 1868 is generally referred to as the Meiji Restoration. Sakamoto Ryōma, who had arbitrated the secret agreement between Satsuma and Chōshū, had been assassinated the year before, but the Charter Oath (or Oath in Five Articles) based on his ideas and completed by Kido Takayoshi was promulgated at the time of the Restoration. This stated the government policy to abandon the policy of national seclusion, abolish anti-foreign sentiment, unite the people, and gain knowledge from the rest of the world to restore the country's economy.

Japan had been divided up into lands belonging to the emperor, shogun, and domains, but now this feudal system was discarded and a single nation-state was born.

た100万都市江戸が、戦火を被らずにすんだのです。

　しかし、それからおおよそ一年間、徳川幕府と結びつきの深かった会津藩を中心とした東北地方で戦いが続き、会津が降伏したあとは、北海道の函館に旧幕府軍が立てこもり抵抗しました。これら一連の戦争を、中国式の年号に基づいて、**戊辰戦争**と呼んでいます。日本が明治天皇を長とする新政府に統一されたのは、函館の旧幕府軍が壊滅した1869年5月のことでした。

　徳川幕府が滅び、1868年に日本が近代国家として正式に生まれ変わったことを**明治維新**と呼びます。薩摩と長州とを調停し密約を結ばせた坂本龍馬は、その一年前に暗殺されましたが、彼の案をもとに、**木戸孝允**がまとめた「**五箇条の御誓文**」が明治維新に際して発表されます。そこには、鎖国や攘夷を廃して、国民が一丸となって世界から知識をもとめ、国の経済を再興するこという施政方針が明記されています。

　天領と藩に分割されていた日本が、その封建的な政治体制を捨て、国民国家として生まれ変わったのでした。

ひとくちメモ
五箇条の御誓文
明治元年3月14日（1868年4月6日）に明治天皇が公卿や諸侯などに示した明治政府の基本方針

木戸孝允

木戸孝允

61 The Historical Significance of the Meiji Restoration

The Meiji Restoration was a landmark political reform that put an end to continuous military rule since 1192. Furthermore, compared to the European and American history of transition from absolute monarchy to constitutional monarchy or democratic government by means of popular revolution, the change from the Edo period to Meiji was unique in one respect.

The absolute monarchies of Europe were all-powerful, and although the aristocracy were wealthy landowners, the country was governed by the king or queen as the supreme ruler, assisted by bureaucrats and a permanent army. Even after the monarch's position changed by popular revolution, the new regime inherited the old system of bureacrats and army, and used the existing infrastructure.

In Japan's case, in the Edo period the country was governed by the shogun in concert with the daimyo. The daimyo had full power of government, legislation, and justice in their own domain, and the shogunate had the role of managing the daimyo. The shogunate's power was absolute and the shogun the highest authority in the land, but the state structure was essentially a feudal system that respected the regional sovereignty of the daimyo.

As the monetary economy spread throughout the country during the Edo period, it affected the shogunate and domain administration, and they were desperate to respond to this new social change. They both carried out numerous reforms of the taxes on merchants, development

明治維新の歴史的意義とは？

　明治維新は、1192年以来続いてきた**武家政権**に終止符を打った画期的な政治改革です。しかも、欧米の**絶対君主制**から市民革命を経て**立憲君主制**、あるいは**民主主義**の政体へと移行してきた歴史と比べるとき、江戸時代から明治時代への変化は、ある面ではユニークです。

　欧米の絶対君主制の場合、王の権利が強く、貴族は自らの所領と富を持ってはいるものの、国の統治という意味ではあくまでも国王が主権者でした。そして国王のもとに全国を統治する官僚と常備軍が整備されていたのです。市民革命の後も国王の位置づけは変化しても、制度としての官僚と常備軍は継承され、新たな政権はそのインフラをそのまま使用できました。

　日本の場合、江戸時代は、征夷大将軍と藩主との連携で国が統治されました。藩主は自らの領地への行政、立法、司法の全ての権利を有し、幕府はそうした藩主を管理統率する役割を担っていました。幕府の権力は絶対で、国家としては将軍が最高権力者でした。しかし、国家の構造はあくまでも**地方領主の主権**を尊重する封建制度に依っていたのです。

　江戸時代、**貨幣経済**の全国規模での浸透によって、それが幕政や藩政の維持にも影響し、幕府も藩も、この新たな社会的変化に対応しようと必死でした。商人からの冥加金、農村の開発など、幕府も藩も何度も改革を行いま

🔍 **ひとくちメモ**
全人口の7％を占める武士は、官僚的・軍事的な存在であり、非生産者であるため、納税もしなかった。貨幣経済の浸透にともなう社会の混乱の中、このような支配層のリストラが急務であった

of farming communities, and so forth, but the fact remained that seven percent of the population consisted of samurai. The samurai were soldiers and bureaucrats who did not produce anything, and furthermore did not pay any taxes.

In establishing the modern state, it was essential to restructure this ruling class. The samurai government had been founded in the Kamakura period and perfected in the Edo period, and was something of a compromise between the western European absolute monarchy and feudal system. Having taken on the mission to destroy that system, the Meiji Restoration was burdened with the prospect of popular revolution as had happened in Europe.

We usually lump together the entire period since Meiji Restoration and call it the present era. So if we consider this present era in the same way as past eras, each lasting several centuries, what kind of period is it, and where is it headed? This also has implications for the future.

However, the history of destroying and replaying the past that started in the Meiji period was interrupted by World War II, eighty years after the Meiji Restoration. I shall attempt to situate this divided present era within the historical context.

す。しかし、全人口の7％を占める武士はあくまでも官僚的、軍事的存在で、非生産者でした。しかも武士は納税者ではありません。

　近代国家の建設には、**この支配層のリストラ**が必要不可欠です。西欧の絶対君主制度と封建制度の折衷案のような武家政権が鎌倉に始まり、江戸時代に完成したわけですが、明治維新は、その制度そのものを破壊しなければならないという使命を負った点で、西欧での市民革命以上の課題を背負うことになります。

　我々は、一般的に明治時代から現在までをひとくくりにして、**現代**といっています。では、現代とは過去の数百年ごとに区切られる時代区分で読み取ると、どのような時代のどこにかかっているのでしょうか。これは未来学とも関連したテーマです。
　ただ、明治時代にはじまった過去の破壊と再生の歴史は、第二次世界大戦で一区切りします。明治維新から80年と、その後現在までの60年を区切って、現代を長い歴史の中に位置づける方法を模索したいものです。

62 The Reforms of the Meiji Government

The reforms of the Meiji Restoration encompassed all aspects of politics, economy, culture, and so forth. They were wide-ranging and led to major changes in society in a short period of time, making it an unusual case in the world. The Meiji government's basic policy was *fukoku kyōhei*, or "enrich the country, strengthen the military" and *shokusan kōgyō*, "the promotion of industry." First, it was necessary to develop an environment in which this would be possible.

Following the surrender of Edo castle in 1868, the Tokugawa shogun was sent to Sunpu (modern-day Shizuoka) where he became a daimyo. Also, Edo was renamed Tokyo, and the following year Emperor Meiji took up residence in Edo castle and moved the seat of government, making Tokyo the capital city of Japan.

The Meiji government first created a Council of State under the emperor, and then below that a Justice Ministry. They also abolished the feudal class system under the principle of equality, awarding special treatment to daimyo and court nobles as peers.

Next they abolished the domain system and set about creating a system of equal government throughout the country.

As the first stage, in 1869 they enacted the return of the domain registers, bringing the land belonging to daimyo under national ownership, and then appointing the daimyo as governors. Later they dismissed the daimyo and reorganized the domains into a prefectural system administered by governors appointed by the central government. This major reform was effected in 1871 in return for the government

明治政府はどのような方針で改革を行った？

　明治維新での改革は、政治経済文化等あらゆる面に及びます。内容は多岐で、社会そのものを短期間で変化させた、世界的にも珍しいケースとなりました。明治政府の基本方針は、**富国強兵**と**殖産興業**（産業の振興）です。まずはそれを可能にする環境整備が必要です。1868年の江戸城の開城後、徳川家は駿府（現在の静岡）に移され、一大名になりました。

　そして、江戸を東京と改めて、翌年に明治天皇が江戸城に入り、行政府が移され、東京が日本の首都になったのです。

　明治政府は、まずは天皇の親政の元に**太政官**をおき、その下に**刑部省**を設置します。そして、士農工商の身分制度を廃止し、四民平等の原則のもと、大名や公家は華族として特別に遇します。

　次に、藩を廃止し、全国を均一に統治するシステム造りが始まります。

　第一段階として、大名の土地である藩を国の所有に変え、改めて国が大名を藩知事に任命する版籍奉還を1869年に実施します。次に、大名を藩知事から解任し、藩を県と改め、国から県令を送る制度を構築します。多くの藩は膨大な債務に苦しんでおり、債務を藩主から切り離し、政府が引き受けることを条件に、1871年に実行したのが**廃藩**

assuming responsibility for the crippling debts facing most daimyo.

The individual paper currencies issued by each domain were abolished, and replaced by a new currency issued by the government. Also, the abolition of the domains and establishment of a new prefectural system with the land under government control made it possible to establish a uniform land tax based on the land price nationwide. In order to instigate the change to a monetary economy, payment in kind made with rice was discontinued in favor of tax payments made in paper currency, with taxes being applied to all land without exception instead of just farmland. This was the Land Tax Reform.

The Land Tax Reform meant that the land formerly belonging to the feudal lords or the state could now be under individual ownership. Land was thus considered an asset, and investment on real estate as well as real estate as security, essential to capitalism, was permitted. Parallel to these reforms were others such as the edict forcing the former samurai to cut off their emblematic topknot, and the Ban on Christianity was revoked out of solicitude for Westerners.

These reforms were astonishingly all undertaken within ten years of the collapse of the shogunate, thanks to which Japan was able to reinvent herself as Asia's first modern nation state.

置県の大改革です。

　藩が独自に発行していた藩札という紙幣も廃止され、政府の発行する貨幣と交換されます。また、廃藩置県によって、政府は全国の土地を把握できるようになり、全国の地価に対して一律に地租という税金をかけることを可能にしたのです。貨幣経済の実情への転換のために、従来の米を中心とした物納から、貨幣による納税方式に変更し、農地のみならず、全ての土地に例外なく税金が付加されます。**地租改正**の実施です。

　地租改正は、従来領主や国が所有していた土地を個人所有できるようになったことを意味し、土地が資産と考えられ、資本主義の根幹である**不動産**への投資や**不動産担保**が認められるようになったのです。この改革と平行し、例えば武士の時代の象徴であった**髷**を結った髪型を廃止する断髪令を公示し、欧米の反発を配慮して、キリスト教禁教令を廃止するといった改革も実行します。

　こうした改革が幕府崩壊から 10 年以内に実施されたことは驚くべきことで、この改革があってこそ、日本がアジアではじめての近代国家へと脱皮してゆくことができたのです。

Imperial Japan
大日本帝国の興亡

63 The Satsuma Rebellion

In 1871, the new Meiji government made its diplomatic debut as Iwakura Tomomi, Kido Takayoshi, and Ōkubo Toshimichi left domestic affairs up to Saigō Takamori and visited the great powers of Western Europe. Their main objective was the amendment of the unequal trade treaties concluded with various countries in the Edo period. Under these treaties, Japan had ceded tariff autonomy and granted extraterritorial rights to other countries.

However, they were unable to persuade the countries they visited to renegotiate the treaties, and seeing the overwhelming economic and military power of the West, they returned home more than ever aware of the urgent need to continue with domestic reforms and military build-up.

While they had been away, Saigō Takamori's government had continued with the reforms, establishing Ministries for the Army and Navy, and introducing the solar calendar. On the other hand, an official request to establish diplomatic relations had been rejected by the Joseon dynasty of Korea. Having just returned from their round tour, Iwakura Tomomi and Kido Takayoshi considered domestic policy a priority, and rejected Saigō Takamori's insistence on a hardline policy towards Korea (the *seikanron*, or Debate to Conquer Korea).

However, the radical domestic reforms had been disadvantageous for some people in the country. There was particular discontent among the former samurai, who had originally been a privileged class. For example, the new government was founding a regular army with conscripts from the general population, and the samurai saw this as usurping their

西南戦争までの状況は？

1871年に、明治政府は岩倉具視、木戸孝允、そして大久保利通は、内政を西郷隆盛にまかせ、西欧列強を訪問し、新政府としての外交デビューをしました。一行の主な目的は、江戸時代に諸外国と締結された不平等条約を改正してもらうことでした。江戸時代に結ばれた通商条約には、日本に**関税自主権**がなく、相手国に**治外法権**がみとめられたものだったのです。

しかし、欧米を訪問した一行は、条約改正交渉は受け付けてもらえず、欧米の圧倒的な経済力と軍事力を目の当たりにして、国内の改革と国力増強がいかに急務かを思い知らされて帰国します。

一行の留守中に、西郷隆盛による政府は、**陸軍省**、**海軍省**を設置し、**太陽暦**を採用するなどの改革を進めますが、外交面では李氏朝鮮から国書の受理を拒絶され、国交を開くことができないといった問題に直面します。朝鮮への強硬政策（**征韓論**）を主張する西郷隆盛派に対して、欧米歴訪を終えて帰国した岩倉具視や木戸孝允は、内政を優先させる考えから西郷の提案を拒絶します。

しかし、内政の急激な改革は、一方で国内に様々な不利益を受ける人々を生み出します。特に元々特権階級であった旧武士階級、すなわち士族の不満には著しいものがありました。例えば、新政府は一般の国民から徴兵し、常備軍を創設しますが、これは戦闘集団としての武士の特

🔍 **ひとくちメモ**
岩倉具視、木戸孝允、大久保利通らは、治外法権、関税自主権などの不平等条約を改正しようと諸外国をまわるが、交渉は受け付けてもらえなかった

Imperial Japan
大日本帝国の興亡

prerogatives as soldiers. Also, the antagonism between the victors of the Boshin War — Satsuma, Chōshū, Tosa, Hizen (Saga prefecture) — and the losers had deep roots. Added to this, with the transition from the domains to the prefectural system many samurai had lost their jobs.

Saigō and Etō Shinpei sympathized with these dissatisfied samurai families and as a result in 1873 they resigned from the government. Etō returned home to Saga and organized the Saga Rebellion in 1874 with discontented samurai, for which he was executed.

Citing the principle of equality, the new government subsequently abolished the samurai stipend and promulgated the law banning swords, prohibiting samurai from wearing this symbol of the samurai.

Even though Satsuma was on the side of the victors, the circumstances there were similar. When Saigō returned home, the discontented samurai rallied around him and eventually this flared up into the large-scale Satsuma Rebellion of 1877.

At the end of this war, which engulfed most of Kyushu for nine months, Saigō Takamori's army was cornered in Kagoshima and Saigō committed suicide. With the conclusion of the Satsuma Rebellion, the Meiji government gradually emerged from the turmoil surrounding its inception.

権を奪うものです。また、戊辰戦争の勝ち組である薩摩、長州、土佐、肥前（佐賀県）と負け組との対立も根深いものがありました。それに加えて廃藩置県で、多くの武士が職を失います。

　これら不満を持つ士族に同情的であった西郷や江藤新平は、その結果1874年に政府を去ります。江藤新平は地元佐賀に帰ると不平士族と共に1867年に**佐賀の乱**を起こし処刑されました。

　その後さらに、新政府は**四民平等の原則**に従い、武士への報禄支給を廃止し、**廃刀令**も発布し、武士のシンボルであった刀を帯びることを禁止します。

　薩摩も勝ち組とはいえ、状況は似ていました。彼らのリーダー的存在であった西郷が帰郷すると、不満を抱く士族が西郷を押し立てて、それがついに大規模な反乱へと発展します。1877年、**西南戦争**の勃発です。

　9ヶ月に及ぶ九州の大半を巻き込んだ戦争の後、西郷軍は鹿児島に追いつめられ、西郷隆盛は自決します。西南戦争の終結をもって、明治政府はその創世記の混乱を脱してゆくのでした。

ひとくちメモ
西南戦争
1877年西郷隆盛らがおこした新政府に対する反乱。熊本に達するが城を攻略できないうちに政府軍に討たれ敗退

64 The Freedom and People's Rights Movement and the Constitution

The Satsuma Rebellion was a civil war that erupted out of the dissatisfactions of the discontented samurai class, while the government forces that suppressed the rebellion were a regular army drawn from the general population following the abolition of the four-class system. Amongst the commissioned officers were samurai that had fought on the side of the former shogunate in the Boshin War.

There has not been a civil war in Japan since the Satsuma Rebellion. When the attempt to overthrow the government by military force foundered, the discontented samurai developed into a movement demanding a voice in the political arena. Particularly people like Itagaki Taisuke, who had originally been part of the Meiji government and later withdrew from the political world along with Saigō Takamori and cohorts, insisted that the government should establish a National Diet and determine policy through a party political system. Together with Ōkuma Shigenobu and others who had left the government, he promoted the Freedom and People's Rights Movement throughout the country.

The government tried to suppress it with laws controlling meetings and the press, but given that the government was seeking the revision of the unequal trade treaties with the West, they were also under pressure to demonstrate at home and abroad that Japan was a constitutional monarchy and under the rule of the law.

In order to reform the extraterritoriality of foreigners, who were immune from prosecution under the national laws, and lack of authority to impose customs duties on imported products, it was necessary to create

自由民権運動から憲法発布までの経緯は？

西南戦争は、**不平士族**の不満が噴き出した内戦でした。そして、西南戦争を鎮圧した政府軍は、士農工商を撤廃し、一般から集めた正規軍でした。将校の中には、戊辰戦争で旧幕府側で活躍した武士も加わっています。

板垣退助

西南戦争以来現在まで、日本では内戦は起きていません。不平士族は、武力での政府転覆は困難として、政治の場での発言権を求める運動を展開します。特に元々明治政府に参画し、その後西郷隆盛たちと政界を去った**板垣退助**などは、政府が国会を開設し、政党政治をもって政策を決定すべきであると主張し、同じく政府を去った**大隈重信**などと共に、**自由民権運動**を全国に広めます。

大隈重信

🔍 **ひとくちメモ**
自由民権運動
明治時代前期に、憲法制定、議会の開設、言論と集会の自由の保障など求めた国民運動

政府は、新聞条例や集会条例などによって、弾圧を加えようとしますが、一方で、欧米との不平等条約の改正などを考えた場合、日本が**立憲君主国**であり、**法治国家で**あることを内外に示す必要性にも迫られていました。

外国人を自国の法律で裁くことのできない**治外法権**や、自らが輸入品に関税をかけられない**関税自主権**のない取引関係を改善するためには、例えば日本で外国人が不当

a system that would demonstrate that foreigners would not be unjustly subject to cruel punishments and that changes in circumstances would not lead to the sudden imposition of high tariffs. In other words, Japan had to demonstrate at home and abroad that it was a country under the rule of laws that the rest of the world could approve of.

Night after night, Foreign Minister Inoue Kaoru invited foreigners to balls at the Rokumeikan, completed in 1883, as a symbol of Japan's Westernization, but many foreigners could not trust Japan, which until a short while before had conducted such cruel punishments as beheading.

With the situation thus, the repression of the Freedom and People's Rights Movement in itself lowered the image of Japan for foreign countries.

Finally, in 1889, the government promulgated the Meiji Constitution, and the following year gave voting rights to males over the age of twenty-five who paid taxes of fifteen yen or above, held a general election, and established the National Diet. Previously, in 1885, they had abolished the system of the Grand Council of State and started the Cabinet system, appointing Itō Hirobumi from Chōshū as the first Prime Minister.

However, under the Meiji Constitution, both the prime minister and ministers of state were appointed by the emperor, rather than a cabinet system whereby the government was formed by the biggest party in the Diet. Under the Meiji Constitution, the emperor was sovereign, and Japan was a monarchal system in which the emperor was supreme commander of the army and navy.

で残酷な刑に処されることがないことや、状況の変化で高関税をいきなり適応することがないといったことを証明できる制度の構築が必要になります。すなわち、日本という国が、世界が納得する法律で運営されている法治国家であるということを、内外に示さないといけないのです。

　1883年に完成した**鹿鳴館**で、当時の外務大臣井上馨は、外国人を連夜舞踏会に招き、欧米化した日本を印象づけようとしますが、多くの外国人は、少し前まで斬首などの残酷な刑が執行されていた日本のことを信用できません。

　そうした観点からみた場合、自由民権運動を弾圧すること自体、諸外国へのイメージダウンにつながってしまいます。

　政府は最終的に、1889年に**大日本帝国憲法**を発布し、翌年には、国税を15円以上納税する25歳以上の男子に**選挙権**を与え、総選挙を実施、**国会**を開設しました。それ以前1885年には**太政官**制を廃止して、内閣制度がスタートし、長州出身の伊藤博文が初代内閣総理大臣に任命されています。

　しかし、大日本帝国憲法では、内閣総理大臣も国務大臣も等しく天皇が任命することになっており、国会の最大政党が組閣する責任内閣制は採用されていません。大日本帝国憲法は天皇が主権者であり、日本は、天皇が内閣とは独立した陸海軍の統帥権を持った君主制国家であることを規定した憲法だったのです。

鹿鳴館

🔍 **ひとくちメモ**
鹿鳴館
現在の千代田区内幸町に、お雇い外国人であるジョサイア・コンドルの設計により建てられた。レンガ創り2階建てで、1階に大食堂、談話室、ライブラリーがあり、2階が開け放つと100坪にもなった舞踏室であった

伊藤博文

65 The Economy in the Meiji Period

Long ago, people from the continent had introduced advanced Chinese culture into Japan.

Likewise, the Meiji government invited many intellectuals and experts from abroad in order to make Japan a strong, wealthy, and industrialized nation.

In some cases, even people at the center of the regime went abroad to observe and learn about Western systems and society. Before the Meiji constitution was promulgated, Itō Hirobumi had gone to Germany to study the German constitution, the closest thing to a constitutional monarchy at the time. He also invited a military adviser from Germany to train officers.

Meanwhile, for the criminal and civil law codes, France's Gustave Boissonade came to Japan as an advisor to help make Japanese legal codes along the lines of France's laws.

Japan thus rapidly established a social system, but after the Satsuma Rebellion the national finances were strained. The high land tax to compensate for this led to increasing numbers of farmers going bankrupt as well as substantial price rises, and the consequent social instability further spurred the anti-government cause of the Freedom and People's Rights Movement.

In the Imperial Diet, following the amendment of the Constitution, the political party formed by Itagaki Taisuke and others of the Freedom and People's Rights Movement trounced the governing party and, holding the majority, opposed the Cabinet policy. The Cabinet increased military

明治時代の経済状況は？

　はるか昔、日本には大陸からの帰化人が中国の進んだ文明を持ち込みました。

　それと同じように、明治政府は、外国から多くの知識人や技術者を招き、富国強兵、殖産興業に努めます。

　時には政権の中枢の人間までが海外に赴き、欧米の制度や社会を学び、参考にします。大日本帝国憲法を制定する前、伊藤博文はドイツに赴き、より**立憲君主制**に近い当時のドイツ憲法を学んでいます。同じドイツからは軍事顧問を招聘し、将官の育成にあたります。

　一方、刑法と民法については、フランスの**ボアソナード**が顧問として来日し、フランスの法律を参考にした法律の作成にあたりました。

　日本はこのようにして急速に社会制度を整えますが、西南戦争以来、国家財政は決して潤沢ではありませんでした。それを補うための高い地租に、農村では経済破綻する農民が増え、物価が高騰し、社会不安が**自由民権運動**による反政府運動をさらに刺激します。

　憲法改正後の**帝国議会**では、板垣退助などの流れを組む自由民権派の政党が、政府系政党を破り、過半数を占め、内閣の政策と対立します。内閣は、ロシアなどからの脅威、不安定な朝鮮半島への対策などから、軍事費を増

🔍 **ひとくちメモ**
ギュスターヴ・ボアソナード
フランスの法学者、明治初期に来日、日本の国内法の整備に貢献した。
1825–1910

🔍 **ひとくちメモ**
自由民権運動では、憲法制定、議会開設、地租の軽減、言論・集会の自由などの要求をかかげた

spending and raised taxes to fund measures to counter the threat from countries like Russia and the instability of the Korean peninsula. In the original Meiji Constitution, the Cabinet was responsible to the emperor and could exercise a strong authority that transcended the Diet. Accordingly, the Cabinet dissolved the Diet, but the result of the general election was again a victory for the Freedom and People's Rights Movement faction. At the same time, added to the discontent over economic hardship, there was also opposition to politicians from Satsuma, Chōshū, Tosa, and Hizen who had served in the Meiji Restoration, holding sway in the key positions of state.

Against the background of a surge in morale of the Freedom and People's Rights Movement, there was economic disparity caused by the rapid modernization following the Meiji Restoration. The shortfall between the costs necessary to establish the country's infrastructure, including military spending, and the tax revenue from the nation's economic development, put a strain on people's livelihoods. And many people had not yet realized that this shortfall was a serious issue affecting Japan's modernization as a whole.

Discontent over this shortfall and the standoff between the Diet and the government was alleviated the fact that people's attention turned to the external threat posed by the friction with Qing China. This had started out as a squabble between Qing China and Japan over the Korean peninsula, and developed into contemporary Japan's first all-out war with a foreign country.

やし、増税をもくろみます。もともと大日本帝国憲法では、内閣は天皇に対して責任を持つことになっており、内閣は議会を超越した強い権限を行使できたのです。従って、内閣は議会を解散しますが、総選挙の結果は再び自由民権派が勝利します。当時、経済的な困窮への不満に加え、明治維新の功労者である薩摩、長州、土佐、肥前出身の者が、国の中枢で幅をきかせていたことへの反発もあったのです。

　自由民権運動が高揚した背景には、明治維新以降の急速な近代化がもたらす経済矛盾があります。軍事費を含む国のインフラ整備に必要なコストに、国家の経済発展による税収が追いつかないというアンバランスが、国民生活に無理を強いたわけです。そして、このアンバランスこそが、日本の近代化の歴史全てに影響する重大な課題だとは、多くの人はまだ気付いていませんでした。

　その矛盾からくる不満を沈静化し、議会と政府との対立が緩和されてゆく過程にあったのが、清との軋轢という外からの脅威に国民の目を向けることだったのです。それは、朝鮮半島を巡る日本と清との利権争いに端を発した、現代日本で初めての本格的な対外戦争に発展するのです。

66 The Sino-Japanese War

Around this time, superpower Russia was laying the Trans-Siberian Railroad and was on the lookout for opportunities to acquire concessions across the north and east of the continent. It had already acquired the concession from Qing China to directly connect the Trans-Siberian Railroad to the Chinese Eastern Railway that ran through Manchuria, and was looking to expand its interests.

Under the 1875 Treaty of Saint Petersburg, Japan gained sovereignty over the Kuril Islands in exchange for surrendering Sakhalin, to which its rights of possession were unclear, thereby settling the issue of its border with Russia. However, given the future threat posed by Russia, the Meiji government was keen to bring the Korean Peninsula under Japanese influence.

The Korean peninsula was under the conservative rule of the Joseon dynasty, who paid tribute to Qing China. Japan was negotiating with China for equal of opportunities in the Korean peninsula when the Donghak Peasant Revolution, reminiscent of the "revere the Emperor and expel the barabarians" movement of the late Edo period, broke out and both China and Japan sent troops to quell it. Afterwards, the Japanese troops remained stationed in the Korean Peninsula, which eventually led to the start of the Sino-Japanese War in 1894.

Japan had been modernizing its military ever since the Meiji Restoration, and by the following year had defeated the Qing's northern squadron, captured strategic places in the Shandong Peninsula, and won the war. Since the peace treaty was signed at Shimonoseki in Japan, it is also called

日清戦争とは？

当時、強国ロシアが**シベリア鉄道**を敷設し、北から極東での利権獲得の機会を狙っていました。すでに、清とは、シベリア鉄道と直結して満州に伸びる**東清鉄道**の敷設権を獲得し、権益の拡大を狙っていました。

日本は、1875年にロシアと交渉し、領有権が曖昧であった樺太を放棄するかわりに、**千島列島**を日本が領有する**樺太千島交換条約**を締結し、ロシアとの国境問題は解決していました。しかし、将来のロシアの脅威を考えたとき、朝鮮半島を日本の影響下に置くべきであると、明治政府は考えます。

当時、朝鮮半島は李氏朝鮮王朝の保守的な統治のもと、清に対して隷属していました。日本は朝鮮半島の機会均等を求めて清と交渉し、朝鮮にちょうど江戸末期の尊王攘夷を思い出させるような**東学党の乱**が起きると、清と共に出兵してそれを鎮圧します。そして、その後も日本が朝鮮半島に軍隊を駐留させたことから、ついに1894年に清との全面戦争となったのです。**日清戦争**の勃発です。

明治維新以来、軍の近代化に積極的に投資をしていた日本は、翌年までに清の北洋艦隊を撃破し、**山東半島**の要衝も占領し勝利します。講和条約は日本の下関で締結されたことから、**下関条約**と呼ばれています。

ひとくちメモ
シベリア鉄道
ロシアの国内を東西に横断する鉄道で、東アジアへの進出も目的のひとつだった。さらに東清鉄道の敷設権も獲得した

ひとくちメモ
千島列島
根室海峡からカムチャッカ半島の南の千島海峡までの間に連なる列島

樺太・千島交換条約
日本とロシア帝国との間で国境を確定するために結ばれた条約。1875

ひとくちメモ
東学党の乱
この朝鮮半島での内戦が、日清戦争に発展する。東学とは儒・仏・道教を折衷した宗教で、内戦の関与者に東学の信者が多かった。甲午農民戦争とも言う

ひとくちメモ
山東半島
渤海湾を隔てて遼東半島に向かい合う中国最大の半島

the Treaty of Shimonoseki.

As a result, Japan secured a large amount in compensation from Qing China, as well as possession of Taiwan, the Penghu islands, and Liaodong Peninsula. The Sino-Japanese Commerce and Navigation Treaty signed the following year was very much like the earlier unequal treaties between Japan and the West.

However, just after the Treaty of Shimonoseki was signed, Russia, bent on expanding their concessions into China, joined France and Germany in demanding that Japan return the Liaodong Peninsula to China. Japan bowed to the pressure from these three powerful countries, but their meddling excited national sentiment and foreshadowed the war with Russia ten years later.

When the Sino-Japanese War broke out, the standoff between the Freedom and People's Rights Movement and the government ceased and the country united behind the government. Indeed, it diverted attention from the domestic conflict to matters abroad.

Japan's modernization appears to have succeeded due to the fact that Japan learned from other countries. Just as in the past Japan digested this foreign culture to create its own, but this time the process happened within a very short space of time. Amidst the subtle interaction of this imbalance and the economic shortfall created by rapid investment, Japan took an unprecedented aggressive stance overseas.

その結果、日本は清国から多額の賠償金を獲得し、台湾と澎湖島、**遼東半島**の領有を認めさせます。そして翌年、**日清通商航海条約**を締結しますが、これは以前、日本が欧米と締結した不平等条約と酷似したものでした。

ところが、下関条約締結直後に、中国への利権の拡大をもくろむロシアが、フランスとドイツを伴って、遼東半島の中国への返還を日本に要求します。列強3国の圧力に屈した日本は、その要求をのみますが、この三国干渉が国民感情を刺激し、10年後のロシアとの戦争の伏線になるのです。

日清戦争がおきると、日本国内での自由民権派と政府との対立はなくなり、国民はこぞって政府の後押しをします。まさに、国内の矛盾を外に目をやることでそらしたわけです。

日本の近代化は、急速な西欧化の歴史で、諸外国が参考にするほど成功したかに見えます。しかし、それは過去の日本のように海外の文化を消化し、自らの文化を形成するには、あまりにも短期間で急速な異文化の導入でした。そのアンバランスと、急速な投資によって生じた経済的矛盾が微妙に影響し合いながら、日本はかつてない積極的な対外進出へと自らを追いやるのです。

ひとくちメモ

遼東半島
中国遼寧省の南部に位置する半島

日清通商航海条約
1896年7月21日に北京において日本と清の間に締結された、日本に有利な不平等条約

The Russo-Japanese War

Following the Sino-Japanese War, the government saw Russia as a potential adversary and pumped up to half the national budget into building up the military. The Diet aimed to establish a cabinet system of government, and after a certain amount of maneuvering, the Rikken Seiyūkai (Friends of Constitutional Government party) set up by members of the Freedom and People's Rights Movement and outstanding statesmen from the Meiji Restoration such as Itō Hirobumi took charge of government while Katsura Tarō, who insisted on a hardline against Russia, became prime minister.

At the time, Russia was in league with the anti-Japanese influence in Joseon dynasty Korea. In Qing China, amidst the advance of the world powers, there was a standoff between the modernizing faction under the emperor and the emperor's aunt Empress Dowager Cixi who effectively ruled the country, and in 1898 the emperor's faction was defeated. The same year the Righteous Harmony Society (known as "Boxers" in English), an ultranationalist religious group that held that the colonialism of the European powers was the cause of disorder within the country, started an uprising. Since this was supported by the Qing government it became an international dispute, and allied forces from various countries including Japan and Russia dispatched troops to Beijing to quell them. Even after this was settled, Russian troops remained in Beijing.

There was a reason behind Russia's advance on the Far East. In 1853 Russia had gone to war with Turkey and Crimea as it sought to expand its interests into the Middle East, but Britain, France, and Turkey had formed an alliance and defeated them. Consequently Russia changed the focus of

日露戦争とは？

　政府は日清戦争のあと、ロシアを仮想敵国とし、国家予算の半分までをつぎ込んで、軍備を増強します。議会は、政党内閣を目指し、様々な駆け引きの末、自由民権運動家の一部と伊藤博文などの明治維新以来の元勲による、立憲政友会が政権を担当し、その後対ロ強攻策を主張する桂太郎が首相となります。

桂太郎

Imperial Japan
大日本帝国の興亡

　当時、ロシアは、李氏朝鮮内の反日勢力と連携していました。清では列強の進出の中で、皇帝を擁して近代化を進める一派と国を実質上支配していた皇帝の叔母にあたる西太后（せいたいごう）とが対立し、1898 年に皇帝派が一掃されます。同年、国の混乱の原因が欧米列強の植民地主義にあるとして、排外主義をかざす宗教団体、**義和団**が争乱をおこします。その活動を清国政府が支援したため**国際紛争**となり、日本とロシアを含む各国連合軍が北京に出兵するという事件がおきました。ロシアは事件解決後も兵を引きません。

🔍 ひとくちメモ
西太后
清末期の権力者で、咸豊帝の后で、同治帝の母。1835–1908

　ロシアの極東進出には理由がありました。1853 年に、ロシアは中近東への権益の拡大を狙ってトルコとクリミア戦争をおこしますが、イギリスやフランスとトルコが連合し、戦いに破れます。そのため、ロシアは領土拡大の矛先を

its territorial expansion from the Middle East to the Far East.

Britain, who had invested in China since early on, was wary of this move by Russia. In order to oppose Russia, Britain promptly approached Japan and just before the Sino-Japanese War amended the outline of the unequal treaty. The Anglo-Japanese Alliance was concluded after Katsura Tarō's cabinet was formed in 1901. Meanwhile, Russia formed an alliance with Britain's rival France, and Japan became increasingly caught up in the complicated fetters of such international relations.

In 1903, Japan went to war against Russia. Japan attained major victories in this war, and ultimately Russia surrendered their stronghold in Port Arthur and then conceded defeat in the Battle of Mukden. Finally, to the amazement of the world, Russia's flagship Baltic Fleet was annihilated in the Japan Sea. However, Japan was already at the limits of its strength, and having spent an enormous amount of money on the war the country's finances were on the verge of collapse. The unprecedented injection of 1,100,000 troops had resulted in over 84,000 casualties. In Russia, amidst the various conflicts of the closing years of the Tsarist government, morale in the military was low. The incident known as Bloody Sunday, when the army opened fire on workers who were marching to petition parliament in the capital of St Petersburg, exacerbated the acute political situation.

In view of the sorry plight of both countries, the U.S. president Theodore Roosevelt mediated a peace treaty that was signed in Portsmouth, America, in 1905.

中東から極東に変えたのです。

　このロシアの動きを、早くから中国に投資していたイギリスは警戒します。イギリスは、ロシアと対抗するために、日本に急速に接近、日清戦争直前に不平等条約を大筋で改正し、1901年に新英派の桂太郎内閣が成立すると、**日英同盟**を締結します。一方、ロシアはイギリスのライバルであるフランスと同盟しており、日本はこうした国際関係の複雑なしがらみに捉えられてゆきます。

　1903年、日本はロシアと開戦します。日本は主要な戦争では勝利し、最終的に**旅順**のロシア要塞が陥落、**奉天の会戦**で勝利、そしてロシアの誇る**バルチック艦隊**を日本海で壊滅させ諸外国を驚嘆させます。しかし、国力はすでに限界で、膨大な戦費を使い果たし、国家財政は**破綻寸前**でした。110万人という前代未聞の兵力を注入し、戦死者は8万4000人以上になります。そして、ロシアはロシアで帝政末期の様々な矛盾の中で兵の士気も下がり、首都ペテルスブルグでは、国会の開設を請願して行進していた労働者に、軍隊が発砲し多数の死傷者をだす、**血の日曜日**事件がおき、政情が極度に緊迫します。

　こうした両国の窮状を背景に、アメリカのセオドア・ルーズベルト大統領の仲裁で、1905年、アメリカのポーツマスで、講和条約が締結されたのでした。

68 Japan's Standing after the Russo-Japanese War

The Russo-Japanese War was a major turning point for Japan.

The aim of the United States in brokering the Treaty of Portsmouth lay in their Asian Pacific policy post-Perry. America had annexed Hawaii in 1898, just before the Russo-Japanese War. Subsequently they had extended their interests to the Philippines and China. Meanwhile, due to the Anglo-Japanese Alliance and the Russo-Japanese War, Britain had not only placated the threat from Japan but had been able to drive Russia northwards.

From the point of view of the European powers, the Far East was a long way away. Being at its furthest extreme, Japan had managed to maintain its independence. However, from the point of view of both the U.S. and Britain, Japan had become an important strategical point for the huge market of China. In ancient times, Japan had been located "east" of China. Now, since modernization, its position had changed to "ahead of" China. It was unclear at this stage whether it would prove to be a dangerous thorn or a friendly sponge.

Aware of Japan's straitened circumstances, Russia was unyielding and negotiations for the Portsmouth Treaty were difficult. Eventually, the plenipotentiary for Russia, Sergei Witte ceded the southern half of Sakhalin to Japan, Japan's preeminence in the Korean Peninsula was guaranteed, and the transfer of the southern half of the Eastern Chinese Railway (the Manchuria Railway) and southern Liaodong Peninsula to Japan was agreed. However, Japan did not receive any war indemnity from

日露戦争後の世界と日本は？

　日露戦争は、日本の大きな転換点になりました。

　ポーツマス条約を斡旋したアメリカの意図は、あのペリー以来のアジア太平洋政策にありました。日露戦争直前、1898年にアメリカはハワイを併合しました。そこからフィリピン、そして中国へと自らの権益を伸ばしてゆきます。一方、イギリスは、日英同盟と日露戦争によって、日本という脅威を懐柔しながら、ロシアを北方に追いやることができました。

　極東は、西欧列強からみれば遠隔地です。日本は、その一番端にあるという特異性によって、その黎明期から独立を保ってきました。ところが、アメリカにとってもイギリスにとっても、日本は中国という広大な市場へつながる重要な戦略ポイントとなったのです。太古、中国の「東」という風に日本は位置づけられていました。それが、近代から現代には、中国の「前」という位置へと変化したのです。それが危険な釘となるか、友好的なスポンジとなるか、列強はまだ判断できずにいたのです。

　ポーツマス条約では、日本の窮状を知るロシア側は強硬で、交渉は難航します。結局、全権大使の**ウィッテ**は、樺太の南半分を日本に割譲し、朝鮮半島の日本の優越権が保証され、東清鉄道の南半分（満州鉄道）、遼東半島南部の日本への譲渡などに同意します。しかし、**賠償金**は獲得できませんでした。

　ひとくちメモ
ポーツマス条約で日本が得たもの—樺太の南半分、朝鮮半島の優越権、東清鉄道の南半分（満州鉄道）、遼東半島南部

Russia.

The fact that the depleted national finances were not offset by any indemnity was a major blow. Considering that Japan had won the war after making major sacrifices, the people were extremely dissapointed by to this result. Komura Jutarō, who had conducted negotiations as Japan's plenipotentiary, was strongly criticized, and there was even a major protest against him in Hibiya, Tokyo.

Meanwhile, under the Taft-Katsura Agreement, a secret understanding made in 1905, Japan recognized America's advance in the Philippines, while America posed no objections to Japan's control of the Korean Peninsula. At the same time, America planned a full-scale entry into the Chinese market, but when they presented a proposal for joint management of the Manchurian Railroad, Japan rejected it. Japan and America gradually became polarized over concessions in China.

After the Russo-Japanese War, the small country in the Far East called Japan had a sense of national greatness and actively participated in international politics as a major power. The discrepancy between this confidence and the impoverished economic situation drove Japan to acquire concessions in Korea and China. The Russo-Japanese War was a major turning point following which Japan challenged the world with an unprecedented arrogance.

枯渇した国家財政を賠償金で補えなかったことは大きな痛手です。国民は、多大な犠牲を強いられた末、戦争に勝利したものと思っていただけに、その結果に強く反発します。日本の全権大使として交渉に臨んだ小村寿太郎は強い非難を浴び、東京の日比谷などでは大規模な暴動が起きたほどでした。

　一方、アメリカは、**桂タフト協定**で、アメリカのフィリピンへの進出を日本に認めさせ、日本の朝鮮半島支配には異を唱えないとの密約を1905年に結びます。同時にアメリカは、中国市場への本格的な参入を目論んでおり、日本が獲得した満州鉄道の共同経営案を提示しますが、日本はそれを拒否します。日本とアメリカは中国への利権を巡り、次第に対立するようになるのです。

　日露戦争以降、極東の小さな国日本は、大国意識をもって列強として国際政治に積極的に参加します。その自信と国家経済の破綻という矛盾が、日本を朝鮮半島と中国への利権獲得に駆り立てます。日露戦争は、日本が今までにない傲慢さで世界に挑む、大きな転換点となった戦争なのです。

🔍 **ひとくちメモ**

当時の総理大臣（兼外務大臣）の桂太郎と、ウィリアム・タフト陸軍長官の間で交わされた桂タフト協定の内容

日本はアメリカのフィリピン政策を認め、代わりにアメリカは日本の韓国における指導的地位を認める。また極東の平和維持を日米英の同盟で行うこと

Imperial Japan
大日本帝国の興亡

69 Annexation of Korea

Meiji Japan started with the reforms of the Restoration, and ended with the annexation of Korea.

Having secured the support of the United States in the Taft-Katsura Agreement, the same year Japan negotiated to extend the Anglo-Japanese Alliance and managed to gain Britain's approval for Japanese rule in Korea. This enabled Japan to colonize the Korean Peninsula without any diplomatic obstacles. Gradually Korea was deprived of its autonomy and diplomatic authority. The Korean people protested against such moves and Itō Hirobumi, the Resident-General of Korea, was assassinated by a Korean youth in Harbin, China. In 1910, upon signing the Japan-Korea Annexation Treaty, Korea formally became a colony of Japan. The Governor-General of Korea was installed in Seoul, initiating colonial control under the military.

The European powers had undergone dramatic growth from the nineteenth to the early twentieth centuries with the industrial revolution, and had pursued an aggressive colonialization of Asia and Africa to expand trade. This policy is known as imperialism.

In other words, Japan had undergone the Meiji Restoration in the midst of this imperialism, and by the time of Emperor Meiji's death in 1912 had become an imperial power in its own right.

Even when Japan and Russia had been battling each other in the Russo-Japanese War, the battlefield had been northeastern China. Also, in 1907, just before the Annexation of Korea, the Korean emperor sent secret emissaries to the Hague Peace Convention to demand action against

日韓併合とは？

　明治の日本は、維新の改革にはじまって、**日韓併合**に終わります。

　桂タフト協定で、アメリカの支持を取り付けた日本は、同年、日英同盟の延長交渉する中で、日本の朝鮮半島支配をイギリスに認めさせることができました。これによって、日本は外交的な障害なく、朝鮮半島を植民地化することができるようになりました。次第に韓国の自治権、外交権を奪います。こうした動きに韓国民衆は反発し、韓国総監に就任していた伊藤博文が中国のハルピンで、韓国人青年に暗殺されるという事件も起きました。そして、1910年に**日韓併合条約**の調印をもって、日本は韓国を正式に植民地とします。ソウルに朝鮮総督府を設置し、軍人による武断的な植民地支配をはじめたのでした。

　西欧列強は、19世紀から20世紀初頭にかけて、産業革命によって飛躍的に成長した自国の商圏の拡大を求め、アジアやアフリカで積極的な植民地経営に乗り出していました。この列強の考え方を**帝国主義**と呼びます。

　日本は、帝国主義のまっただ中で明治維新を迎え、明治天皇が亡くなった1912年には、自らが帝国主義の担い手となったわけです。

　日露戦争も、日本とロシアとが交戦しながら、戦場は中国東北地方でした。また、日韓併合直前の1907年に、ハーグでの国際会議に韓国皇帝が日本の横暴を訴える密使を送りますが、日本の韓国支配を認めていた欧米列強は、

🔍 **ひとくちメモ**
日韓併合
当初反対の立場を取っていた伊藤博文だが初代の総監になったことで、韓国人からの恨みを買い、朝鮮の独立運動家だった安重根にハルピン駅で暗殺された

Japanese tyranny, but they were ignored by the Western powers who sanctioned Japanese rule in Korea. This incident was symbolic of the fact that in Asia, Japan alone was treated by the Europeans as a fellow colonial power. Incidentally, in 1910 the unequal treaties with the West that had been so disadvantageous for Japan were extensively amended.

In Asian countries far from Japan, such as Turkey and India, there were many leaders who praised the country's dramatic growth. However, for Japan's neighbors, includeing Korea and China, Japan was a callous aggressor.

In order to stimulate its economy, impoverished by the Russo-Japanese War, Japan wanted to extend its management of Korea as quickly as possible into northeastern China. This deepened the rift with the United States, who demanded equal opportunities in the same territory, and even Britain began to be wary of Japan's intentions.

Having concluded its treaty with Russia, with whom it had been at war a few years earlier, Japan ignored this opposition and continued its advance into northeastern China. At the start of the twentieth century, the map of alliances and rivalries between the world powers in the Far East was being largely redrawn.

それを黙殺します。これは、アジアにおいて、日本だけが、欧米列強と同じ立場で植民地獲得について渡り合えることを象徴した事件といえます。ちなみに、日本を苛んでいた列強との不平等条約も1910年には全面的に改正されています。

　例えばトルコやインドなどのように、日本に遠いアジアでは、日本の飛躍的な成長を賞賛した指導者も多くいました。しかし、韓国や中国など、日本に近いアジアでは、日本は冷酷なる侵略者として位置づけられるようになるのです。

　日本は、日露戦争によって疲弊した国家経済を活性化させるために、一刻も早い朝鮮半島経営と、その延長にある中国東北地方の経営を進めようとします。これは、同地への機会均等を主張するアメリカとの溝を深め、イギリスもそうした日本の動きに警戒感を持つようになります。

　日本は、数年前に戦ったロシアと日露協約を締結し、こうした動きに対抗し、中国東北地方への進出をさらに進めます。20世紀初頭、極東を巡る列強の提携と対立の絵図面は、大きく塗り替えられてゆくのです。

🔍 ひとくちメモ
英米への牽制のためもあり日本はロシアと互いに権益を認めあう協約を結ぶ。しかし1917年にロシア帝国が滅亡すると、協約はソビエト政府に破棄された

70 The Development of Industry in the Meiji Period

In the Meiji period, the Japanese people received a rude awakening from the "peace" of the Edo period. Alarmed at the imperialistic ambitions of the world powers, they felt compelled to throw in their lot with Western civilization.

Before long they had cornered themselves into the Sino-Japanese and Russo-Japanese Wars, and entered the club of imperialistic nations. The direct threat from Russia disappeared, they formed an alliance with Britain, and ultimately escaped the threat of becoming a colony themselves.

This was an unnaturally impetuous course of action for the Japanese, entirely at odds with the people who had slowly assimilated continental culture from China and elsewhere over many centuries.

During the forty-five years of Meiji, Japan underwent its own industrial revolution, first centered on light industries such as textiles, and then around the time of the Russo-Japanese War it took the leap to heavy industries, with the founding of the Yawata Iron and Steel Works in 1901.

The first railway between Tokyo's Shinbashi district and Yokohama opened in 1872, and the network of major lines was expanded early on in the twentieth century. Around the same time major companies such as Nippon Yūsen (Japan Mail Shipping Line) started regular shipping services to locations in Asia and Europe, and later went on to develop important infrastructures on the mainland.

After the Russo-Japanese War, there was a temporary economic boom occasioned by wartime special procurements. However, in 1907 the

明治時代の産業の育成とは？

　明治時代、日本人は江戸時代の「和」に浸りきった眠りからおこされ、列強の帝国主義の野望に驚愕し、西欧文明を無理矢理その胃袋に放り込みました。

　そして、それを消化する間もなく、日清、日露戦争へと自らを追い込み、帝国主義国家の仲間入りをしました。ロシアの直接の脅威はなくなり、イギリスと同盟し、ようやく自らが植民地にされる脅威から逃げ切ったのです。

　それは日本人が中国などの大陸文化を数百年かけてゆっくりと消化してきた過程とは全く異なる、性急で不自然なまでの焦りに駆り立てられた行為でした。

　産業面では、明治という 45 年間に、日本は繊維など**軽工業**中心の第一次産業革命を成し遂げ、日露戦争前後には、1901 年の**八幡製鉄所**の創設など、一気に**重工業**の拡大による第二次産業革命を遂行しました。

　1872 年に、新橋と横浜に最初に開通した鉄道は、20 世紀初頭には主要幹線が開通し、さらにネットワークを広げていました。海運業も、同じ頃日本郵船など大手によるアジア、欧米との定期航路が開かれ、後の大陸経営への重要なインフラ整備が進みます。

　日露戦争のあと、民間は**戦争特需**で一時的に好景気を迎えます。しかし、国家財政の逼迫などとのアンバランス

🔍 **ひとくちメモ**
日本初の鉄道が新橋駅から横浜駅間で開通したのが1872年のこと。日本の近代化の象徴的なできごとだった

country's straitened finances turned to panic. This led to mergers between small and medium enterprises to form large companies with monopolies on certain industries. This was not just with manufacturing, but also in the finance sector as the major conglomerates that had maintained a cozy relationship with the Meiji government, such as Mitsui, Mitsubishi, Sumitomo, Yasuda, and Daiichi, pooled loan capital and the roots of industry continued to extend under their umbrella.

The growth of capitalism in Japan is characterized by a tactic whereby the people take over a package created by the government and make it grow.

Japanese industry developed in leaps and bounds on the model of government-run factories being established by the government after initially learning the skills from the West, and then being transferred to influential members of the public.

Japan's modernization was guided by the government, which in turn trained the people. Furthermore, many of these people were aristocrats or influential figures in cahoots with the government, and the rapid modernization under their leadership depended on cheap labor from rural areas.

The textile factories producing the raw silk that became one of Japan's leading exports famously exploited female employees, and this social issue is linked to the sudden rise of the socialist movement. Japan's impatience to catch up with the West created new social problems.

が原因で1907年には恐慌となります。これによって、中小資本が統合され、さらに大資本による産業の独占が進むことになったのです。それは一般産業のみならず、金融財務界も同様で、明治政府と緊密な関係を保ってきた三井、三菱、住友、安田、第一などといった**財閥**が、金融資本を統合し、その傘下に産業の根を広げてゆきます。

　日本の資本主義の成長には、一つの特徴がありました。それは、官によって育てられたパッケージを民が受け取り、それを成長させるという仕組みです。
　当初は、政府の指導で技術を欧米から学び、官によって設立される**官営工場**が民間の有力者に払い下げられる形式で、一気に日本の産業が発展したのです。

　日本の近代化は、官が指導し、民間を育成していったのです。しかも、この民間も、多くの場合官と深く関わった華族や有力者で、彼らによる急激な近代化は農村などの安価な労働力に依存したものでした。

　日本の代表的な輸出産業となった生糸などの繊維工業は、女工を酷使したことで有名ですが、この社会問題が、日本での**社会主義運動**の勃興へと繋がります。西欧に追いつこうとした日本の焦りが、社会に新たな矛盾を造ったのです。

71 Meiji Ideology and Social Movements

Westernization naturally had a major effect on people's cultural activities.

At the start of Meiji, when the ideology of reverence for the emperor was used to promote newly established centralized state under the emperor's rule, Shinto gained prominence while Buddhism was persecuted as an imported religion. The movement to eradicate Buddhism called *haibutsu kishaku* (abolish Buddhism and destroy Shakyamuni), led to much of Japan's cultural heritage being either destroyed or sold abroad at cheap prices. Ironically, this informed the West about Japanese art and led to the Japonisme boom.

For ordinary people, the influx of Western culture meant a new lifestyle. The Europeanization phenomenon in Meiji is referred to as "civilization and enlightenment," and in Tokyo it was fashionable to cut off one's topknot, wear Western clothes, and go to restaurants specializing in beef hotpot (and later sukiyaki).

Major proponents of Western ideology included Fukuzawa Yukichi, the founder of Keio University who introduced Western rationalism into Japan; Niijima Jō (known in English as Joseph Hardy Neesima), the founder of Dōshisha University who brought Protestantism to Japan; and Nakae Chōmin, who introduced the ideology of the French Enlightenment.

The Freedom and People's Rights Movement made ordinary people aware that they could participate in politics. The mass media, including newspapers, actively joined in the developing discussions.

明治時代の思想、社会運動とは？

　西欧化は当然のことながら、人々の文化活動にも大きな影響を与えます。

　明治の初頭、**尊王思想**を引き継ぎ、天皇による中央集権国家の建設を国が宣伝する中で、神道が統合され、仏教が外国からの宗教として迫害されるという現象が起こりました。この**廃仏毀釈**という活動で、日本の多くの文化遺産が破壊されるか、海外に安価に流出しました。これが西欧に日本美術が伝わり、ジャポニズムブームが起きたことは、皮肉なことです。

　西欧文化の流入は、一般の国民にとっては、新しいライフスタイルでした。明治の欧風化現象は、**文明開化**と呼ばれ、東京では、髷を切り、洋服を着て、牛鍋（すき焼きに進化）屋に行くことが流行ります。

　西欧の思想は慶応義塾大学の創始者で、西欧流の**合理主義**を日本に紹介した**福沢諭吉**や、同志社大学を開講し、プロテスタントの思想を日本に伝えた**新島襄**、さらにフランスの啓蒙思想を紹介した中江兆民などがその代表です。

福沢諭吉

🔍 ひとくちメモ
新島 襄
キリスト教の布教家で、同志社大学の前身となる同志社英学校の創立者。
1843–1890

　自由民権運動の高揚は、国民に政治参加の意識を植え付けます。言論活動を展開する中で、新聞などマスコミの活動も活発になります。政治活動は多様に拡大し、西欧

Political activity became broader, embracing Western democracy and even socialism, with more support for workers and farmers who suffered from the demanding labor conditions and poverty that was the dark side of industrial development. A prime example of this was the support given by Tanaka Shōzō and others to the farmers worried about mineral pollution from the Ashio Copper Mine.

Kōtoku Shūsui and Abe Isoo, who had originally studied Western liberalism, also turned to socialism from around the time of the Russo-Japanese War and were closely linked to the labor movement. However, the government used the Peace Preservation Law to crack down on this, and in 1910 Kōtoku Shūsui and other activists were charged with plotting to assassinate Emperor Meiji, and executed the following year. Known as the High Treason Incident, this was a major blow to socialism in Japan.

The Russo-Japanese War had been an ambitious war that necessitated the mobilization of the entire nation. The well-known Christian ideologue Uchimura Kanzō, the writer Yosano Akiko and others took a public anti-war stance. However, the majority tended towards extreme patriotism, and many scholars and ideologues went along with the government. The fact that Fukuzawa Yukichi became an advocate of war towards the end of his life is of particular note.

流の**民主主義**に加え、社会主義も紹介され、殖産興業の陰で貧しさと過酷な労働に苦しむ農民や労働者への支援活動も展開されます。代表的な例としては、足尾銅山の鉱毒に悩む農民を支援した田中正造などが揚げられます。

　また、もともと西欧の**自由主義思想**を学んだ幸徳秋水や安部磯雄などは、日露戦争前後から**社会主義**へと傾斜し、**労働運動**などに深く関わりますが、政府は**治安維持法**などをもって弾圧し、幸徳秋水をはじめとした活動家が1910年に明治天皇を暗殺しようとした嫌疑で翌年には処刑されます。この事件は**大逆事件**として、日本の社会主義活動に大きな打撃を与えました。

　日露戦争は、国民を総動員した大掛かりな戦争でした。キリスト教の思想家で有名な内村鑑三や、文筆家の与謝野晶子などは反戦の立場から、世論に訴えます。しかし、大方の国民は**国粋主義**に傾斜し、多くの学者や思想家が政府に迎合します。福沢諭吉が晩年こうした主戦論者の一人になったのも興味深い事実といえましょう。

内村鑑三　　　　与謝野晶子

72 Artistic Activity in the Meiji Period

Tsubouchi Shōyō was critical of the poetic justice employed in traditional narrative literature, including Kabuki, and theorized on the importance of the individual in Western literature. Under his influence, Futabatei Shimei wrote his novel *Ukigumo* (Drifting Cloud) in a new, colloquial literary style.

There were various artistic movements in the West during the nineteenth century, with numerous famous works of literature published particularly in France and Russia, and many musical works considered classics composed at this time.

People had been liberated from the shackles of the Middle Ages and early modern period, and were enjoying greater freedoms than ever before. However, this was offset by the turbulence and anxiety of the modern period with its revolutions and conflicts. People began looking inward, and seeking to express their conflicting emotions and contradictions.

Such artistic activity came to be known in Japan from Meiji onward, and by the end of the period Japanese writers were already publishing works reflecting a move away from classical techniques in favor of a colloquial literary style portraying daily events and the finer points of human emotions. Futabatei Shimei himself had been influenced by Russian literature, and had even translated works by Turgenev and others. Aided by the development of new media such as newspapers in which writers could serialize their works, Japan's literary scene subsequently produced many authors who still enjoy a large readership today, such as

明治時代の芸術活動は？

　歌舞伎などにも採用される勧善懲悪の伝統的な物語文学を批判し、西欧流の「人」そのものにスポットをあてた文芸活動を説いたのは、**坪内逍遥**という人物でした。彼の影響を受けた**二葉亭四迷**は、**言文一致体**で『浮き雲』という小説を発表します。

坪内逍遥

　19世紀は欧米においても、様々な芸術活動があり、文学ではフランスやロシアなどを中心に名作の数々が発表され、音楽の上でも現在クラシック音楽とされている作品の多くがこの時期に作曲されています。

　その背景には、人が中世や近世の束縛から解放され、今まで以上に自由になったことと、その代償として近現代社会の動揺や不安、そして革命などの争乱が多発したことがあげられます。人間が自らを見つめ、人の持つ葛藤や矛盾を率直に表現することができるようになったのです。

二葉亭四迷

　こうした芸術活動が、明治以降日本にも伝えられ、明治時代の後半には早くも古典的な技法を離脱し、口語文体で日常の出来事や人の心の機微を描いた作品が発表されるようになりました。二葉亭四迷自身、ロシア文学の影響を受け、ツルゲーネフなどの翻訳も発表しています。その後、日本の文壇は新聞など、文章を連載できる新たなメディアの発展の影響もあって、**夏目漱石**、**森鷗外**など、現在でも多くの読者に支持されている作家が輩出されます。夏目漱石はイギリスへ、森鷗外はドイツに留学経験があり、海外

Natsume Sōseki and Mori Ōgai. These writers had both studied abroad, Natsume Sōseki in England and Mori Ōgai in Germany, where they were directly influenced by the new literary trends.

Around the same time Masaoka Shiki, a friend of Natsume Sōseki's, reformed traditional waka and haiku, to incorporating a sense of realism that revitalized Japanese poetry, which had become increasingly formulaic.

The way these writers looked at people and events has had a major impact on contemporary literature. Their objective approach, distancing themselves from the object, enabled them to see people as individuals regardless of their position in society and to portray the worries and emotional turmoil shared by all people, as well as the contradictions in society. This approach is evident not just in novels but also in the theater movement known as *shingeki*, or new drama, and even in contemporary drama. It makes use of journalistic techniques of expression to appeal to audiences and readers, informing them candidly of the facts.

The phenomenon of Europeanization in the Meiji period was crystallized in the most refined, digested form by many sensitive artists.

での新たな文芸活動から直に影響を受けたのです。

夏目漱石

　同じ頃、夏目漱石などとも交友関係のある正岡子規が、日本古来の和歌や俳句を写実の精神をもって改革し、ともすれば形骸化しつつあった詩歌の世界に新風を吹き込みます。

　彼らに共通した、人間や事象を見つめる精神は、そのまま現代文学へと受け継がれています。そして対象を突き放して、客観的に描く考え方は、たとえ地位のある人間でも一人の人として捉え、万人に共通した悩みや葛藤、時には社会の矛盾を描くのです。この考え方が、小説のみならず、当時新劇と呼ばれた演劇活動などでも表現され、その延長に現在のドラマや、事実をありのまま伝え、視聴者や読者に訴えるジャーナリズムでの表現方法があるのです。

森鷗外

　明治時代の**欧化現象**は、多感で多彩な芸術家の中に、最も洗練され、消化された形で結晶していったのです。

73 The Early Taishō Period

Emperor Meiji died in 1912, bringing the turbulent 45-year era to an end. The Crown Prince acceded to the throne and became Emperor Taishō.

Historical periods since Meiji seem to be marked by every change of emperor and era name. These periods do not correspond to events in world history, however. The last years of Meiji through the first half of Taishō was a period of major transition in which the hostilities between Western powers over imperialistic diplomatic policy led to the First World War, and the collapse of the Russian empire under the Romanov dynasty.

By shrugging off the imperialist threat to itself, and being politically outside these upheavals in the world, Japan was able to push for hegemony in Asia. As a preliminary step, the army took advantage of the change to the Taishō era to push for large-scale expansion in order to deal with the threat from Russia following the Russo-Japanese War, further Japan's push for hegemony in China, and to confront America's ambition for economic advancement in China.

However, in view of the fact that Japan was in recession and public finances were strained, Prime Minister Saionji Kinmochi resisted these moves by the military.

In the second year of Taishō (1913), when the antagonism between the army and the cabinet came to a head, the army bypassed the prime minister and made the Minister for War resign, and ultimately the entire

大正初期の国内情勢は？

　明治天皇は 1912 年に亡くなり、激動の明治は 45 年で終焉します。天皇の死去と同時に、皇太子が**践祚**し、大正天皇となります。

ひとくちメモ
践祚
天子の位を受け継ぐこと

　歴史の教科書などでは、明治以降、天皇がかわり、元号がかわるごとにあたかもひと時代が終わったかのように区切りをつけますが、世界史的にみるならば、明治の終盤から大正時代前半までは、欧米列強の帝国主義的な外交方針による利害関係の対立が**第一次世界大戦**へと発展し、オスマントルコやハプスブルグ家のオーストラリア・ハンガリー帝国、そしてロマノフ王朝下のロシア帝国が崩壊する歴史上の重要な過渡期にあたる一つの時代です。

　日本は、自らが帝国主義の脅威をはねのけたことにより、政治的にはこうした世界の動乱の枠外で、アジアへの覇権の追求を押し進めることができたのです。その前段階として、大正時代にはいるや否や、**日露戦争**以後のロシアの脅威の払拭と、中国への覇権をもくろむ日本と、中国への経済進出を強く望むアメリカとの対立を意識し、陸軍が規模の増強を画策します。

　一方、日本は不況のまっただ中で、国家財政も逼迫していることから、当時首相になった**西園寺公望**は、この陸軍の動きを牽制します。

　大正 2 年（1913 年）、陸軍と内閣との対立が表面化すると、陸軍は内閣総理大臣を無視する形で陸軍大臣を辞任させ、最終的に内閣を総辞職に追い込むという事件がおこ

西園寺公望

cabinet was forced to resign. This confrontation occurred because the chain of command in the army and navy was independent of the cabinet, answering directly to the emperor.

After Saionji's cabinet fell, the Chōshū clan official Katsura Tarō was reinstalled as prime minister, and Inukai Tsuyoshi and Ozaki Yukio, advocates of parliamentary democracy ever since the mobilization of the Freedom and People's Rights Movement, staged a protest against the despotism of the military. This touched a chord with the people and a mass demonstration surrounded the Diet building, forcing the collapse of the Katsura cabinet after only fifty days. This is known as the Taishō Political Crisis, a landmark event in the pro-democracy movement after the Freedom and People's Rights Movement. The *goken undō*, or Movement in Defense of the Constitution, sought to uphold the aims of the Imperial Diet established under the Meiji Constitution.

The Taishō period saw the start of the tug-of-war between the Movement in Defense of the Constitution and the militarists who were to lead Japan to destruction. From the start the Meiji Constitution had not been a constitution for popular sovereignty, and the Diet and cabinet were restricted in what they could do. It was these very restrictions that ended up being one of the causes of the rise of militarism.

ります。これは、陸海軍が内閣から独立して天皇の指揮系統に属することに起因した対立でした。

　西園寺内閣の後に、長州藩の藩閥官僚である桂太郎が総理大臣に返り咲くと、陸軍の行動を横暴として、自由民権運動運動が起きて以来、議会制民主主義を標榜してきた**犬養毅**や**尾崎行雄**が抗議行動を起こします。これに民衆が呼応し、デモ隊が国会を取り巻き、桂内閣が50日で崩壊するという事件が起こりました。これを**大正の政変**と呼びますが、こうした自由民権運動からの政治活動が民主化運動として結実したことは、画期的なことでした。大日本帝国憲法での帝国議会設立の趣旨を守ろうというこうした運動を**護憲運動**と呼んでいます。

　大正時代は、この護憲運動とその後日本を破滅に導く軍部との綱引きが始まった時代です。そもそも大日本帝国憲法は、国民主権の憲法ではなく、議会や内閣の活動にも制限がありました。その憲法上の制限こそが、将来軍部が台頭する原因の一つとなるのでした。

犬養毅

74 Japan and World War

The period spanning end of the nineteenth century and start of the twentieth century was marked by the collapse of three major empires. These were all large Asian empires that ruled until the early-modern era.

The first to go was the Mughal Empire, which had been started in 1526 by descendants of the Mongol Empire and ruled most of the Indian subcontinent until the colonization of India by the British. With India as its colony, Britain enjoyed trading interests throughout Asia.

Next was the Empire of the Great Qing sustained by the Manchu for over 260 years, which fell in 1912 after the rise of the general Yuan Shikai.

Finally, there was the decline of the Ottoman Empire, which had ruled the Middle and Near East for centuries since the fall of the Byzantine Empire, and collapsed after World War I.

The decline of these three major empires in Asia enabled Japan to advance into the continent, while Western powers fought bitterly over the interests left by the dying empires.

The Ottoman territory had included the southern part of what is now Eastern Europe, where Muslims, Catholics, and Orthodox Greeks lived together. The nationalism and independence movement against the Ottomans in this area was tied up with the interests of surrounding countries such as Russia and the Austro-Hungarian Empire, as well as the German Empire then rapidly acquiring power, which contributed to the complex political chaos.

第一次世界大戦での日本は？

19 世紀末から 20 世紀への世界をみるときに、3 つの大国の崩壊に注目する必要があります。それらは全て近世まで世界に君臨したアジアの大帝国でした。

最初に起きたのは、**モンゴル帝国**の末裔によって 1526 年に建国され、インドのほとんどを統治していた**ムガール帝国**の滅亡とその後のイギリスによるインドの植民地化です。このインドの植民地化によって、イギリスはアジア全体への強い利権を享受するようになります。

次は、満州族によって 260 年にわたって維持されてきた**清帝国**が、軍人として台頭した**袁世凱**によって 1912 年についに滅亡したことです。そして、最後に注目したいのが、**東ローマ帝国**の滅亡以来、長年中近東を支配してきた**オスマントルコ帝国**の衰退と、第一次世界大戦後の帝国の滅亡です。

このアジアに君臨した 3 大帝国が衰亡してゆく過程に、日本の大陸進出があり、死にゆく大帝国に残された権益をめぐった欧米列強の熾烈な争いがあるのです。

オスマントルコの場合、版図の中に現在の東ヨーロッパ南部が加わっており、そこにはイスラム教徒とカトリック教徒、そしてギリシャ正教徒が同居していました。その地域でのオスマントルコからの独立運動と民族の自立は、そのままロシアやオーストリア・ハンガリー帝国、当時急速に国力を蓄えたドイツ帝国など周辺の国々の利権と絡み合い、複雑な政治的混沌を生み出します。

ひとくちメモ
モンゴル帝国
チンギス・カンが創設した遊牧国家。1206–1634

ムガール帝国
インド南部を除くインド亜大陸を支配したモンゴル系イスラム王朝。1526–1858

ひとくちメモ
清
中国最後の王朝。1644–1912

袁世凱
中国清末民初期の軍人・政治家。大清帝国第 2 代内閣総理大臣、中華民国臨時大総統、及び大総統。1859–1916

東ローマ帝国
東西に分割統治されて以降のローマ帝国の東側の領域を指す。395–1453

オスマン帝国、トルコ帝国
東ローマ帝国滅亡後、東南ヨーロッパ、トルコ、アラビアを席捲した。1299–1923

Imperial Japan
大日本帝国の興亡

In 1914 the assassination of the Austro-Hungarian Crown Prince in Serbia led to war between Austria and Serbia, which was joined by various political alliances and war rapidly spread through Europe.

As allies of Britain, which had declared war on Austria, Germany, and the Ottomans, Japan occupied the German colonies of Quingdao in China and various islands in the Pacific.

Having dispatched its troops, Japan presented the Twenty-One Demands to Chinese President Yuan Shikai. This included the demand to transfer German interests in China to Japan, which was conceded by Yuan Shikai under threat of military force. Naturally, this was one of the causes of anti-Japanese sentiment in China.

Having seen how Japan used the upheaval of World War I in Europe to determinedly expand its sphere of influence in China and the South Pacific, Britain and America began to be view it as a threat. Needless to say, this cast a shadow on the situation and subsequent developments.

1914年にセルビアでオーストリア・ハンガリー帝国の皇太子が暗殺され、オーストリアとセルビアとが戦争状態になると、様々な同盟関係に縛られていた列強がそれに加わり、たちまち戦火がヨーロッパに拡大します。

　日本は、オーストリアとドイツ、そしてオスマントルコに対して戦線を布告したイギリスと同盟関係にあり、ドイツの中国での権益の拠点であった青島（ちんたお）と、太平洋のドイツ領であった島々を占領しました。

　日本は、袁世凱の指導する中華民国への派兵の後、軍隊を撤収せずに、ドイツの中国における権益の日本への譲渡などを盛り込んだ**対華21カ条要求**を突きつけ、軍事力を背景に無理矢理、袁世凱の承諾を得ます。もちろん中国の中で**反日感情**が根付きます。

　欧州の動乱であった第一次世界大戦を利用し、したたかに中国と南太平洋へ影響力を拡大した日本に、イギリスやアメリカが強い警戒感を抱き始め、その後の世界情勢に陰を落とすことになったことはいうまでもないことです。

ひとくちメモ
サラエボ事件
1914年、オーストリア・ハンガリー帝国の皇太子が、セルビアで暗殺された。これによりオーストリアとセルビアが戦争状態に入ると、たちまち戦火がヨーロッパに拡大した

ひとくちメモ
青島
ドイツ帝国が中国北部の山東半島南海岸に所有していた膠州湾（こうしゅうわん）租借地の行政中心地

対華21カ条要求
1915年（大正4年）1月18日、山東支配の確立と、従来の権益の拡大を求めて、日本が中華民国に行った要求

Imperial Japan
大日本帝国の興亡

大日本帝国の興亡 | 323

75 Post-World War I Japan

World War I resulted in the collapse of Europe's absolute monarchies and their empires, and the birth pains of the new order for the twentieth century.

In 1917, the Russian Empire was toppled by revolution, and was replaced by the Soviet Union under Lenin's leadership. Then following the end of World War there was revolution in the German Empire, which was succeeded by the Weimar Republic. The federal system of the Austro-Hungarian Empire, too, collapsed following internal moves for independence.

There had been signs of major shifts in Europe in the nineteenth century, especially in eastern Europe and Russia, where wars and social unrest produced many refugees that headed for America. America grew quickly with the abundant workforce and diverse knowledge provided by these migrants, and at the end of World War I America became the world's biggest creditor nation.

World War I spelled economic recovery for Japan. Saionji Kinmochi attended the conclusion of the Treaty of Versailles at the end of the War as plenipotentiary for Japan, and managed to protect Japan's rights to the territory in China acquired during the war.

However, while overseas demand for light and heavy industries increased, the price of rice shot up due to stockpiling by traders anticipating further demand for raw materials because of the Russian Revolution and other events. This led to nationwide rice riots in 1918.

第一次世界大戦後の日本の状況は？

　第一次世界大戦の結果、ヨーロッパでも絶対王朝以来の帝国が崩壊し、世界は 20 世紀の新しい秩序への産みの苦しみがはじまります。

　1917 年に、ロシア帝国が革命で倒れ、その後**レーニン**の指導する**ソビエト連邦**が興ります。世界初の共産主義国家の成立です。次に、第一次世界大戦終了とともにドイツ帝国にも革命がおき、**ドイツ共和国**（ヴァイマル共和国）が誕生します。また、連邦制を維持していたオーストリア・ハンガリー帝国も、内部での独立運動などにより、もろくも崩壊します。

　欧州大変動の予兆は 19 世紀からあり、特にロシアを含む東欧では、戦火や社会不安で大量の難民が生まれています。難民の移住先はアメリカでした。そうした移民による豊富な労働力と多様な英知によって、アメリカ社会は急速に成長し、第一次世界大戦の終了時、アメリカは世界最大の債権国へと成長します。

　第一次世界大戦は、日本に景気回復をもたらしました。戦争終結にあたって締結された**ヴェルサイユ条約**では、日本から西園寺公望が全権として出席し、大戦で獲得した中国などでの日本の権益を守ることもできました。

　しかし、戦争で軽工業、重工業双方の海外での需要が高まる中、**ロシア革命**などでさらなる物資の需要を当て込んだ商人による米の買い占めなどで米価が高騰します。これが原因で、1918 年には全国的に**米騒動**という暴動がお

🔍**ひとくちメモ**

第一次世界大戦中の敗北で社会不安が深まると、1917年、帝政が倒れて、レーニン指揮のもとソビエト政権が成立した。

レーニン
ロシア・ボルシェビキの創立者、ロシア革命主導者、旧ソ連の最初の指導者。1870-1924

ドイツ共和国
1919年8月に制定・公布されたヴァイマル憲法に基づいた戦間期ドイツの政治体制。1919-1933

🔍**ひとくちメモ**

ヴェルサイユ条約
1919年6月28日にフランスのヴェルサイユで調印された、第一次世界大戦の講和条約

ロシア革命
1917年にロシア帝国で起きた社会主義国家樹立につながった2度の革命

Imperial Japan 大日本帝国の興亡

At the end of the war, when world demand returned to normal, surplus production led to rising stocks and put pressure on corporate businesses. Contrary to expectations, this economic recession accelerated after the war.

Being an island nation, Japan is faced with the dilemma that its manufacturers must depend largely on demand from abroad. In order to stabilize its market, Japan had planned to annex the Korean peninsula and advance into China. However, the Chinese people protested against this policy and in 1919 led a mass boycott of Japanese products that developed into the May Fourth Movement calling for political reform. Then when the Russian Revolution started, Japan joined the anti-Communist drive by western powers and dispatched soldiers to Siberia, but in 1922 were forced to withdraw by the revolutionary army. Behind this dispatch of troops was Japan's plan to expand its interests into Siberia as well as China.

Looking to foreign expansion in order to resolve economic problems and maintain markets became the main thrust of Japan's policy up to World War II.

きてしまいます。戦争が終結すると、世界の需要が元に戻り、過剰生産に投資した分だけ、在庫が増えて企業の経営を圧迫します。戦後の景気後退が予想に反して加速します。

　島国日本は、海外の需要に国内の産業が大きく依存せざるを得ないというジレンマを持っています。その市場を安定して獲得するために、日本は朝鮮半島を併合し、中国への進出を目論んだのです。しかし、この政策はさらなる中国民衆の反発につながり、1919年には大規模な日本製品の不買運動と、国内の政治改革を叫ぶ**五・四運動**へと発展します。また、ロシア革命がおきると、日本は欧米列強と共産主義政権の抹殺のために、シベリアに出兵しますが、数年間にわたる戦争の末、革命軍の抵抗にあい、1922年に撤兵します。この出兵の背景も、中国に続き、シベリアへの日本の権益の拡大が意図されていました。

　経済問題の解決と市場維持のための海外への進出は、**第二次世界大戦**までの日本の根本政策となってゆくのでした。

ひとくちメモ
五・四運動
1919年5月4日、北京の学生のデモを契機に起きた中国の民族運動。日本商品のボイコットなど、最後にはヴェルサイユ条約の調印拒否にいたった

ひとくちメモ
第二次世界大戦
ドイツ、イタリア、大日本帝国の三国同盟を中心とする枢軸国陣営とイギリス、フランス、アメリカ、ソ連、中華民国などの連合国陣営との間で戦われた、全世界的規模の戦争。
1939–1945

76 The Taishō Democracy

The Taishō period saw vigorous political activity.

Under the provisions of the Meiji Constitution, the prime minister and ministers of state were appointed by the emperor, but the emperor's decision was customarily influenced by the elder statesmen from the Meiji Restoration, especially those from Satsuma and Chōshū.

With the Taishō period came a change in government with the fall after just half a year of the cabinet formed by Katsura Tarō, a former army general from Chōshū, one of the major han that had dominated politics. After this, politics was increasingly influenced by public opinion, with a strong tendency to respect the political heavyweights and the Diet.

For a long time, Japan had been dependent on farming, and especially rice cultivation. After Meiji, however, it underwent an industrial revolution and the population of factory workers and company employees increased. By the Taishō period these outnumbered the farming population. Politicized citizens calling for human rights and better labor conditions began to take leading roles in society.

This was in keeping with world trends, which were beginning to reflect a rise in socialist and democratic movements around the time of World War I, as revolutions toppled the despotic monarchies of Russia and Germany.

After the cabinet of Terauchi Masatake resigned en masse following the rice riots, at the urging of Chōshū statesman Yamagata Aritomo, in 1918 Hara Takashi of the Rikken Seiyūkai (Friends of Constitutional Government) was made prime minister. The Hara Cabinet was Japan's

大正デモクラシーとは？

　大正時代は政治活動が盛んな時代でした。

　大日本帝国憲法の規定で、内閣総理大臣および国務大臣は天皇が任命することになっていますが、天皇の判断には常に明治維新以来の薩摩、長州を中心とした**元老、元勲**が影響を及ぼしていました。

　大正の政変によって、軍部よりで、藩閥政治を代表する長州藩出身の桂太郎による内閣が半年で倒れて以来、日本でも国民の意見が政治に影響を与え、政界の大物も議会の意向を尊重する傾向が強くなります。

　日本は長い間、稲作を中心とした農業を土台とした国でした。それが明治以降産業革命を経験し、工場労働者や企業関係者などの人口が増え、大正時代には農業人口を上回るまでに伸長します。**労働条件**や**人権**に敏感で政治にも関心のある市民が社会を担うようになったのです。

　加えて、第一次世界大戦の頃に、ロシアやドイツに革命がおき、各地で**専制君主制度**が崩壊してゆくなか、世界的な傾向として**社会主義運動や民主化運動**が高揚していたことも背景にあります。

　特に、米騒動で長州藩出身の大物である山県有朋が推す寺内内閣が総辞職すると、民意に押されて、1918年に立憲政友会の原敬が首相となります。原内閣は日本ではじめての本格的な政党内閣です。このとき、日本は第一次

first true party cabinet backed by public opinion. It was at this time that Japan participated in the peace treaty at the end of World War I, and subsequently became a permanent member of the League Council.

Following Hara Takashi's assassination in 1921 there was a return to politics dominated by the major han factions. This saw a resurgence in the Movement in Defense of the Constitution, and eventually a new cabinet was formed by their leader Katō Takaaki.

This cabinet enacted the General Election Law that had been pending, under which all males over the age of twenty-five were given voting rights, and all males over the age of thirty were qualified to run for election. However, the same cabinet also approved the Peace Preservation Law, ostensibly to crack down on Communism. This would later be a weapon to suppress freedom of speech during the rise in militarism in Japan.

Socialist activity also flourished in the Taishō atmosphere of democratization, and although Communism was illegal, in 1922 the Japan Communist Party was formed. Activists for women's suffrage and the advancement of women in society, including Hiratsuka Raichō, succeeded in getting women admitted into the political process — an enormous achievement for the time.

These movements are generally referred to as Taishō Democracy.

世界大戦の講和条約に参加し、その後、**国際連盟の常任理事国**に就任しています。

　その後、原敬は 1921 年に暗殺され、再び藩閥政治へと揺れ戻しがあったとき、立憲政治を守ろうとする護憲運動が再燃し、その立役者の加藤高明を首班とする内閣が成立します。

　この内閣のときに、懸案であった**普通選挙法**が成立し、25 歳以上の全ての男子に選挙権が、30 歳以上の全ての男子に被選挙権が与えられたのです。ただ、同時に共産主義の取り締まりを名目に**治安維持法**も可決され、それが後の日本の軍国主義化の中での**言論弾圧**への武器となるのでした。

　大正時代は、こうした民主化の動きの中で、社会主義活動も活発で、1922 年には非合法ながら**日本共産党**も結党しています。また、女性の社会進出と婦人参政権の獲得を目指した平塚雷鳥などの活動は、女性の政治活動が認められるにとどまりましたが、当時としては大きな飛躍でした。

　これら大正時代の民主化の動きを、**大正デモクラシー**と呼んでいるのです。

平塚雷鳥

77 The Great Kanto Earthquake

On September 1, 1923, the Tokyo area was struck by a magnitude 7.9 earthquake. The Great Kanto Earthquake resulted in over a hundred thousand victims, both of the quake itself and of the numerous fires that spread rapidly in strong winds.

Tokyo and other major cities like Yokohama and Chiba suffered devastating damage.

While the city was paralyzed and the publication of newspapers was delayed, wild rumours circulated. These included misleading stories of Koreans rioting, which led to mob attacks and murders of Koreans, reportedly with hundreds, possibly even thousands of victims. It was also in the chaos after the quake that the Communist activist Ōsugi Sakae, his lover, and six-year-old nephew were beaten to death by the military police, an incident that shocked the nation.

These events exposed the darker side of the Taishō Democracy, and foreboded the gradual undermining of the democracy movement by the despotic military and resultant swing to the right amongst the general population.

Reconstruction after the Great Kanto Earthquake necessitated enormous government spending. This expenditure once again cast a dark shadow over Japan's economy.

Incidentally, in the Taishō period the phrase *Tenpō atama* (Tenpō head), was in current usage. Tenpō was the name of the era from 1830 to 1843 in the late Edo period, and this phrase was a comical expression

関東大震災とその後の
日本は？

　1923年9月1日に、東京周辺はマグニチュード7.9の
大地震に見舞われます。風の強い日であったこともあり、
各所から失火し、地震とその後の火災のために、10万人
以上が犠牲になるという関東大震災がおきました。

　東京をはじめ、横浜や千葉など主要都市が壊滅的な打
撃を受けてしまいます。

　都市機能は麻痺し、新聞などの発行も遅れる中、流言
飛語が駆け巡ります。その中で、朝鮮人が暴動を起こして
いるという噂に惑わされ、朝鮮人への集団暴行、殺害事件
がおこり、数百人とも数千人ともいわれる犠牲者が出てい
ます。また、震災のどさくさの中で、憲兵隊によって、共
産主義の活動家である大杉栄が、愛人と6歳の子供ととも
に殺害されるという事件もおこり、全国に衝撃を与えまし
た。

　それらは、民主化が進んだ大正デモクラシーという時代
の暗部が、浮き彫りにされた事件でした。その暗部は軍
部の横暴とそれに煽動され右傾化する大衆が、民主化運
動を切り崩してゆくことを予感させるものといえましょう。

　関東大震災はその復興に多額の財政出動が必要でし
た。ここでの出費が再び日本経済に暗い影を落としてゆき
ます。

　ところで、大正時代に、「天保頭(あたま)」という言葉が流行り
ました。天保とは、江戸時代後期の年号で、1830年から
1843年までの期間を指します。ペリー来航直前のこの時

describing the bewilderment at the new age of the now-elderly people born in this era before the arrival of Perry's ships.

The last shogun, Tokugawa Yoshinobu, born in 1837 (eighth year of Tenpō) and deceased in 1913 (second year of Taishō) was a prime example.

In Taishō, the Edo period already seemed long distant, with advances in newspapers and magazines enabling information to be shared nationwide. With the commencement of radio broadcasts in 1925, people's lifestyles changed enormously. Compulsory education also meant that the literacy rate had substantially improved.

Japan had also been affected by Western lifestyles, and lifestyle customs fostered at that time have directly affected contemporary Japan's blend of traditional Japanese and Western cultures.

The Great Kanto Earthquake destroyed the last vestiges of pure Edo culture. Two years after the quake, the sickly Emperor Taishō passed away, and in 1926 was succeeded by Emperor Shōwa.

代に生まれた人が、大正時代には老人となり、新しい時の流れにあたふたとすることを滑稽に表したのが「天保頭」という言葉でした。

　徳川幕府最後の将軍である徳川慶喜もその年齢に該当する一人で、生まれたのが 1837 年（天保 8 年）で他界したのは 1913 年、大正 2 年のことでした。

　大正時代は、江戸時代が遠くなり、新聞や雑誌などのさらなる進化によって、全国で情報が共有されるようになりました。1925 年には**ラジオ放送**もはじまり、人々のライフスタイルも大きく変化します。義務教育も普及し、日本人の**識字率**も大幅に向上しました。

　文化の上では、西欧風のライフスタイルが日本人にも定着し、和と洋が混ざり合った現代の日本に直接通じる独特の生活習慣が育まれます。

　関東大震災で破壊されたのはまさに明治以降も残された純粋な江戸の世界でした。関東大震災の 2 年後にもともと体の弱かった大正天皇が亡くなり、昭和天皇が即位します。1926 年のことでした。

78 Cultural Activity in the Taishō Period

One prominent author in the Taishō period was Arishima Takeo.

In his novel *Aru onna* (A Certain Woman), the protagonist is a woman called Yōko who is on a passenger liner headed for the United States where she is due to marry when she falls in love with the ship's purser. Instead of disembarking at Seattle, she dumps her fiancé and returns to Japan to live with her new lover.

With his outspoken protagonist, who dared to fly in the face of societal values and wisdom, it seems clear that Arishima was deliberately commenting on the conflict between "emotional turmoil and rage" and "the wall of society" that he saw in the society around him at the time.

Arishima and other authors like him are known as the Shirakabaha (White Birch Group). The Shirakabaha is usually defined as being the group of authors behind the magazine *Shirakaba* that openly portrayed the lives of people caught up in the tide of the Taishō democracy. However, *A Certain Woman* heralded a spirit challenging society and its conventional wisdom. Some also maintain that the author voiced his own feelings in his protagonist of the opposite sex, connecting it to the autobiographical confessionary genre of the I-novel that was fashionable in Taishō and early Shōwa.

Meiji and Taishō also saw a surge in proletariat fiction influenced by the socialist movement, especially in mass-market popular fiction. The same period also produced Akutagawa Ryūnosuke, known for his many highly literary short stories on classical subjects. His story Rashōmon was

大正時代の文化活動は？

大正時代に、**有島武郎**という作家がいます。

彼の作品、『或る女』の主人公である葉子は、結婚のために渡米する船中で、客船の事務長と恋をし、シアトルに上陸することなく、婚約者をおいて帰国し、その事務長と同棲をはじめます。

有島武郎

世間の常識や価値観にあえて逆らうように生きてゆく主人公の赤裸々な姿は、明らかに有島武郎が自らの生きる時代を見つめ、人と社会、そして「心の葛藤や怒り」と「世の中の壁」との歪みを強く意識しつつ、描き上げたのではないかと思われます。

有島武郎のような作家を**白樺派**と呼びます。雑誌「白樺」のもと、大正デモクラシーの風潮の中で、人の生き様を自由に描いた作家たちというのが、白樺派への通常の定義です。しかし、この『或る女』からは、そうした常識を越えた、社会に挑戦する魂の呻きを感じることができます。そして、作家自身の思いを異性の主人公に演じさせているようにみえる点も、大正から昭和にかけて流行した、自らをテーマに人間を描く**私小説**にもつながっているように思えます。

明治から大正にかけて、日本の文学はこうした純文学に加え、社会主義運動の影響を受けたプロレタリア文学、さらには大衆小説も多く発表されています。質の高い文章で、古典などをテーマにした短編小説を多く残した**芥川龍之介**

later adapted to film by Kurosawa Akira and is known worldwide.

Many people judge the Taishō period to be one of unprecedented liberty and democratic activity. However, the democratic activity itself meant that there was something to protest against — and this was the feudal values inherited from the Edo period that ultimately grew into the monster of nationalism during the Shōwa period.

The Shirakabaha itself was a literary movement started by students from the Gakushūin (Peers School). Their headmaster was General Nogi Maresuke, who famously committed ritual suicide in order to follow Emperor Meiji in death. Their magazine, the *Shirakaba*, was banned from the Gakushūin. Incidentally, General Nogi was from Chōshū and a typical member of the military elite. We can see how these authors were motivated by a dislike of his feudal militarism as they experimented with literature as a means of resistance against the existing Japanese society.

At the start of the Shōwa, as Japan plunged headlong into war, such literary activity acquired even greater depth as it was further tested by repression.

も、この時代の人です。彼の書いた「羅生門」は後に黒澤明によって映画化され、世界中に紹介されました。

　大正時代を、かつてない自由で民主的な活動のできた時代と評価する人は多くいます。しかし、民主的な活動とは、活動しなければならない対象があったからで、その対象とは昭和になって怪物のように成長する国家主義であり、江戸時代から受け継がれた封建的な価値観でした。

　白樺派も、実は明治天皇の後を追って殉死した軍人乃木希典が校長であった学習院の学生が始めた文芸運動です。彼らが刊行した雑誌「白樺」は、学習院では購読禁止の扱いを受けています。ちなみに乃木希典は、長州出身の典型的な軍人エリートで、そんな封建的な軍人を嫌い、文学に走った作家たちの動機を考えるとき、既存の日本社会への反抗の試みをみてとることもできるのです。

　昭和に入り、日本が戦争に突入してゆく段階で、こうした文学活動そのものが、弾圧の中でさらに試され、深みを帯びてくるのです。

芥川龍之介

The Early Shōwa Period

Right at the start of Shōwa, the discounted government bonds issued by the government to aid businesses damaged by the Great Kanto Earthquake became nonperforming loans as the depression known as the Shōwa Financial Crisis hit. Then two years later, in 1929, shares on Wall Street crashed and the world was plunged into the Great Depression.

While Tanaka Giichi's cabinet had managed to control the crisis through government intervention, it had also attempted to silence social dissent by rounding up all the Communist Party in a crackdown under the Peace Preservation Law. Then, when war broke out between the wavering administration in Beijing and the Kuomintang led by Chiang Kai-shek in the confusion following the collapse of the Qing dynasty, it initiated a hardline against China with the aim of further expanding Japan's interests on the continent. In order to protect its interests in Shandong, acquired from Germany, it dispatched troops to the area. It then took advantage of the warlord Zhang Zuolin's return from Beijing to blow up the railroad and assassinate him, with the aim of placing the entire northeastern region of China under Japan's influence.

Tanaka Giichi's cabinet blamed Zhang Zuolin's assassination on the Kuomintang, but when it became known it was the act of a Japanese army officer Emperor Shōwa ordered the entire cabinet to resign.

The worldwide Great Depression started two months later, on October 24, 1929.

Having been through the temporary economic boom of the Russo-

昭和初期の政治情勢は？

昭和に入るや否や、関東大震災での被災企業を救済するために政府が保証し、支払いが猶予された手形が**不良債権**化し、日本は**昭和の金融恐慌**とよばれる大恐慌に見舞われます。そして、2年後の1929年には、ニューヨークのウォール街で株の大暴落がおこり、世界的な**大恐慌**がはじまります。

その前年、当時の田中義一内閣は、金融恐慌を政府の保証行為で沈静化する一方で、社会不安を払拭する目的で共産党を一斉に検挙し**治安維持法**を強化します。また、大陸への権益のさらなる拡大を目的に、清朝滅亡後の混乱の中で迷走する北京政権と**蒋介石**率いる国民党との戦争がはじまると、対中強攻策を打ち出します。ドイツから引き継いだ**山東省**（さんとうしょう）の権益を守るために、現地に派兵したのです。加えて、中国東北地方を完全に日本の影響下におくために、同地の軍閥、**張作霖**（ちょうさくりん）が北京から帰郷するときに、鉄道を爆破して彼を暗殺します。

田中義一内閣は、張作霖爆殺事件を中国国民党のせいにしますが、それが日本軍部の犯行とわかると、昭和天皇の不審をかい、総辞職に追い込まれます。

その2ヶ月後の1929年10月24日に世界恐慌がはじまったのでした。

日本は日露戦争以降、戦争による一時的な**好景気**と、

ひとくちメモ

昭和金融恐慌
日本で1927年3月に発生した経済恐慌。中小銀行を中心として取り付け騒ぎが発生した

大恐慌
1929年10月24日にニューヨーク証券取引所で株価が大暴落したことを端緒として世界的な規模で各国の経済に波及した金融恐慌

ひとくちメモ

山東省
中国の省の一つ。東は黄海、北は渤海湾、黄河の下流に位置する

張作霖
中華民国初期の軍閥政治家。1875–1928

Japanese War and recession from the stagnating markets, compounded by the Great Kanto Earthquake and the bungling of the subsequent financial crisis, Japan was hard hit.

In the recession, small and medium sized banks were culled, while the five big banks that had grown dramatically around the time of the Russo-Japanese War — Mitsui, Mitsubishi, Sumitomo, Yasuda, and Daiichi — grew even bigger, and used their enormous resources to bring manufacturing under their control, ruling as the conglomerates known as *zaibatsu*. These zaibatsu mobilized politicians that would further the expansion of their own interests and markets. This stimulated Japanese investment in the continent, and was behind Tanaka Giichi's cabinet's advance into China.

The economic issues and Japan's aggression on the continent were two sides of the same coin.

Awareness of the threat from Japan in the aftermath of the fall of the Qing dynasty spurred a surge towards unification in China. Anti-Japanese sentiment was linked to the May Fourth Movement and the development of the two influential parties, the Kuomintang and the Communists, which merged to form the First United Front to overthrow the dithering government in Beijing.

This United Front collapsed in 1927, due to scheming by Western powers fearful of the advance of Communism, and the revolt by Chiang Kai-shek. However, following the assassination of Zhang Zuolin and Japan's subsequent aggression towards China, ten years later China again rallied under the Second United Front.

戦争の需要の沈静化による**不景気**を繰り返し、最終的に
関東大震災とその後の金融政策の不手際から、さらなる
不況に見舞われます。

　不況の中で、中小の銀行は淘汰され、日露戦争前後に
急激に成長した三井、三菱、住友、安田、第一の5大銀
行がますます肥大化し、これら巨大資本の下に産業を統
合し、財閥として君臨します。財閥は政治家を動かし、自
らの利権と市場の拡大を求めます。この構図が日本の大
陸への一層の投資を刺激し、田中義一内閣の中国進出の
背景となったのです。

　経済問題と日本の大陸への侵略行為は、コインの表と
裏だったのです。

　中国は、清朝末期とその後の混乱から、日本という脅
威を意識することで逆に統一に向かってうねりだします。
反日運動が**五・四運動**を通して国民党と共産党の2大勢
力の発展につながり、混乱する北京政府を打倒するために
第一次国共合作が成立したのです。

ひとくちメモ
国共合作とは中国国民党と
共産党の協力体制。1回目は
1924年、2回目は日中戦争
の勃発によりその後1937年
に成立

　この国共合作は、共産主義の進出を懸念する欧米列強
の画策と蒋介石の反乱がもとで1927年に崩壊します。し
かし、張作霖爆殺事件とその後の日本の中国への侵略行
為は、その10年後に**第二次国共合作**へと中国をまとめて
ゆくのです。

80 The Manchurian Incident

There was one flaw in the Meiji Constitution.

This was to place the army and navy, with its enormous military force, under the direct command of the emperor, and not under the management of the cabinet.

Also, just as the army was dubbed Chōshū and the navy Satsuma, they were closely linked to the clan factions and linked to statesmen from the Meiji Revolution who were close to the emperor, and were thus able to bring enormous pressure to bear on the cabinet.

This issue only came to light at the time of the London Naval Treaty in 1930.

Originally, in the mood of peace and fears of a costly arms race following World War I, the major powers including Japan gathered in the U.S. capital to conclude the Washington Naval Treaty in 1922. This fixed the number of ships permitted in the main fleets of America, Britain, and Japan at a ratio of 5:5:3.

However, this had not covered support ships like cruisers, and so in 1930 under the London Naval Treaty the ratio of permitted warships and other vessels was set at 10:6.97 for the U.S. and Japan.

The military were fiercely opposed to Japan signing this treaty. The reason they gave was that despite their opposition the cabinet had persisted with negotiations on behalf of the military, which was under the supreme command of the emperor. This was known as the Problem of the

満州事変と当時の情勢は？

大日本帝国憲法には一つの欠陥がありました。

それは、甚大なる武力を持つ陸海軍が**天皇の指揮下**に置かれ、内閣の管理のもとに置かれていなかったことです。

また、日本の陸海軍は、陸軍が長州、海軍が薩摩といわれていたように、藩閥が幅をきかせ、それぞれ天皇に近い明治維新以来の元勲とつながり、内閣の運営に強い圧力をかけることもできたのです。

この問題が顕在化したのが、1930年の**ロンドン軍縮条約**の時でした。

もともと、第一次世界大戦の後、お互いの軍拡競争が国家財政を圧迫させることへの懸念と、戦後の和平ムードの高まりの中で、アメリカの首都ワシントンD.C.に日本を含む主要国が集まり1922年に**海軍軍縮条約**が締結されます。これで、アメリカ、イギリス、日本の戦艦など主力艦船の保有比率が、それぞれ5対5対3と規定されました。

しかし、その会議では巡洋艦などの補助艦が対象外であったために、1930年に改めてロンドン軍縮会議が開かれ、該当する艦船の保有比率がアメリカを10とした場合、日本は6.97とすることが決定したのです。

この軍縮条約に日本が調印したことに、軍部が強く反発します。天皇の統帥権下にある軍隊の戦力の交渉を、内閣が軍の反対を無視して行ったというのが彼らの反発の理由でした。これを**統帥権干犯問題**といいます。

🔍 ひとくちメモ
ロンドン軍縮条約
1930年に開催された列強海軍の補助艦保有量の制限を主な目的とした国際会議。アメリカ、イギリス、日本、フランス、イタリアで会議がもたれた

ワシントン海軍軍縮条約
1921年11月11日から1922年2月6日までアメリカ合衆国のワシントンD.C.で開催された「ワシントン会議」のうち、海軍の軍縮問題について採択された条約。アメリカ、イギリス、日本、フランス、イタリアの戦艦・航空母艦（空母）等の保有の制限が取り決められた

🔍 ひとくちメモ
統帥権干犯問題
ロンドン海軍軍縮条約の強硬反対派は、統帥権（統帥権は天皇大権とされていた）を拡大解釈し、浜口雄幸内閣が海軍軍令部の意に反して軍縮条約を締結したのは、統帥権の独立を犯したものだとして攻撃した

Infringement of Independence of the Supreme Command.

Prime Minister Hamaguchi Osachi followed the government policy of cooperative diplomacy and somehow shrugged off this pressure to ratify the treaty. However, this enraged extreme rightwingers and on November 11, 1930 Hamaguchi was shot at Tokyo Station, and died the following year.

In 1931, persisting with the expansion of interests in northeastern China, the Kwantung Army blew up the Japanese-run Manchuria Railway and, blaming it on the Chinese government, launched military action and imposed military rule on Mukden. This was the infamous Manchurian Incident. At the time Japan also attempted to occupy Shanghai but were forced to withdraw by resistance from China and Western settlers.

Hamaguchi Osachi's successor, Wakatsuki Reijirō tried to prevent the military action from spreading, but was ignored by the Kwantung Army and eventually his government ratified the military's policy. The fact that the government had no control over the military aggravated the situation.

Subsequently, the Kwantung Army installed Emperor Puyi, the last of the Qing dynasty, as ruler of the puppet state of Manchukuo in northeastern China.

時の首相浜口雄幸は海外との協調外交を政府の方針としており、この圧力をなんとかはねのけ、条約を批准します。しかし、このことが右翼の反発を招き、浜口首相は、1930年11月に東京駅で狙撃され、翌年死亡してしまいます。

　1931年、中国東北部の権益拡大に執着する陸軍は、現地の**関東軍**によって日本が運営する満州鉄道を爆破し、それを中国政府の行為として軍事行動をおこし、奉天を軍政下におきます。**満州事変**の勃発です。同時に、上海でも同市の占領を試みますが、中国側の抵抗と居留地を持つ欧米の反発で撤退します。

　浜口雄幸のあとをついだ若槻礼次郎内閣は、軍事行動の不拡大を求めましたが、関東軍はそれを無視し、結局は内閣も軍部の方針を追認する形となったのです。内閣が軍を管理できないことが、傷口を拡大したのでした。

　その後、関東軍は清の最後の皇帝**溥儀**を擁立し、東北地方に、**満州国**という傀儡政権を打ち立てたのでした。

🔍ひとくちメモ
満州事変
日本と中華民国との間の武力紛争。1931–1932

🔍ひとくちメモ
溥儀
清朝の第12代皇帝（在位1908–1912）、満洲国の初代皇帝（在位1934–1945）

満州国
満州（現在の中国東北部）に存在した国家。1932–1945

81 The Aftermath of Manchurian Incident

The Manchurian Incident deepened the rift with America and Britain.

Needless to say, Manchukuo was a puppet state of Japan: according to the protocol signed by Japan with Manchukuo, Japanese officials were highly involved in government, Japanese troops were of course stationed there, and important communications within the country were ceded to Japan.

This aggression by Japan was possible because the West already had colonies in the Far East and was not as eager as before to intervene. The Western powers had also turned their attention to domestic matters as it struggled to control the global financial crash. Expanding the economy through trade rather than territorial expansion was both cost effective and more diplomatically expedient.

At the same time, China was in turmoil following the downfall of the Qing and was not militarily capable of taking on Japan.

And there was a further issue at play: the might of the Communist Soviet Union. The U.S., Britain, and other powers, had to bury the hatchet with Japan in order to hold the Soviet Union in check, yet they could not permit Japan to have a monopoly on interests in northeastern China. This situation revealed a contradiction in diplomatic policy.

Eventually, China's case came before the League of Nations, and the Western powers sent the British Earl of Lytton as the head of a factfinding mission to Manchukuo. His report was a highly political compromise with

満州事変の影響は？

　満州事変はアメリカやイギリスとの溝を深めます。

　いうまでもなく、満州国は日本の**傀儡政権**です。日本は満州国との間に日満議定書を締結し、国政には多くの日本の官吏があたり、軍隊の駐留はもちろん、主要な国内交通も日本の権益下に置かれました。

　こうした日本の侵略行為が可能であった背景には、まず欧米がすでに植民地主義による極東の運営に、以前ほど熱心でなかったことがあげられます。世界恐慌の収拾という重要な課題の中で、欧米列強の目はむしろ国内に向けられていました。領土拡張よりも商業的なつながりの中で経済を拡大していく方が、コスト面でも外交面でも有利だったのです。

　同時に、中国も清国の崩壊のあと、国内は混乱状態で、日本と総力戦を行うほど国力も充実していませんでした。

　そして、そこにもう一つの課題があります。それは、共産主義勢力であるソ連の存在です。イギリスやアメリカなど列強は、ソ連を牽制しながら日本にうまく矛を収めてもらわなければならず、かといって、日本が中国東北地方の権益を独占することは許されません。この思惑が、外交政策の矛盾となります。

　結局、中国の**国連**への提訴を受け、欧米列強はイギリスの**リットン卿**を代表とする調査団を満州国に送ります。その報告書は、満州国が傀儡政権であることを記し、中

ひとくちメモ
日満議定書
1932年、日本の満州国承認についての両者での取り決め。リットンの報告書が公表される前に日本が既成事実として先行させた

Imperial Japan
大日本帝国の興亡

ひとくちメモ
リットン卿
ギリスの第2代リットン伯爵ヴィクター・ブルワー＝リットン。1930年代初めにリットン調査団の団長として満州事変の調査を行なった

Japan, finding that Manchukuo was a puppet regime and recommending establishing an autonomous government in northeastern China under an international administration, principally Japanese.

In February 1933, by unanimous resolution with the exception of Japan, the League of Nations declared the founding of Manchukuo to be invalid and urged Japan to withdraw its troops. Japan's representative, Matsuoka Yōsuke walked out in protest, and the following month Japan resigned its membership of the League of Nations.

The League of Nations had no power to impose military sanctions, and considering it a fait accompli Japan continued to manage Manchukuo as before. However, by stubbornly rejecting the Lytton Commission's compromise, Japan found itself increasingly isolated internationally.

Thus left to confront alone the threat posed to the Chinese border by the Soviet Union, while also having to suppress resistance within China, Japan sent reinforcements to the Kwantung Army in Manchukuo and made its commanding officer ambassador plenipotentiary. The military grew into a powerful independent war machine, not just in Manchukuo but in Japan too.

国東北地方に自治政府を設け、日本を中心とした列強の官吏下におくことを求める、日本にも妥協した政治色の強いものでした。

1933年2月に、国際連盟で、満州国の建国を無効とし、日本軍の撤兵を求める勧告が、日本をのぞく全会一致で決議されました。日本の国連代表であった松岡洋右は、これに抗議し退席、翌月に国連を脱退します。

国際連盟には**軍事的な制裁力**がなかったため、日本はそのまま満州国の運営を**既成事実**化してゆきます。しかし、**リットン調査団**の妥協案を頑に拒んだ日本は、これをさかいに国際的に孤立してゆくのです。

このことで日本は、中国との国境にあるソ連との脅威に自力で対峙し、同時に中国の抵抗を武力で抑え込まなければならなくなります。そのため、満州国内の関東軍は、大幅に増強され、関東軍司令官は、満州国への全権大使となり、満州国のみならず、日本国内に向けても独立した強力な軍事マシーンとして成長するのです。

🔍 ひとくちメモ
リットン調査団
国際連盟によって満州事変や満州国の調査を命ぜられたリットン卿を団長とする国際連盟日支紛争調査委員会より派遣された調査団

Imperial Japan
大日本帝国の興亡

State Socialism

The birth of the Communist state in Russia posed a major threat to the West. The Communist movement proposed to replace the ruling classes by expanding the rights of workers and farmers to create an egalitarian society. With the founding of the Soviet Union, in order to convert people to the Communist ideal, Lenin pushed the philosophy of the dictatorship of the proletariat in which the people assumed state power.

Looking back at Japan's frequent economic recessions since Meiji and consequent growth of the major conglomerates and spread of wealth and poverty, something similar to this Communist movement was already happening.

Ostensibly, Communism holds that there are economic contradictions the world over, and for that reason the workers and farmers should unite to overthrow the current state through class struggle.

So, away from this theme of "global unity," what would happen if we merge the philosophy with state history and tradition?

Unlike the Soviet Communists, the philosophy of State Socialism in Japan aimed to create an ideologically pure state of integrity headed by the emperor. It had nothing to do with either the suffering of the poverty stricken farmers and workers, or the major conglomerates that controlled the Japanese economy and the government made up of the political parties they backed, which had together plunged the state recession.

Military officers who shared this philosophy, particularly the young

日本での国家社会主義の動向は？

1917年にロシアに**共産主義国家**が産まれたことは、欧米にとっては大きな脅威でした。**共産主義運動**は労働者や農民の権利拡大によって支配階層にとってかわり、平等な社会を築こうとする運動です。レーニンは、ソ連成立にあたって、人々の意識を共産主義の理想に近づけるため、強力に国家が国民を指導管理する**プロレタリアート**独裁という考え方を打ち出します。

日本を振り返れば、明治以降の度重なる経済不況と、それによる財閥の成長、貧富の拡大により、常にこうした共産主義運動がおきていました。

共産主義の建前は、経済矛盾は世界中にあり、そのために世界の労働者や農民が団結し、現存する国家を**階級闘争**によって壊滅させてゆくことです。

では、その「世界レベルの団結」というテーマをはずし、それを国家の歴史や伝統と融合させて考えればどのようになるでしょう。

日本経済を支配する財閥と、その財閥に支援支持される政党による内閣が、国家を不況に放り込み、貧しい農民や労働者が苦しんでいると考え、そうしたものを排除し、日本本来の天皇を頂点にした清廉な国家に改造しようというのが、ソ連型の共産主義とは全く異なる**国家社会主義**の考え方だったのです。

日本の軍部、特に陸軍の若手を中心に、こうした考え

bloods of the army, got together and in 1930 formed the Sakurakai, or Cherry Blossom Group.

Civilian thinkers who backed the philosophy were the rightwingers Ōkawa Shūmei and Kita Ikki. Also the nationalist Nichiren Buddhist, Inoue Nisshō set up the Ketsumeidan (League of Blood) with the stated purpose of assassinating leaders of the conglomerates and politicians under the motto "One Man, One Assassination," and a former finance minister and a conglomerate head were actually murdered.

On May 15, 1932, similarly minded young naval officers conspired with army cadets to shoot dead Prime Minister Inukai Tsuyoshi at his official residence. The attempted coup failed and in the end the officers were arrested, but the assassination led to the collapse of the government and Admiral Saitō Makoto formed a new cabinet. It was during his tenure that Japan withdrew from the League of Nations.

After the May 15 Incident, as it was known, the internal standoff in the army intensified between the Kōdōha (Imperial Way Faction) that favored direct action, and the Tōseiha (Control Faction) who advocated taking political power within the existing structure of the bureaucracy and financial conglomerates.

This was also a conflict between young officers fanatical about the ideals of State Socialism, and the upper echelons of the army who wanted to merge their interests with the prominent figures of the political and financial worlds who had a grip on power.

方を持つ将校が集まり、1930年に**桜会**というグループを結成します。

　この考え方を支援した民間の思想家が、大川周明や北一輝という右翼の大物でした。そして、日蓮宗の国家主義者である井上日召は、**血盟団**を組織して、一人一殺をもって、財閥や政治家を暗殺しようとし、実際に蔵相経験者や財界の大物が殺害されました。

　1932年5月15日に、海軍で同様の考え方を持つ青年将校は、陸軍若手と結託し、当時の首相犬養毅を官邸で射殺します。連携した決起行動は失敗し、結局将校たちは逮捕されますが、これにより、政党内閣が崩壊し、海軍大将の斎藤実が組閣します。この斎藤内閣のとき、日本は国際連盟を脱退したのでした。

　この事件を**五・一五事件**と呼びますが、陸軍ではその後、こうした直接行動を支持する**皇道派**と、政財界との関係の中で、政権をとっていこうとする**統制派**との対立が激化してきます。

　それは、国家社会主義の理想に燃える青年将校と、より軍部の実権を握り従来の政財界の重鎮と利害をともにする陸軍上層部との対立でもあったのです。

🔍 **ひとくちメモ**
血盟団とは、井上日召らが結成した右翼思想の団体。「一人一殺」を唱え、財閥や政治家を暗殺した

🔍 **ひとくちメモ**
五・一五事件
1932年5月15日、当時の犬養毅首相が官邸内で軍の青年将校によって暗殺された

皇道派は天皇中心の国体至上主義を唱え、統制派は財閥・官僚とつながり軍部勢力の樹立を目指した

83 Japan's Prewar Economy and Diplomatic Policy

At the time of the global depression, the colonial powers of Britain and France attempted to overcome the financial crisis by protecting their own economic zones, or blocs. It could also be said that by establishing Manchukuo Japan was attempting to set up its own economic bloc.

The United States, under President Franklin D. Roosevelt, facilitated recovery from recession with the New Deal programs to stimulate domestic demand through public works and regulation of the domestic economy.

Japan promoted exports and incited a weak yen and inflation by stopping the export of money and issuing nonconvertible bank notes, and boosting munitions manufacturing through deficit-covering bonds. These moves caused new economic friction between Japan and the West.

Firstly, America was the biggest supplier of the scrap iron needed by the heavy industries pivotal to munitions manufacturing. Also, the textiles that were Japan's main export were controlled by demand in Western countries such as America and Britain.

The world economy was already starting to forge links beyond political ideology. However, the low value of the yen meant that Japanese exports were cheap, which led Britain and America to accuse Japan of dumping, aggravating the friction between Japan and the Western economic bloc.

On February 26, 1936 the young army officers of the Kōdōha staged a coup d'état (the so-called February 26 Incident), killing, amongst others,

戦前の日本経済と外交方針の関係は？

　世界恐慌の当時、元々植民地を世界に持つイギリスやフランスなどの大国は、自らの経済圏をしっかりと保持したブロック経済の中で、恐慌から立ち直ろうとします。そうした見方をすれば、日本は満州国を建国し、新たなブロック経済圏を造ろうとしたことになります。

　またアメリカは、フランクリン・ルーズベルト大統領の指導のもと、国内経済の統制と公共事業などによって内需を促進する**ニューディール政策**によって、経済危機からの離脱を促進します。

　日本は、金の輸出を停止し、**不換紙幣**を発行することと、**赤字国債**による**軍需産業**の大幅な育成で、インフレと円安を誘導し、輸出を促進していました。こうした日本の動きは欧米列強との新たな経済摩擦を産み出してゆくのでした。

　まず、軍需産業の要となる重工業においては、その原料となる鉄くずの最大の輸入元はアメリカでした。また、日本の代表的輸出製品である繊維製品はアメリカ、イギリスなどの欧米諸国の需要に左右されます。

　世界経済は、すでに政治的な立場を越えてリンクをはじめていたのです。しかし、イギリスやアメリカは、日本の円安による安価な輸出製品を**ダンピング**として非難し、日本と欧米のブロック経済との摩擦が深刻化します。

　1936年2月26日に、皇道派の陸軍青年将校が決起する**二・二六事件**というクーデターが起こり、前首相の斎

the former prime minister Saitō Makoto and Takahashi Korekiyo, who had been in charge of the financial recovery following the crash, and placing Tokyo under martial law. The emperor was furious, and the coup was quashed, and the leaders sentenced to death by court-martial.

After this the army purged Kōdōha, and increased their influence in politics and industry. They placed China and the Soviet Union into the mainstream of foreign policy, and changed course to policies that kept in mind the possibility of war with Britain and America due to the worsening political and economic standoff.

In Europe the Nazi party, leaders of the National Socialist movement in Germany, came to power in 1933. In Italy, too, Mussolini's National Fascist Party had come to power after World War I, and was making inroads into North Africa. Japan quickly approached Germany and Italy, and in 1938 concluded the Anti-Comintern Pact.

When Japan attempted to expand its own economic bloc by bringing not just Manchuria but all of China and even South East Asia under its control, the United States, Britain, and others imposed economic sanctions on Japan.

藤実や恐慌後の財政の立て直しを指導してきた高橋是清などが殺害され、東京に**戒厳令**がしかれます。天皇がこれに激怒したこともあり、クーデターは鎮圧され、首謀者は**軍法会議**で死刑となります。

陸軍は、その後皇道派を一掃し、政財界への発言力を増し、従来のソ連と対中政策を主流に置いた外交方針から、日本との政治的、経済的対立が深まるアメリカやイギリスとの戦争をも視野に入れた方針へと舵をきってゆくのでした。

当時、ヨーロッパでは、1933年にドイツで国家社会主義運動を指導する**ナチス**が政権をとっていました。またイタリアでも第一次世界大戦後に**ムッソリーニ**の**ファシスト党**が政権をとり、北アフリカなどへ進出していました。日本は急速にドイツ、イタリアに接近し、1938年には**日独伊防共協定**を締結します。

日本が自らの経済圏の拡大のために、満州のみならず、中国全体、さらに東南アジアを自らの権益下に置こうとしたとき、アメリカ、イギリスとの対立がついに日本への**経済制裁**へと発展するのでした。

ひとくちメモ
日独伊防共協定
1936年の日独防共協定が1937年イタリアの加入によって三国に拡大した「反ソ」「反共」を目的とした協定

ひとくちメモ

ナチス
国家社会主義ドイツ労働者党。ドイツ国の政党。
1919-1945

（ベニート・）ムッソリーニ
イタリアの独裁者。ファシスト党党首。1883-1945

ファシスト党
イタリア王国における政党。一党独裁体制を確立。
1921-1943

ヒトラー　　　　　　　ムッソリーニ

大日本帝国の興亡

Imperial Japan

84 The War with China

After the Manchurian Incident, anti-Japanese sentiment spread throughout China as the United Front Movement.

Japan continued with its incursions into China, and in July 1937 engaged in battle with the Chinese army at the Lugou (Marco Polo) Bridge in the outskirts of Beijing. In anticipation of a rapport between the military and the political parties, Prince Konoe Fumimaro had been made prime minister less than a month before.

In the end, Prince Konoe's cabinet was forced to accept the army's expansion of the war front to capture Beijing and Tianjin, and in August the army advanced from Shanghai onto Nanjing, the capital of the Kuomintang Government. Then over a two-month period, civilians in Nanjing were systematically slaughtered in the Massacre of Nanjing, condemned the world over. The Kuomintang government took refuge in Chongqing, Sichuan province, from where it continued the war with Japan.

Then Zhang Xueliang, the son of Zhang Zuolin killed by the Japanese army just before the Manchurian Incident, detained Chiang Kai-shek of the Kuomintang government in Xi'an, pushed for a peaceful settlement with the People's Liberation Army based at Yan'an, and in 1937 a new Kuomintang-Communist collaboration was formed. Japan welcomed Wang Jingwei, who opposed Chiang Kai-shek, and founded a puppet government in Nanjing in order to gain a foothold in China, but it could not control the entire extended area of China and the war turned into a quagmire.

日中戦争のなりゆきは？

　満州事変以来、中国の反日感情は、抗日運動として中国全域に拡大します。

　日本は、中国へのさらなる進出を目論み、1937 年 7 月に、北京郊外の盧溝橋で中国軍と交戦します。軍部と政党との融和を期待され、公家出身の近衛文麿が内閣総理大臣に就任して 1 ヶ月足らずのことでした。

　結局、近衛内閣は、軍部に押されて戦線を拡大し、北京、天津を攻略し、8 月には上海から当時の国民政府の首都南京に軍を進めます。このとき、南京で一般市民を 2 ヶ月にわたり組織的に虐殺した南京大虐殺は、世界中の非難を浴びることになります。国民党政府は四川省の重慶に避難し、日中戦争を継続します。

　その頃、満州事変直前に日本軍に殺害された張作霖の息子、張学良が国民党政府の蒋介石を西安に拘束し、当時延安に本拠地をおいていた中国共産党軍との和解を迫り、1937 年に再び国共合作が成立します。日本は、蒋介石と対立する汪兆銘を迎え、南京に傀儡政権を樹立して、中国への足場を造ろうとしますが、広大な中国全土を制圧することはできず、戦争は泥沼化します。

ひとくちメモ
盧溝橋
中国北京市の南西、豊台区を流れる盧溝河（現在は永定河）に架かる石造りの橋

ひとくちメモ
南京大虐殺
日本軍が中華民国の首都南京市を占領した際、中国軍の捕虜、敗残兵、便衣兵及び一般市民を不法に虐殺したとされる事件

ひとくちメモ
張学良
中華民国の軍人・政治家。1901–2001

汪兆銘
中華民国の政治家。1883–1944

大日本帝国の興亡 Imperial Japan

As part of the war effort, Prince Konoe's cabinet promoted wartime education, issued propaganda on surmounting the national crisis to rally the nation behind emperor, and suppressed free speech. In 1938 the National Legislation Law was approved, which granted the government unconditional powers to mobilize the people and national assets, and by 1940 all political parties were brought under the organization called Taisei Yokusankai (Imperial Rule Assistance Association) to create a totalitarian single-party state. This marked the end of party politics in Japan.

Meanwhile, from 1938 into 1939, Japan clashed twice with the Soviet Union, in the Battles of Lake Khasan and Khalkhyn Gol (Nomonhan), and were defeated both times. As a result they reviewed their strategy against the Soviet Union, and in July 1939 announced the annulment of the US-Japan Trade Treaty. When economic sanctions against Japan were intensified, there began to be calls among the military to go to war against the United States.

And so, after the Manchurian Incident, Japan found itself in the grip of totalitarianism rushing headlong into an insane war with no exit in sight.

Meanwhile in Europe, Germany and Italy were growing in power and becoming a threat to Britain and France, but just as with the Manchurian Incident, Britain saw such moves as a restraint on the Soviet Union and adopted an appeasement policy towards Germany.

However, Britain and France finally declared war on Germany in 1939, after Germany invaded Poland. World War II had started. Japan sided with Germany, and in 1940 the Tripartite Pact between Germany, Italy, and Japan was signed.

近衛内閣は、戦争遂行のために、戦時教育を強化し、挙国一致で天皇のために国難を克服するという宣伝を徹底し、言論統制も進めます。1938年には国民とその資産を政府が無条件で動員できる**国家総動員法**を可決し、1940年になると、全ての政党を**大政翼賛会**という組織にまとめ、政治的にも全体主義の基盤造りを行います。日本の政党政治はここに完全に終焉したのでした。

　一方、1938年から39年にわたって、日本軍は**張鼓峰事件、ノモンハン事件**と、2度にわたってソ連軍と紛争をおこし、2回とも敗北しています。これにより、対ソ戦略は見直され、1939年7月に**日米通商航海条約**の破棄をアメリカに通告され、日本への経済制裁が強化される中、対米開戦が軍部の中で叫ばれ始めます。

　このように、満州事変以降、日本は**全体主義**のなかで、狂気ともいえる出口の見えない戦争に突入したのでした。

　その頃ヨーロッパでは、ドイツとイタリアの勢力拡大が、イギリスやフランスの脅威となっていましたが、満州事変と同様、イギリスはこうした動きをソ連への牽制として、ドイツとは宥和政策をとっていました。
　しかし、1939年にドイツがポーランドに侵攻したことから、ついにイギリス、フランスがドイツに宣戦を布告します。**第二次世界大戦**が勃発したのです。日本はドイツに接近し、1940年に**日独伊三国軍事同盟**を締結しました。

ひとくちメモ
国家総動員法
総力戦遂行のため国家のすべての人的・物的資源を政府が統制運用できる（総動員）旨を規定した法。
1938–1946

ひとくちメモ
張鼓峰事件
1938年の7月29日から8月11日にかけて、満州国東南端の張鼓峰で発生したソ連との国境紛争

ノモンハン事件
1939年5月から同年9月にかけて、満州国とモンゴル人民共和国の間の国境線をめぐって発生した日ソ両軍の国境紛争事件

日米通商航海条約
日本・米国間の通商および航海に関する条約。1939年の日本の中国侵略に抗議してアメリカは破棄を通告。
1911–1940

ひとくちメモ
日独伊三国軍事同盟
1940年9月27日に日本、ドイツ、イタリアの間で締結された「日独伊三国間条約」に基づく日独伊三国の同盟関係

85 War with America

It cannot be said that there were no voices of caution with regard to policy towards America. For example, Yonai Mitsumasa, who came to power between the three cabinets formed by Konoe Fumimaro, tried to take a pro-American line.

However, none of the cabinets were able to check the military's recklessness. Within the military, the only voices of caution came from one part of the navy, and the majority was optimistic about the war with China, although the claim that war with the United States was inevitable appears to have been ideological.

With the conclusion of the Tripartite Pact Japan had made its position clear by joining the fascist Axis of Power. Both Germany and Japan were playing the diplomatic card of a deterrent for the Soviet Union and, lacking a strategy for negotiating successfully with Britain and others, dragged the cautious Western powers into the war.

In order to secure strategic materials, oil first and foremost, Japan kept a watchful eye on Germany's invasion of France, and in 1940 sent troops to French Indochina (present-day Vietnam), completing their occupation of the entire territory the following year. Also, since Germany had a nonaggression pact with the Soviet Union, Japan signed the Soviet-Japanese Neutrality Pact in order to secure the northern regions. However, given that Germany broke the pact and invaded the Soviet Union just three months later, there was clearly disarray between the Axis powers.

In retaliation for Japan's advance into French Indochina, America

対米開戦への道のりは？

　歴代の内閣の中には、対米政策を慎重に進めようとする動きがなかったわけでもありません。例えば、3回にわたって組閣された近衛文麿内閣の間に政権を担当した米内光政などは親米路線をとろうとします。

　しかし、いずれの内閣も、結局軍部の暴走をとめることができなかった点では共通していました。軍部は軍部で海軍の一部に慎重論があったに過ぎず、大勢は日中戦争を楽観しながら、最終的には日米開戦もやむなしという、場当たり的な対応をしていたことが現実のようです。

　日独伊三国軍事同盟の成立で、ファシズム3大国を**枢軸**とする日本の立場は鮮明になります。ドイツも日本の場合も、ソ連への抑止力という外交カードを使用し、イギリスなどとうまく掛け合ってゆくという戦略を持てず、そのまま自分の方から戦争に慎重だった欧米列強を戦争に引きずりこんでゆきました。

　日本は、石油をはじめとした戦略物資を確保するために、ドイツがフランスに侵攻する状況をにらみながら、1940年に現在のベトナムにあたる**フランス領インドシナ**（仏印）に軍を進め、翌年には仏印全土への進駐を完了します。また、ドイツがソ連と**不可侵条約**を締結していることから、北方の安全のために**日ソ中立条約**を締結します。しかし、その3ヶ月後にドイツが条約を破りソ連に侵攻したことからみても、枢軸間での足並みの乱れをみることができます。

　アメリカは日本軍の仏印進出の報復として、アメリカ国

ひとくちメモ
枢軸国
第二次世界大戦時に連合国と戦った諸国（日本、ドイツ、イタリア）

ひとくちメモ
フランス領インドシナ
1887年から1954年までフランスの支配下にあったインドシナ半島東部地域。現在のベトナム・ラオス・カンボジアを合わせた領域に相当する

日ソ中立条約
1941年に日本とソビエト連邦（ソ連）の間で締結された中立条約

froze Japanese assets within the country, and also reached agreement with Britain, China, and Holland, including its colony Indonesia, to tighten the noose of economic sanctions on Japan.

In a last attempt by the Japanese government to avoid war, Nomura Kichisaburō was sent as ambassador to the United States to negotiate, but America took a hardline against the Japanese army's occupation of French Indochina and the negotiations failed to progress.

In October 1941, a central figure in the army's Tōseiha, Tōjō Hideki, was made prime minister, and in December, the war against the United States was sanctioned at an Imperial Conference attended by the emperor.

The Americans, too, issued an ultimatum to Japan in the form of the Hull Note, delivered by Secretary of State Cordell Hull, demanding Japan's withdrawal from French Indochina and China, and annulment of the Tripartite Treaty.

On December 8, 1941, Japan launched its surprise attack on the American military base at Pearl Harbor on Oahu Island, Hawaii, starting the Pacific War. According to the Tripartite Treaty, Germany and Italy had also thus declared war on America, and the war spread worldwide.

内の日本資産の凍結を断行し、イギリス、中国、インドネシアを領有するオランダによる**経済制裁包囲網**を造り上げます。ABCD 包囲網です。

　日本政府は、最終的な開戦を回避しようと、野村喜三郎を全権大使に任命し日米交渉を進めますが、日本軍の仏印進駐はアメリカ側をさらに硬化させ、交渉は進展しません。

　1941 年 10 月に陸軍の統制派の中心人物であった東条英機が内閣総理大臣に就任し、12 月の対米開戦が天皇の出席する**御前会議**で決定されます。

　アメリカ側も、国務長官**ハル**が、**ハル・ノート**と呼ばれる日本の仏印や中国からの撤退や、三国軍事同盟の破棄などの強硬な要求を日本に提示します。

　1941 年 12 月 8 日に、日本軍がハワイのオアフ島真珠湾のアメリカ軍基地を奇襲したことから、**太平洋戦争**がはじまったのです。条約によってドイツとイタリアもアメリカに宣戦布告し、戦火は世界に拡大したのでした。

🔍ひとくちメモ
ハル・ノート
太平洋戦争開戦直前の日米交渉において、1941 年 11 月 26 日にアメリカ側から日本側に提示された交渉文書

コーデル・ハル
アメリカ合衆国の政治家。1933 年から 1944 年まで国務長官を務めた。1871–1955

86 The Pacific War

From the point of view of the Japanese people, the Pacific War was the most momentous, disastrous ordeal of Japan's recorded history.

At the start of the war, the Japanese army gained control over Singapore and Indonesia, and also America's stronghold in the Philippines, but after defeat in the Battle of Midway in June 1942, Japan was exposed to the counterattack of the Allies, particularly the Americans, and was gradually driven out of the South Pacific starting from the island of Guadalcanal.

Japan was still at war with China, and had 1,000,000 troops stationed there. Also, in Europe the Soviet Union started its counterattack of Germany, and then in 1943 Italy surrendered. This was unexpected for Japan, which had intended to gain the advantage in the war through the Axis powers forcing Britain to surrender.

When Saipan fell in June 1944, it became the base for U.S. air raids on the Japanese mainland, and the major cities all over Japan were exposed to bombings. At the same time the Japanese army suffered tremendous losses in the Philippines and Burma in the counterattacks by allied forces. In April 1945 Germany surrendered, and in the same month American forces landed on Okinawa, gaining control of the whole island by June.

Through the Japanese army's strict moral education of its soldiers, many officers and men were forced to die an honorable death rather than surrender to the enemy, and to undertake suicidal attacks as Kamikaze and human torpedoes. Civilians, too, under the government's instructions for all-out resistance, were mobilized to work in factories, and even when

太平洋戦争の成り行きは？

太平洋戦争は、文字で記されている日本の歴史の中で、日本人にとって、最も悲惨で深刻な試練でした。

開戦当初は、日本軍はシンガポールからインドネシア、そしてアメリカの拠点であったフィリピンを制圧しますが、1942 年 6 月の**ミッドウェー海戦**での敗北以来、アメリカを中心とした連合軍の反撃にさらされ、南太平洋の**ガダルカナル**諸島からはじまり、じわじわと日本軍は駆逐されていきました。

日本は、中国と依然、戦争状態で 100 万人の兵力を割いています。また、ヨーロッパでもソ連のドイツに対する反撃が開始され、1943 年にはイタリアも降伏し、ヨーロッパで**枢軸側**がイギリスを屈服させることで、戦争を有利に導こうとする日本の思惑は外れてしまいます。

1944 年の 6 月に**サイパン島**が陥落すると、同島から本土への空襲がはじまり、日本全国の主要都市が爆撃に晒されます。同時に、**フィリピン**、**ビルマ**方面も**連合軍**の反撃によって日本軍は甚大な損害を受けます。1945 年 4 月、ドイツは降伏し、同じ月にアメリカ軍は沖縄に上陸、6 月までに全島を制圧します。

日本軍は兵士への厳しい精神教育で、多くの将兵が敵に降伏すること無く、玉砕を強いられ、神風特攻隊や人間魚雷のような**自殺行為による攻撃**まで展開します。一般市民も徹底抗戦という政府の指導のもと、工場などに動員され、戦局が悪化し、日本の主要都市が焼土と化しても、**本**

the war took a turn for the worse and Japan's major cities were burned to the ground, there were calls for people to prepare for fighting on the mainland.

In many territories not on the Japanese mainland, including Okinawa, noncombatants were forced to die along with military personnel and there were countless victims, both military and civilian.

In these circumstanes, the leaders of the allied forces in 1943 adopted the Cairo Declaration, demanding that Japan return its overseas colonies, and urging Japan to surrender. And in February 1945, with the imminent collapse of Germany, the U.S. president Franklin D. Roosevelt, British prime minister Winston Churchill, and Soviet leader Joseph Stalin met in Yalta on the Crimean peninsula, and signed the secret treaty that the Soviet Union would join the war against Japan after Germany's surrender in return for the ceding of the Kuril Islands and Sakhalin to the Soviet Union.

However, Japan indicated its intention to continue the war to the bitter end. America feared the casualties that would be incurred by landing on the Japanese mainland, or further protracting the war by the Soviets advancing south into Japan. For America, the most desirable outcome would have been Japan's unconditional surrender.

土決戦が叫ばれていました。

　沖縄など日本国外の多くの地域では、非戦闘員も軍隊と共に死ぬことを強いられ、軍民共々、数えきれない犠牲者を出します。

　こうした状況の中、連合国首脳は 1943 年に**カイロ宣言**を採択し、日本の海外植民地の返還を求め、降伏を勧告します。そして、ドイツ崩壊が目前に迫った 1945 年 2 月に、アメリカのルーズベルト大統領、イギリスのチャーチル首相、ソ連のスターリン首相がクリミア半島の**ヤルタ**で会談し、千島と樺太のソ連への返還を条件に、ドイツの降伏後、ソ連が日本に参戦する**密約**が結ばれました。

　しかし、日本はあくまでも戦争を継続する意思を示しており、アメリカとしては、日本本土に上陸した場合の被害、さらに戦争が長引いた場合の、ソ連の日本への南進を深く懸念するようになります。アメリカの影響下での日本の無条件降伏がアメリカにとって、最も望ましい結論だったのです。

🔍 ひとくちメモ
1943年11月、ルーズベルト、チャーチル、蒋介石がカイロで会談し発表したカイロ宣言。後日、連合国の対日基本方針となった

87 Japan's Surrender

In July 1945, President Harry S. Truman, who had come to office following the death of Franklin D. Roosevelt, Prime Minister Winston Churchill of Britain, and Prime Minister Joseph Stalin of the Soviet Union, met at Potsdam in the outskirts of Berlin, and defined the terms for Japan's surrender in the Potsdam Declaration. This included eliminating militarism in Japan and punishing war crimes, and reducing Japanese territory to the four main islands and surrounding islands as specified by the Allies. However, it also included provisions not to enslave Japan, but to reform it as a democracy. This was to be Japan's fundamental postwar policy.

Japan took responsibility for the fall of Saipan, and in 1943 the entire cabinet of Tōjō Hideki resigned, only to be succeeded by the army general Koiso Kuniaki, who continued the war. However, when admiral Suzuki Kantarō became prime minister after the Battle of Okinawa, he attempted to maneuver an end to the war, albeit unsuccessfully.

The Potsdam Declaration did not guarantee the emperor's sovereignty and this, coupled with the opposition of the army who insisted on fighting to the bitter end on Japanese soil, led the government to ignore it.

Meanwhile America, who wished to avoid incurring heavy casualties by fighting on the Japanese mainland, and stressed the strategical value of having Japan under its wing in the Cold War situation after the end war, wanted to end the war as soon as possible. On August 6, 1945 it dropped the atomic bomb on Hiroshima, and on August 9, another on Nagasaki,

日本の降伏とその影響は？

1945年7月に、フランクリン・ルーズベルトが他界すると、次に就任した**トルーマン**大統領、イギリスの**チャーチル**首相、ソ連の**スターリン**首相がベルリン郊外のポツダムに集まり、対日戦争終結の条件を**ポツダム宣言**として発表します。そこには、日本からの軍国主義の除去と戦犯の処罰、日本の領土を本土4島と連合国が規定する周辺の諸島に縮小することが盛り込まれます。しかし、同時に日本を奴隷化せず、民主国家として再生させる条項も盛り込まれていました。これが、戦後の日本の統治の基本政策となったのです。

🔍 **ひとくちメモ**
1945年7月、ポツダムに連合軍のトップが集結し日本に対する共同宣言を出す。軍国主義の一掃、戦犯の処罰、領土の局限などが規定された

日本は、サイパン島陥落の責任をとって、1943年に東条英機内閣が総辞職しますが、同じ陸軍の小磯国昭が首相となり、戦争を継続します。しかし、沖縄戦の時期に海軍出身で、天皇にも近い鈴木貫太郎が首相となり、戦争終結へ向けた工作を、ソ連などを通して開始しますが、思うように進みません。

政府は、ポツダム宣言が発表されると、そこに天皇の地位の保証が盛り込まれていないことや、本土決戦を主張する陸軍の抵抗によって、宣言を黙殺します。

一方、アメリカは甚大な被害が予想される本土決戦を避け、戦後の冷戦状態に日本を傘下に置く戦略的価値を重視し、戦争を一刻も早く終結させようと、1945年8月6日に広島に、8月9日には長崎に**原爆**を投下します。これによって、非戦闘員33万人が死亡、街は灰燼に帰します。

killing 330,000 civilians, and reducing both cities to ashes. At the same time, on August 9, despite the Soviet-Japanese Neutrality Pact still being in force, the Soviet Union declared war on Japan and invaded Manchukuo.

The Japanese government had again requested America to guarantee the position of the emperor, but received no response, and in the end, on August 14 in Imperial Conference, it was decided to accept the unconditional surrender. The emperor informed the nation of the surrender directly by radio broadcast on August 15. Known as the *gyokuon hōsō*, or Jewel Voice Broadcast, this was the first time the people of Japan had heard the emperor's voice.

With the conclusion of the Pacific War, World War II was also over. Japan was said to have suffered casualties of 3.1 million, but it is not known how many losses Japan inflicted on China and South East Asia. And the Allies, particularly America, lost almost a million men in battle.

The Japanese Instrument of Surrender was signed on September 2, 1945, on the deck of the *USS Missouri* in Tokyo Bay. With this, the Japanese army was disarmed, and the structure of the Japanese empire since Meiji was largely replaced under the guidance of the Allied powers.

同時に、8月9日には**日ソ中立条約**の有効期限を残しながらソ連が日本に宣戦布告し、満州国に侵攻します。

　日本政府は、アメリカに天皇の地位保全を再度申し込んだものの回答はなく、最終的に8月14日の御前会議で**無条件降伏**の受諾を決定します。国民には翌日の8月15日に天皇が直接ラジオを通してそれを通知します。この放送を**玉音放送**といい、国民が初めてきいた天皇の肉声でした。

　太平洋戦争の集結で、世界中を巻き込んだ第二次世界大戦は終わります。日本の犠牲者は310万人といわれますが、中国や東南アジアに日本が与えた損害も計り知れません。また、アメリカをはじめとした連合軍にも100万人近い戦死者がありました。
　降伏文書の調印は、1945年9月2日に東京湾に停泊したアメリカの戦艦ミズーリの艦上で行われました。これによって、日本軍は武装解除され、明治以来の日本帝国の体制は連合国の指導の元で、大きく変換されてゆくのです。

Part 5

Postwar Japan to the Present
戦後から現代へ

戦後から現代へ

　戦後、日本の政治は 180 度変化しました。

　そして、その影響を受けて文化や言論界も変わりました。

　今、そうした戦後の日本を造る原点となった日本国憲法について、改憲の議論があちこちから噴出しています。その議論を進めてゆく上からも、特に敗戦直後から 10 年間の日米関係には注目する必要があります。

　占領下の日本で、どのように民主化が進められたか。さらに独立が認められたあと、日本のあり方がどのような形で選択されたかをしっかりと見詰めてゆくべきなのです。

　海外の人と交流するとき、いまだに日本には女性差別があり、言論の自由や人権が抑圧されているのではという批判に接することがあります。事実無根のこともあれば、冷静にみれば一理あることもあります。

　これらの指摘や憶測に対して日本人が答えるとき、戦後の歴史を正しく踏まえながら答えることができれば、より説得力のある会話が成り立つはずです。また、日本人も心を開き、こうした会話の中から将来の日本のあるべき姿をみつけてゆくことも大切です。英語で世界情勢を語るときにも、現代の日本のスタンスや日本政府の方針などを理解しながら、自分なりの意見を述べてゆきたいものです。

世界的にみるならば、19 世紀から 20 世紀にかけては、欧米の文化を
アジアが吸収する時代でした。

　しかし、現代ではアジアの中で欧米とアジアの文化が混ざり合った結
果でき上がった新たな文化が、逆に欧米に向けて輸出される時代になっ
ています。ここでも、そうした観点から日本文化の輸出というテーマにも
ふれています。

　日本文化が輸出され、世界の人々に受け入れられれば、さらに日本へ
の関心が高まり、観光と文化交流、そしてビジネスなど多方面でも人々の
行き来が活発になるはずです。

　世界に優しい、海外に開かれた日本をアピールするためにも、戦後の日
本の歩みをもう一度振り返り、説得力のある意見を語りましょう。そのた
めにも、英語で日本を正しく紹介する能力を持つように努めたいものです。

88 The Postwar Period

There were major changes in the Shōwa period before and after World War II, and the events of the postwar period directly shaped present-day Japan.

Compared to Germany, which was divided into East and West due to the influence of the Cold War, Japan was lucky. Japan's administration was overseen by the Far Eastern Commission, consisting of eleven countries against whom Japan had fought in the War, and instigated by the United States. The Allied Council of Japan set up by America, Britain, the Soviet Union, and China, decided on the occupation policy, but the actual operation of the occupation fell to the Supreme Commander of the Allied Powers (SCAP), generally refered to as GHQ, headed by Douglas MacArthur. Domestic affairs were carried out as before by the cabinet, under the guidance of GHQ for the duration of the occupation.

The reforms carried out at this time were the most sweeping since the Meiji Restoration. Political prisoners were released, freedom of speech at public meetings was guaranteed, and pro-democracy education was instigated. Labor unions were also restored. Improvements in the status of women were guaranteed, and under the reform of agricultural land the tenant farmer system was abolished. The major industrial conglomerates formed against the backdrop of Japan's advance into China were abolished, and antitrust laws enacted to prevent the concentration of wealth in the market.

The Meiji Restoration had been achieved by loyalists espousing the Sonnō jōi (revere the emperor and expel the foreigners) ideology, and they had been directly involved with building up the nation afterwards.

戦後の始まりとは？

　昭和という時代は、戦前と戦後とで大きく変化します。そして戦後は直接現在の日本に繋がる時代です。

　ドイツが**冷戦**の影響で東西に分割したことに比べると、日本は幸運でした。日本の統治はアメリカが中心で、日本と交戦した 11 カ国による**極東委員会**がアメリカにおかれました。日本にはアメリカ、イギリス、ソ連、中国の４カ国による**対日理事会**がおかれ、その下で占領政策が決定されますが、実際の占領業務は、**連合国軍最高司令官総司令部(GHQ)** があたり、最高責任者にはダグラス マッカーサーが就任します。内政は、今まで通り日本の内閣が実施しますが、占領期間中は GHQ が行政のありかたを指導します。

　そこで行われた改革は、明治維新以来の大々的な改革でした。思想犯が釈放され、言論思想集会の自由が保証され、**民主化教育**が徹底されます。労働組合の活動も復活します。婦人の地位向上が保証され、農地改革により、小作人制度も撤廃されました。経済活動では、日本の中国進出の背景となった財閥が解体され、経済活動における富の集中を避けるために、**独占禁止法**が制定されます。

　明治維新は、尊王攘夷思想の志士によって実現され、彼らは以後の国家建設に直接関わりました。その中で産業が育成され、政治も経済も志士たちのつながりの中で

🔍 ひとくちメモ

極東委員会
太平洋戦争に敗北した日本を連合国が占領するに当たり、日本を管理する為の政策機関として設けられたもの

対日理事会
太平洋戦争に敗北した日本を、連合国が占領するに当たり、連合国軍最高司令官総司令部（GHQ/SCAP）の諮問機関として設置されたもの

連合国軍最高司令官総司令部
太平洋戦争の終結に際してポツダム宣言の執行のために日本において占領政策を実施した連合国軍の機関

改革の内容
思想犯の釈放、言論思想集会の自由、民主化教育の徹底、労働組合活動の復活、婦人の地位向上、小作人制度撤廃、財閥解体、独占禁止法制定

This included nurturing industry, which means that both politics and the economy developed under these loyalists. When the upsets and contradictions in society caused by these rapid changes eventually became manifest, Japan had attempted to resolve this situation through expansion onto the continent.

Ironically, it was this policy that eighty years later led Japan to self-destruction in the Pacific War. The West had eradicated imperialist policies in World War I and had started searching for a new framework of international cooperation. By rejecting this and instead pursuing the old imperialist path, Japan's tragedy was that it had missed the boat in the nineteenth century.

And, just as the arrival of Perry's ships had changed Japan, once again Japan was forced to change direction by being occupied for the first time in its history.

From 1946, GHQ used Japan's police force to prosecute and punish war criminals. Class-A criminals, who had conducted the war, were tried at the International Military Tribunal for the Far East in Tokyo. Seven, including Tōjō Hideki, were sentenced to death, while eighteen others were given either life or fixed-term sentences. Also, for wartime atrocities, a further 5,416 were tried both in Japan and elsewhere, with 937 sentenced to death, although there is some controversy about the fairness of these overseas trials.

発展し、やがて急激な変化の中にあった不消化と矛盾が顕現化したとき、日本は大陸へ進出し、自らを拡大することで矛盾を吸収しようとしました。

　この日本の80年にわたる政策自体が太平洋戦争という自己破滅へと国を導いたのは皮肉でした。欧米は、第一次世界大戦で、帝国主義政策を払拭し、新たな国際協調の枠組みの模索を始めました。その動きに同調せず、旧来の帝国主義の道を模倣したことに、19世紀に遅れて世界に出た日本の悲劇があったのです。

　そして、ちょうどペリーが来航して日本が変わったように、日本は再び占領という過去にない経験の中で無理にハンドルを切らざるを得なくなったのです。

　GHQは、1946年から日本の警察を通して戦争犯罪人を裁判にかけ、処罰します。戦争を指導した**A級戦犯**は、**極東軍事裁判**にかけられ、東条英機をはじめ7名が死刑に、他の18名が終身刑や禁固刑に処せられました。また、各戦場で残虐行為を行ったとして、裁判が公正であったかどうか議論されながらも、日本内外の裁判で5416名が裁かれ、937名が処刑されました。

🔍**ひとくちメモ**
極東軍事裁判
第二次世界大戦で日本が降伏した後、連合国が戦争犯罪人として指定した日本の指導者などを裁いた裁判
東京裁判とも呼ばれる

The Constitution of Japan

The occupation of Japan presented many contradictions.

By this I mean that America's political intentions were at odds with the original purpose of the occupation policies.

To begin with, the Allied Powers had thought to indict the emperor for war crimes, and also to hold the leaders of the major conglomerates to account. However, GHQ was both wary of the possible resurgence of Communism with rapid democratization, and also planned to use the emperor to rehabilitate Japan as a stable state with close ties to America. It therefore prevented the prosecution of the emperor for political responsibility.

As a result, in 1946 the emperor retained his position as sovereign while at the same time renouncing his divinity.

Also at the Tokyo War Crimes Tribunal, it was pointed out that the victorious nations were unilaterally passing judgement on the losing nation, while wartime atrocities committed by the victorious nations were ignored. For example, Judge Pal from India and others raised the issue of discrimination and aggression by the West in Asia, but in the end only Japan was prosecuted.

In order to hasten Japan's democratization, America instructed GHQ to enact a new constitution. After discussion with Japan, a constitution was drafted based on the fundamental pillars of the renunciation of war, popular sovereignty, and basic human rights, while the emperor was installed as a symbol of the unity of the nation.

The Constitution of Japan was promulgated on November 3, 1946,

日本国憲法の制定とその後の動きは？

　日本の占領政策はいくつかの矛盾をはらんでいました。

　それは、アメリカの政治的意向と、占領政策の当初の目的とのずれを意味します。

　最初の矛盾は、戦争犯罪人の処罰にあります。当初、連合国は、天皇の戦争犯罪を訴追し、財閥の大物にもその責任を負わせようと考えました。しかし、急激な**民主化**で、日本に**共産主義が台頭**することを警戒すると同時に、日本を、アメリカよりの安定した国家に再生させるために、天皇を利用しようと GHQ は考え、天皇の**政治責任**の追求を中止しました。

　その結果、1946 年に天皇が人間宣言を行った上で、天皇の**地位を温存**します。

　また、**極東軍事裁判**では、戦勝国が敗戦国を一方的に裁くことや、戦勝国による残虐行為が取り上げられないことなどが指摘され、例えばインドから裁判に派遣された**パール判事**などは、欧米によるアジアへの差別と侵略行為についての指摘もなされましたが、結局日本側のみが裁かれます。

　アメリカは、日本の民主化を急ぐために、GHQ を通し新憲法の制定を指示します。日本側とのやりとりのあと、GHQ の指導で、**戦争放棄**、**国民主権**、**基本的人権**を柱とした憲法案を作成し、天皇は国家統合の象徴として位置づけられました。

　新憲法は、大日本帝国憲法を改正する形で**日本国憲法**

ひとくちメモ

パール判事（ラダ・ビノード・パール）
インドの法学者、裁判官。極東軍事裁判において判事を務め、11人の判事の中で唯一被告人全員の無罪を主張した。1886–1967

戦後から現代へ　Postwar Japan to the Present

in the form of an amendment to the Meiji Constitution, and came into effect on May 3 the following year. And in order to give the Constitution coherence, criminal and civil law was also amended. Ever since, the Constitution of Japan has remained in force to the letter, with no amendments, as the world's fairest, most democratic constitution.

The political parties that had been dismantled prior to the war were revived, and even the outlawed Socialist and Communist parties were reformed. In December 1945 the electoral law was amended so that all men and women over the age of twenty were given voting rights, while men and women over the age of twenty-five were eligible for election (thirty for the Upper House and for prefectural governors).

Thus in just two years, Japan was recast from a totalitarian regime to a democratic nation. Ironically, however, the biggest threat to Japan along this course was America and the Cold War. Before long, bringing Japan under its wing for military and economic strategy became GHQ's number one priority.

として、1946年11月3日に公布され、翌年5月3日より施行されました。そして、憲法との整合性を持たせるために、刑法、民法をはじめとする法律も改正されます。その後現在まで、日本国憲法は世界でも最も平和的かつ民主的な憲法として一文も改正されることなく継承されています。

　これより前、すでに戦前に解体されていた政党が復活し、非合法とされていた**社会党や共産党**も改めて組織されます。1945年12月に選挙法が改正され、20歳以上の全ての男女に**選挙権**が与えられ、25歳以上の男女に被選挙権（参議院、都道府県知事は30歳以上）が認められています。

　こうして、日本はほんの2年の間に、全体主義国家から民主主義国家に脱皮します。しかし、皮肉なことに、この急激な変化のその後の成り行きを一番警戒したのはアメリカでした。その原因は、冷戦の進行にほかなりません。やがて、日本をアメリカの軍事経済戦略の傘にいれておくことに、GHQの占領政策の優先順位が置かれるようになってゆくのです。

90 The Peace Treaty

Japan had suffered devastating damage by the end of the War.

The economy was in tatters, its major cities in ruins, and even the infrastructure had been wiped out. Unable to make a living, many people were housed in barracks and procured food on the black market. Towns overflowed with homeless people and orphans barely getting by from day to day on whatever food or clothing they could get hold of.

It was not until the 1950s that these conditions finally began to improve little by little. In 1949, China — with the exception of Taiwan — was again united by the Chinese Communist Party for the first time since the Qing had fallen thirty-seven years earlier. The Kuomintang fled to Taiwan where, by collaborating with the U.S., they managed to maintain power.

On the Korean peninsula, following independence from Japan, the Communists took over the north as the Democratic People's Republic of Korea, while the liberals ruled the southern half as the Republic of Korea. However, in June 1950, the north and south clashed and the Korean War broke out, with the Communist forces at one point reaching as far south as Pusan. America mobilized armed intervention on behalf of the United Nations and temporarily cornered the Communist forces on the border with China. However, China joined the war, and after heavy fighting, both sides remained either side of the thirty-eighth parallel.

With the outbreak of the Korean War, Japan functioned as a rear base for America. Japanese industry was revitalized with the demand for military supplies, which provided a spur for the postwar rehabilitation of Japan.

講和条約に至る道のりは？

　戦争直後の日本は壊滅的な打撃を受けていました。

　経済は破綻し、大都会は破壊され、インフラも壊滅したままで、生活できない人々は**バラック**に住み、**闇市**で食料を調達していました。町には浮浪者や孤児が溢れ、粗悪な食品や衣料品で日々をしのぐのがやっとでした。

　こうした状況が少しずつ改善されていったのは、1950年頃からです。1949年、台湾を除く中国は、清朝滅亡以来37年ぶりに**中国共産党**によって統一されます。国民党は台湾に逃れ、アメリカと連携して政権を維持します。

　朝鮮半島では、日本からの独立後、共産主義勢力が北部を**朝鮮民主主義人民共和国**として、自由主義勢力が南半分を**大韓民国**として統治します。しかし、1950年6月に両者が衝突し、**朝鮮戦争**となり、一時共産主義勢力が釜山に迫ります。これにアメリカが国連を動かして**武力介入**し、一時中国との国境に共産勢力を追いつめます。しかし中国が参戦し、激戦の末、両者は**38度線**で睨み合います。

　朝鮮戦争の勃発で、日本はアメリカの後方基地として機能します。軍需物資の供給によって日本の産業が活性化し、**戦争からの復興**に拍車がかかりました。

In the interests of stability in the Far East, America requested Prime Minister Yoshida Shigeru to remilitarize, and despite this being in contradiction with the Constituion, in 1950 the National Police Reserve was formed, and in 1954 this was upgraded to the Self Defense Forces.

Also, America did a U-turn on occupation policy and reinstated powerful prewar figures who had been purged from public service following the war, and the conglomerates that had been dismantled after the war also began making a comeback as the postwar economic confusion came under control.

Having created the right environment, America hastened to conclude peace with Japan, and after negotiations with Yoshida Shigeru's government, in 1951 forty-nine countries including America signed the peace treaty in San Francisco. Opposing these moves by America, the Soviet Union and other socialist states refused to sign the peace treaty, bringing Japan completely under the influence of the liberal camp.

At the same time, Japan and the U.S. also signed the Treaty of Mutual Cooperation and Security (U.S.-Japan Security Treaty), agreeing to maintain security with American troops stationed in Japan. This security alliance has been the basis of Japan's military foreign policy ever since.

This marked the end of the occupation of Japan, and the start of its revival as an independent nation.

アメリカは極東の安定のため、時の吉田茂内閣に**再軍備**を求め、日本は、憲法上の矛盾を押して**警察予備隊**を1950年に組織、1954年に**自衛隊**に昇格させます。

　また、アメリカが占領政策を転換する中で、戦後公職追放を受けていた戦前の有力者が社会に戻り、解体された財閥も戦後の経済混乱を収拾する中で再び台頭をはじめます。

　こうした環境整備を行った上で、アメリカは日本との講和を急ぎ、吉田内閣と交渉を進め、1951年に**サンフランシスコ**でアメリカをはじめとする48カ国との**講和条約**を締結します。このアメリカの動きに反発し、ソ連など社会主義国は講和を拒否、日本は完全に**自由主義陣営**に組み込まれたのでした。

　講和条約の締結と同時に、日本は**日米安全保障条約**を締結し、アメリカ軍の日本への駐留による安全確保に合意します。日米安保体制という同盟関係は、その後の日本の**軍事外交方針**の基本となります。

　これで日本の占領は終了し、独立国家として再生されたことになったのです。

ひとくちメモ
日米相互協力および安全保障条約（日米安全保障条約）
日本とアメリカ合衆国の安全保障のため、日本にアメリカ軍を駐留することなどを定めた二国間条約。1960

91 Postwar Japan and the International Situation

There was devastation from World War II the world over. Much of Europe sustained damage in both human and physical terms, as had East Asia, particularly in China and Japan. On the other hand, the United States mainland was unscathed, and the U.S. took over the leadership as the European powers busied themselves with postwar reconstruction of the world.

Independence movements had been gaining momentum since before the war in the colonies in Asia, and after the war Vietnam, Indonesia and many others achieved independence. Japan had promoted the wartime doctrine of the Greater East Asia Prosperity Sphere, and supported local movements in order to gain the cooperation of the people in those countries, but their overbearing and high-handed measures had not been at all successful.

The postwar world was divided into the liberal and socialist camps, both of which targeted the newly emergent independent countries, attempting to strengthen their ties and expand their influence to them.

After experiencing two wars, the West developed the former League of Nations into the United Nations, a strong military alliance capable of maintaining peace. The UN was inaugurated in October 1945 with its headquarters in New York, and as permanent members the United States, Soviet Union, China, Britain, and France were all given the right of veto in UN resolutions.

Ironically, however, the UN had to conduct its business caught up in the political bargaining between the United States and Soviet Union, as

戦後の国際情勢と日本との関係は？

第二次世界大戦は世界中を破壊しました。ヨーロッパのほとんどが人的物理的損害を受け、極東でも日本や中国を中心に深刻な被害を受けています。一方、アメリカは国内が無傷のままで、**戦後復興**に悩むヨーロッパ列強に変わって、世界をリードする存在となります。

アジアの植民地では戦争前後に**独立運動**が盛んになり、戦後、ベトナム、インドネシアなど多くの国が独立します。戦争中、日本は**大東亜共栄圏**という理念を掲げて、現地の人々の協力を得ようと、そうした運動の支援を試みましたが、日本を優越視した強圧的な政策は必ずしも成功したとはいえませんでした。

ひとくちメモ
大東亜共栄圏
欧米諸国の植民地支配から東アジア・東南アジアを解放し、日本を盟主とする共存共栄の新たな国際秩序を建設しようという、第二次世界大戦における日本の信念

戦後、世界は自由主義陣営と社会主義陣営に2分されますが、両陣営とも、こうした**新興独立国**との関係の強化を図り、自らの影響力の拡大に努めました。

2度にわたる戦争の体験から、欧米には以前の国際連盟を**国際連合**として発展させ、平和維持のために軍事力も行使できる強力な組織が設立されます。国際連合は1945年10月に発足し、本部はニューヨークに置かれ、常任理事国であるアメリカ、ソ連、中国、イギリス、フランスには、国連決議に対する**拒否権**が与えられます。

しかし、国連も、皮肉なことに、アメリカとソ連の対立の中で、その政治的駆け引きにゆれながら運営されること

the standoff continued between the two countries.

Japan had agreed to peace under the liberal camp, but had not yet resumed diplomatic relations with many countries. The Soviet Union still had in detention many prisoners of war from the former Japanese army, and many were still in the prisons of the Philippines and other countries. This situation continued until 1956, when diplomatic relations were finally resumed with the Soviet Union and the Philippines.

Although diplomatic relations with the Soviet Union resumed, the disputed ownership of the four southernmost Kuril Islands had not been resolved and remains unresolved to this day.

It was also in 1956 that Japan became the eightieth nation to join the United Nations. However, because of the atrocities committed by Japan in Asia before the war, it took time for relations with these member states to improve. Diplomatic relations had resumed with Taiwan in 1952, but it took until 1972 for this to happen with the People's Republic of China. Criticism of Japan's wartime actions is still strong amongst Asian nations, and even today there are still protests over such controversial issues as Japanese history textbooks and cabinet members paying their respects to the war dead at Yasukuni Shrine.

になります。

　日本は、自由主義陣営とは講和を行いますが、多くの国とはまだ国交のない状態が続きます。ソ連には、旧日本軍の捕虜が抑留され、フィリピンなどでもそうした人々が現地の刑務所に残されたままでした。こうした問題は、最終的に1956年にソ連やフィリピンとの国交が回復するまで継続します。

　ただし、ソ連とは、千島列島の南端の4島の帰属を巡り、いわゆる北方領土問題が未解決のままの国交回復でした。これは現在もまだ解決していません。

　同年、日本も80番目の国として、国際連合に加盟しました。しかし、日本は、戦前のアジア諸国への残虐行為のために、該当する国々との関係改善には時間がかかりました。台湾との国交は1952年に回復しましたが、中華人民共和国とは、1972年まで国交がありませんでした。アジア諸国には未だに日本の戦争行為に対する非難が根強く、日本国内での教科書の表記問題や、日本人の戦没者を祀る靖国神社に日本の閣僚が参拝するたびに、抗議活動が起こっていることも、また事実なのです。

🔍 ひとくちメモ

領土問題が起きているのは、ロシアが実効支配している択捉島、国後島、色丹島、歯舞島の4島

92 The War and the Arts

After the Manchurian Incident, the government stepped up their restrictions on the freedom of speech and repression of socialist ideology.

Writers at the time of the financial crash in the early Shōwa period included Kobayashi Takiji, acclaimed for his proletarian literature depicting workers from a socialist perspective. However, the state was determined to suppress the socialist movement, and Kobayashi was tortured to death by police in 1933. Many authors yielded to state repression, and instead became absorbed in the minutiae of their own lives to write the works known as I-novels.

It was risky to be involved in politics at this time, and some authors focused instead on a uniquely Japanese aesthetic of love and beauty, such as Kawabata Yasunari who wrote *Yukiguni* (Snow Country). Tanizaki Jun'ichirō's masterpiece *Sasameyuki* (The Makioka Sisters) was censured by the army, who claimed it went against the tone of wartime Japan, and he had to continue writing it in secret until the end of the Pacific War.

Repression by the military was such that even Minobe Tatsukichi, whose theory that the emperor was an organ of the state, as its sovereign, had been established since the Meiji period, was accused of defying the emperor's divinity and forced to resign from the Diet.

After the end of the war, when political prisoners had been released and freedom of speech restored by the allied forces, socialist movements made a comeback in the political arena.

In the arts, however, the deep scars left by the prewar repression and

戦前戦後の文芸思想活動の変遷は？

　満州事変以降、政府の言論統制、社会主義思想への抑圧が加速します。

　経済恐慌が続く昭和初期には**小林多喜二**など、社会主義的な視点から労働者を描いた**プロレタリア文学**が認知されます。しかし、小林多喜二が 1933 年に警察署で虐殺されたように、国家による弾圧で、社会主義活動の芽が摘まれてゆきます。逆に、作家の中では弾圧に屈して転向する者も多く、彼らは自己の中に埋没し、いわゆる**私小説**を多く発表しています。

　政治との関わりがリスクであった時代、耽美的、日本的な美と恋の世界を描く**川端康成**などが登場し「雪国」などを発表します。**谷崎潤一郎**の名著「細雪」は、軍部から戦時国家の風潮に合わないとの弾圧を受け、その後太平洋戦争末期に極秘に執筆を続けた作品です。

　軍部による弾圧は、明治から大正にかけて定説とされた、天皇が国家という機関の元首であるという天皇機関説まで、天皇の神聖を冒すものとして弾劾され、天皇機関説を説く美濃部達吉が議員辞職に追い込まれることもありました。

　戦争が終結し、連合軍により思想犯が釈放され、言論の自由が戻ったあと、政治思想面では、社会主義活動も復活します。

　ただ、文芸面でみるならば、戦前の弾圧や戦争の悲惨

misery of the war itself had a major influence on authors. Dazai Osamu, who drowned himself together with his lover in the Tamagawa Canal, portrayed the social conditions of the turbulent war years. His destructive, eccentric behavior and literary style, evident in his major works such as *Shayō* (The Setting Sun), which portrayed the decline of the aristocracy, and *Ningen shikkaku* (No Longer Human), written just before his death, is typical of the so-called Buraiha, or Decadent School of writers.

During the war pop culture too was controlled by the army, but later flourished during the American occupation with jazz and various hit pop songs. One massive postwar hit was Satō Hachirō's *Ringo no uta* (The Apple Song), which before the war had famously circulated on the black market after its lyrics were censored.

It was 1950 when Kurosawa Akira adapted Akutagawa Ryūnosuke's novel *Rashōmon* for cinema, and in 1953 Ozu Yasujirō portrayed unremarkable everyday life in his masterpiece *Tōkyō monogatari* (Tokyo Story).

The confusion of the war years provided artists with countless subjects for their creativity.

さによる傷が作家の心に大きな影響を与えたままでした。1948 年に愛人と玉川上水で入水自殺をした**太宰治**は、戦前戦後の激動期に当時の世相を描きます。没落華族を描いた「斜陽」や死の直前に書かれた「人間失格」などが代表作で、その破滅的で奇抜な行動と作風から無頼派作家などと呼ばれています。

　戦争中には軍の統制を受けていた大衆文化も、戦後には一気に拡大し、アメリカの占領により、ジャズなども流行し、様々な流行歌も生まれました。サトーハチローの作詞で知られる「リンゴの唄」が闇市に流れたのは有名な話です。この「リンゴの唄」の詩は、戦前には検閲により発行禁止処分となったものでしたが、戦後には空前のヒット曲になりました。

　映画界では、黒澤明が芥川龍之介の「羅生門」を映画にしたのが 1950 年のことです。また何気ない日常の風景を映画化した小津安二郎が「東京物語」などを発表したのは 1953 年のことです。

　戦前戦後の混乱は、作家にとって、無数の創作テーマを与えたのでした。

93 The Security Treaty and the 1960s

After the war, Japan turned its back on militarism and transformed.

However, when America made occupied Japan into an anti-Communist bastion against China and the Soviet Union, the situation changed subtly.

The U.S.-Japan Security Treaty brought Japan under America's military wing, and many of the former leaders of Japan's business and political circles made a comeback when the postwar purge was rescinded. One of these was Kishi Nobosuke, a leading member of the wartime government with close connections to military and other powerful personnel in former Manchuria.

The reunification of the Rightist and Leftist factions of the Socialist Party in 1955 was seen as a threat by the influential conservative parties, and they settled long years of conflict to reform as the Liberal Democratic Party. Kishi Nobosuke became head of this Liberal Democratic Party and was voted in as prime minister in 1957.

When the U.S.-Japan Security Treaty was revised and renewed in 1960, the existence of a secret pact to waive jurisdiction of American military personnel except in the most serious of cases made the news. This was met by protests all over the country, and even the Diet was surrounded by a mob. The Kishi cabinet's attempt to use extreme rightwing organizations to quell it merely fanned the flames of the mob. Tensions rose further when Tokyo University student Kanba Michiko died in clashes with the police, and after the Security Pact was automatically renewed Kishi's cabinet

安保と60年代とは？

　戦後、日本は軍国主義から180度舵を切った国家に変貌しました。

　しかし、日本の占領政策の担い手だったアメリカが、日本を中国やソ連に対する**反共の砦**として捉えられるようになると、その状況が微妙に変化します。

　日米安全保障条約で、日本はアメリカの軍事力の傘の中に入ります。そして、過去に日本の財界政界を指導した多くの人物が、**公職追放**を解除され戻ってきます。旧満州で軍部や様々な有力者と深い関わりをもち、戦争中は政府の中枢で活動していた岸信介もその一人です。

🔍 ひとくちメモ
日米安全保障条約
日本とアメリカ合衆国の安全保障のため、日本にアメリカ軍を駐留することなどを定めた二国間条約。1960年成立

　1955年に**社会党**の右派と左派が統一されると、それを脅威とした有力**保守党**も長年の確執を解消して**自由民主党**としてまとまります。岸信介が、そんな自由民主党の総裁となり、内閣総理大臣に就任したのは1957年のことでした。

　1960年に日米安保条約を改訂・更新する際に、アメリカ軍兵士への重要事件を除く裁判権を放棄した**密約**の存在などが報道され、全国的な反対運動がおき、国会も群衆に囲まれました。岸内閣が、右翼などの組織を利用してそれを弾圧しようと試みたこともデモ隊を刺激した原因でした。警察との衝突の際に、東大生の樺美智子さんが死亡したことで、状況が緊迫し、日米安保条約が自動更新されたあと、岸内閣は混乱の責任をとって総辞職しました。

🔍 ひとくちメモ
安保条約に反対する全国的規模で展開された日本の近代史上最大の大衆運動。60年の5月から6月には、数万人のデモ隊が国会を包囲した

assumed responsibility for the disturbances and resigned en masse.

This incident represented a clash between the policy to make Japan a bulwark against Communism under America's wing, and people who wanted to protect the Constitution after having suffered terribly in the war. The government no doubt wanted to leave military buildup to the U.S. and avoid the excessive military expenditure of the prewar years, so that they could focus on reviving the country.

Opinion is divided on the Kishi government. He brought a shadow from the past, and the fact remains that under him, Japan has been unable to put its wartime past completely behind it. Kishi Nobosuke's personal network has been connected to influential members of the Liberal Democratic Party ever since.

This prewar shadow on occasion showed itself, such as when Asanuma Inejirō, head of the Socialist Party, was assassinated at a rally by an extreme rightwing youth in October 1960, soon after the Kishi cabinet's resignation.

Kishi Nobosuke's successor, Ikeda Hayato, advocated the "income-doubling plan" and used the special procurement boom occasioned by the Korean War to take Japan from the turbulent powerwar period to the subsequent economic miracle. By raising incomes, people would no longer need to protest, and Japan would be revived as a democratic nation.

Japan did indeed achieve miraculous economic growth worthy of the world's attention.

60 年安保事件は、アメリカの傘の中で、共産主義への防波堤になるという国の方針と、悲惨な戦争経験を元に、護憲を求める人々との衝突でした。政府としては、軍拡をアメリカに任せ、戦前のように軍事に国家予算を極端に使用せず、国の再生にあてようというしたたかな考えもあったのかもしれません。

　戦前の影を引きずる岸内閣の評価はまちまちです。しかし、日本が戦争を完全に清算できずに戦後もそれを引きずってきたことは事実です。岸信介の人脈は、以後、自由民主党の有力者へと繋がってゆきます。

　戦前の影といえば、岸内閣の総辞職間もない 1960 年10 月には、社会党の党首浅沼稲次郎が演説の最中に右翼の少年に刺殺される事件がおこったりもしました。

　岸内閣の後を継いだ池田勇人は、**所得倍増計画**を打ち出し、日本は戦後の混乱期から、朝鮮戦争の特需景気を踏み台に、本格的な高度成長期にはいります。所得が向上することで、国民の不満を癒し、民主主義国家として再生させようというのが政府の方針でした。

　実際、日本は世界が注目する奇跡的な経済成長を遂げるのでした。

94 The Economic Miracle

By 1955 Japan was reaching its prewar standard. The former conglomerates had recovered, and in close concert with government measures, were beginning to expand the economy.

Japan had a cheap labor force, and the government boosted the economy with public works projects to develop infrastructure and heavy industries, which also enabled subcontracting small and medium enterprises to flourish. Many public and private businesses benefitted from the work provided by projects such as the 1964 Tokyo Olympics and the new bullet train link between Tokyo and Osaka, which also boosted national prestige.

Not only was labor cheap, but the yen was fixed at a rate of 360 yen to the dollar, and as the economy grew this low rate enabled Japan to grow into a major exporter.

Most Japanese people were not at all wealthy during this period of economic growth. People were motivated to work and save by the household dream of owning the "three status symbols" of refrigerator, television, and washing machine, and their savings provided the big banks with capital to invest in major enterprises.

It was clearly this strategy of public and private enterprises working to revive the nation that produced the economic miracle.

Diplomatic relations with Korea were restored under the 1965 Treaty on Basic Relations between Japan and the Republic of Korea, while islands under American administration were returned to Japan, the Bonin Islands

高度成長とは？

　日本は 1955 年に戦前の水準に戻っていました。また、旧財閥系の大企業グループも復活し、政府の政策と密に連携をとりながら経済の拡大を進めてゆきます。

　日本には、安価な労働力があり、国が経済を管理、統率する中で、公共事業などのインフラ整備と重工業が育成され、その影響で下請けの中小企業も活気づきます。1964 年に開催された**東京オリンピック**、同時に東京と新大阪間に開通した**新幹線**など、官民一体の公共事業の事例にはことかかず、国民もそうした平和的**国威発揚**を享受します。

　一方、輸出部門では、**安価な労働力**に加えて、**1 ドル 360 円**という固定相場の継続が、経済成長に沿って相対的な円安をうみ、日本は**輸出大国**に成長します。

　多くの日本人は、経済成長が進む中でも決して豊かではありませんでした。従って、当時標榜された冷蔵庫とテレビ、そして電気洗濯機という「**三種の神器**」を家庭に持つ事を夢に、勤労意欲と貯蓄意欲を持ち、そこで貯蓄された資金は、大銀行からさらに大企業への投資に流れます。

　こうしてみると、**高度成長**が、国家をあげての官民一体による戦略であったことがよくわかります。

　外交面では、1965 年に**日韓基本条約**によって、韓国との国交が回復し、施政権がアメリカに帰属していた**小笠原諸島**が 1968 年に、**沖縄**が 1972 年に日本に返還されま

ひとくちメモ
日韓基本条約
1910年の日韓併合以前の条約を無効とした。経済協力や関係正常化などの取り決めをし、さらに朝鮮にある唯一の合法政府として韓国を認め、国交を正常化した

(Ogasawara) in 1968 and Okinawa in 1972.

The return of Okinawa raised the issue of whether the American military had installed nuclear-capable military bases on Japanese territory, and the true details of this remain unclear to this day. The government under Ikeda's successor, Satō Eisaku, had propelled the economic miracle and restored national confidence, as Japan became a major economic power that boasted the second largest GDP in the world.

On the other hand, various social problems were manifest, including the poor quality of urban housing, depopulation of rural areas, a surplus of labor, and lack of equal treatment for men and women in the workplace, environmental pollution caused by rapid industrialization, and so forth. The emergence in Kumamoto Prefecture of Minamata Disease, the serious health problems in a poor fishing village caused by mercury contamination, shocked the world. There were also cases of photochemical smog caused by soot pollution in urban areas and a consequent rise in asthma.

This combination of growth and its downsides continued into the Bubble economy.

した。

　池田内閣の後を受けた佐藤栄作政権は、文字通り高度
経済成長を牽引した内閣でしたが、沖縄の返還にあたっ
て、アメリカ軍が核を日本国内の基地に持ち込んでいるの
ではないかという疑惑に晒されることになり、その真相の
詳細は未だに不明のままなのです。高度経済成長は、国
民に自信を取り戻し、日本が世界第二のGDPを誇る**経済
大国**になったと政府は宣伝します。

　一方で都市での劣悪な住宅事情、農村の**過疎化**、過
剰労働と職場での男女平等の不備、急激な工業化による
公害、環境汚染問題など、様々な**社会問題**も出てきます。
熊本県の水俣での水銀流出による貧しい漁民の深刻な健
康被害は、**水俣病**として全世界を震撼させました。また、
都市部では煤煙による**光化学スモッグ**や喘息の問題など
がおこります。

　成長と矛盾、その二つがその後のバブル経済へと引き
継がれてゆきます。

新幹線

95 The Vietnam War and Relations with Japan

The peaceful, even calm, situation in postwar Japan contrasted with the international situation in surrounding areas where regional conflicts had arisen as a result of the tense relationship between the two superpowers, the United States and Soviet Union.

Following the withdrawal of Japanese troops from Vietnam, there had been an independence movement against the colonial power France and a rise in Communist influence that culminated in a split between north and south. The United States intervened politically, supporting the regime in the south, and in the winter of 1965 began conducting air raids on the north.

In view of Japan's strategic location, the United States made its bases on Okinawa the focal point for prosecuting the Vietnam War, and brought in increasing numbers of troops.

Meanwhile, the People's Republic of China had been formed by the Communist Party of China in 1949, and the Kuomintang's Chiang Kai-shek had fled to Taiwan. The United States thus considered its military bases in Okinawa and elsewhere in Japan the focus of the front line against the Soviet Union, North Korea, China, and Vietnam. The reason America had invested such a huge amount in rehabilitating Japan in return for keeping its military bases was because of the sense of crisis prompted by the resurgence of Communism as Asian countries regained their independence.

Japan had managed to get back on its feet by cooperating with America's strategy, but at the same time it was rearming and building

ベトナム戦争と日本との
関係は？

　日本周辺の国際情勢は、戦後の日本国内の無風ともいえる平和な状態とは対照的でした。それは、アメリカとソ連の2つの超大国の緊張関係が産み出した**地域紛争**にほかなりません。

　特に**ベトナム**は、日本軍が撤退すると、宗主国フランスからの独立運動を経て、共産主義勢力が台頭し、南北に分裂します。アメリカはそこに政治介入し、南部にあった南ベトナム政権を支援し、1965年の冬に北ベトナムへの爆撃を開始します。

　朝鮮戦争において、日本の戦略的な位置を認識したアメリカは、沖縄の米軍基地などをベトナム戦争遂行の重要拠点とし、兵力を投入したのです。

　一方、中国では1949年に中国共産党によって中華人民共和国が成立し、国民党の蒋介石が台湾に追いやられます。これでアメリカにとって、沖縄と日本の基地はソ連、北朝鮮、中国、ベトナムを見据えた**前線**となりました。戦後、アメリカが日本の復興に多大の投資をし、見返りに基地を温存した背景には、アジア諸国が独立する過程での、共産主義の進出への危機感があったのです。

　アメリカの戦略に、日本は協力しつつ、自国の復興を行いますが、それは日本の再軍備と**自衛隊**の増強への道筋

up its own Self Defense Forces. This was prompted by an awareness of the need to relieve the burden on the U.S. military forces and to act as a deterrent in order to keep the peace in East Asia.

Japan is often criticized for not showing autonomy in diplomatic policy and being cagey about its intentions, but this is largely due to it having been placed under America's wing. The process of resolving this issue is behind current issues such as the problem of relocating the bases on Okinawa.

In the 1960s, the friction between China and the Soviet Union over regional supremacy developed into a major clash, further complicating the situation in Japan and surrounding areas. Meanwhile in South Korea, which still had a tense relationship with the Democratic People's Republic of Korea in the north, military rule was established in a coup d'état led by Park Chung-hee.

The Soviet Union still held sway in much of Europe, and in order to maintain their political and economic bloc had cracked down on prodemocracy movements in Hungary and the Czechoslovakia. There was an unspoken agreement between the United States and the Soviet Union that the U.S. would maintain its influence in the Far East after the end of the war. However, America was keenly aware that this balance in Asia could crumble.

でもありました。再軍備は、アメリカの軍事力の負担軽減と極東の安定への**抑止力**になるという認識に基づいたものです。

　よく日本の外交政策には自主性がなく、日本の顔が見えにくいという批判がきかれますが、その背景には、こうしたアメリカの傘の下にある日本という位置づけがあるわけです。この課題をいかに解決してゆくかという道筋の上に、現在問題となっている沖縄の基地移設問題などがあるのです。

　60年代になって、中国とソ連との間に、覇権を巡る軋轢が生まれ、中ソが本格的に対立すると、日本周辺の状況はさらに複雑になりました。そうした背景の中で、朝鮮民主主義人民共和国との緊張関係の続く韓国では、クーデターによって、朴正熙による強力な軍事政権が樹立します。

　もともと、ソ連の影響力の強かったヨーロッパにおいて、ソ連は傘下の国家であるハンガリーやチェコなどの**民主化運動**に介入弾圧し、自らの政治経済圏の維持をはかります。極東は、元々アメリカの影響力を温存するというのが、戦争末期のアメリカとソ連との暗黙の了解でした。このバランスがアジアで崩れることにアメリカは強い警戒感を持ったのでした。

96 The Bubble Years

The United States enjoyed unprecedented prosperity after the war.

With its wealth, the United States led the world and the political theme of America functioning as the bastion of democracy became the slogan for successive presidents.

With the intensification of the Cold War, however, its policy of issuing government bonds to support America's military presence overseas and ensure full employment for a stable economy at home, had a major impact on the country's finances. The ongoing Vietnam War was an especially heavy financial burden.

Furthermore, the industrialization of countries around the world, Japan first and foremost, had been driven by America's consumers and led to a deficit in the balance of trade. In order to solve this problem and stabilize the economy while avoiding runaway inflation, in 1971 President Nixon ended the direct convertibility of the dollar to gold, and sharply devalued the dollar. Then the following year he introduced the floating exchange rate system to rectify America's trade deficit.

Thus the exchange rate of 360 yen to the dollar came to an end, and the brakes were applied to Japan's economic miracle. However, even with low growth Japan's economy continued to expand. Even the setback of the Oil Shock, with soaring oil prices due to the war in the Middle East, was overcome relatively quickly.

When Japan became established as a major economic power in the 1970s, the United States demanded that it ease trade friction. Japan therefore took measures to boost domestic demand, such as reducing taxes

バブルへの道のりは？

アメリカは戦後に空前の繁栄を享受します。

アメリカの豊かさが世界を牽引し、アメリカが**民主主義の砦**として機能するという政治的なテーマを、歴代の大統領も政策のスローガンとします。

しかし、冷戦の激化でアメリカの海外での軍事的プレゼンスを維持し、国内でも景気を安定させ完全雇用を目指して国債を発行してゆくことは、国家財政に少なからぬ影響を与えます。特にベトナム戦争の継続は財政的にも重荷です。

しかも、アメリカの消費に依存した、日本をはじめとする世界各国の工場化は、そのままアメリカの**輸入超過**を招きます。この問題を解決し、財政の立て直しと、過度のインフレ防止のために、時の大統領のニクソンは1971年に、**ドルと金との交換を停止**、ドルを大幅に**切り下げ**ます。さらに、アメリカの貿易赤字を是正する目的から、翌年にさらに**変動相場制**を導入したのです。

これで、日本も1ドル360円の時代が終わり、高度経済成長にもブレーキがかかります。しかし、低成長ながら日本経済は拡大、中東戦争に端を発した石油の高騰（**オイルショック**）による打撃も、比較的短期間に克服します。

戦後アメリカの傘の中にあった日本が、70年代に経済大国として自立すると、アメリカは**貿易摩擦**の解消を日本に求め、日本政府も税金の軽減や、公共事業の促進など

ひとくちメモ
1965年に北爆を開始したアメリカは、73年までベトナムで泥沼の戦争を展開した。その経済的な重荷は計り知れなかった

ひとくちメモ
アメリカは貿易赤字を是正するため、変動相場制（為替レートを外貨の需要と供給の関係に任せて自由に決める）を導入した

戦後から現代へ　Postwar Japan to the Present

and promoting public works projects. This stimulated Japan's domestic economy.

At the end of the 1980s land speculation in Japan exceeded the actual land value and the country's economic power, and asset values soared. Then banks changed their financial strategy from making loans to corporations to boosting private consumption, creating a bubble of unprecedented economic boom.

In 1973 the United States extricated itself from the quagmire of the Vietnam War with wholesale withdrawal. The Vietnam War finally ended in 1975 with the fall of the southern capital of Saigon. Korea's dictatorial president under military rule, Park Chung-hee, was assassinated in 1979. This, and the outrage caused by the later crackdown on students and citizens of the Gwanju Democratization Movement prompted a gradual move to democratization. Diplomatic relations with China had already been restored in 1972 under Tanaka Kakuei's government, and relations between the two countries were stable.

Japan's bubble was also supported by the stability of the surrounding region, and this had the effect of resuming exports of Asian culture to the West. However, the economy was ultimately based on speculation, and when the bubble burst, Japan was in for a rough ride.

で内需拡大政策をとります。これが日本国内の景気を刺激します。

80年代の後半は、日本の**土地への投機**が実際の地価や国の経済力を上回り、日本の**資産価値**が高騰します。そこで、銀行も大企業への融資から個人消費への後押しへと**金融戦略**を切り替え、日本は**空前の好景気**に湧きたったのです。

アメリカは1973年に泥沼化したベトナム戦争から手を引き、撤退を完了していました。そして、ベトナム戦争は1975年に南ベトナムの首都サイゴンの陥落で終結します。また、韓国でも1979年に軍事政権によって独裁体制を維持していた朴正煕大統領が暗殺され、その後の光州事件などでの学生市民運動への弾圧に世界の批判が集まり、次第に民主化が進んでゆきました。すでに中国とは、1972年、田中角栄政権の時に国交を回復し、日中関係も安定してきます。

バブル期の日本は、これら周辺諸国の安定にも支えられ、アジア文化を西欧に再輸出する効果も産み出します。ただ、経済は、あくまでも投機によるもので、そのバブルがはじけたとき、日本は大きな試練に直面したのでした。

🔍 ひとくちメモ
1980年、光州市で、軍部による戒厳令拡大に反対した学生・市民が衝突した

Exporting Japanese Culture

American culture was introduced into Japan during the postwar occupation. However, many of the Americans stationed in Japan at that time also became interested in traditional Japanese culture and actively promoted it in the West.

A pioneer in introducing Japanese culture to America was Edwin O. Reischauer. A U.S. Ambassador to Japan, Reischauer had been knowledgeable about Japan since before the war and made a major contribution to formulating America's policy on Japan.

Also Edward Seidensticker, who translated Kawabata Yasunari's *Yukiguni* (Snow Country) and contributed to Kawabata being awarded the Nobel Prize for Literature, had learned Japanese during the war with the U.S. Navy, and had his first experience with Japan while stationed there with the U.S. Marines. Besides Kawabata, Seidensticker introduced many other of Japan's best known authors to America, including Tanizaki Jun'ichirō and Mishima Yukio.

Donald Keene also studied in Japan after the war, and is known for introducing authors such as Abe Kōbō and Ōe Kenzaburō to the West.

During the Bubble years, Japan had made economic advances overseas, actively pursuing corporate buyouts. Parallel with this, Japan's everyday culture was introduced into America and elsewhere, with Japanese food like sushi and tofu becoming an established feature in cities, and increased interest in the spiritual dimension provided by Zen.

American society was originally rooted in the spiritual culture of

日本文化の輸出とは？

　戦後のアメリカの日本占領は、日本にアメリカ文化を紹介します。しかし、この時日本に駐留したアメリカ人の中には、逆に日本の伝統文化に興味を持ち、それを積極的に西欧に紹介した人も多くいます。

　日本文化をアメリカに紹介した草分けは、**エドウィン・ライシャワー**です。駐日大使でもあったライシャワーは、戦前からの知日派で、アメリカの対日政策の立案にも大きく貢献しました。

　また、川端康成の「雪国」を翻訳し、川端のノーベル賞受賞に貢献した**エドワード・サイデンステッカー**は、戦争中にアメリカ海軍で日本語を学び、海兵隊として日本に駐留したことが日本との出会いです。彼は、川端の他、谷崎潤一郎、三島由紀夫など、日本文学を代表する作家をアメリカに紹介します。

エドワード・サイデンステッカー

　同じく**ドナルド・キーン**も、戦後日本で勉強し、その後安部公房、大江健三郎といった作家を紹介したことで知られています。

　バブル期、日本は海外に経済進出し、海外の企業買収も進みます。それと平行するかのように、日本の日常文化がアメリカなどに紹介され、寿司や豆腐など日本食が都市部に定着し、禅などに代表される精神世界にも興味がもたれます。

　もともと、キリスト教、特にプロテスタントの精神文化に

ドナルド・キーン
© Aurelio Asiain

Christianity, particularly Protestantism, and the contrast between the serenity of Asian culture with Western rationality was probably manifest in the influx of immigrants from Asia.

America is a society founded by immigrants, and this the influx of Asian culture added to the variety and dynamism of American society. Japanese culture, too, was one of the new essences permeating the foundations of American society.

From the 1980s, many Japanese artists from all fields, from music to fashion, have been active the world over. Especially since the 1990s, Japan's visual culture has spread around the world, with English translations of postwar comics popular with children and adults rapidly gaining fans so that now the word manga is world-famous.

Nowadays even the otaku culture of Japanese youth is gaining recognition around the world. Quite independently from the Japanese flag, Japanese culture is organically spreading as it is adopted by young people in many countries and assimilated into their own lifestyles.

根付いていたアメリカ社会が、アジアからの移民を受け入れる中で、西欧流の合理主義とは異なるアジアの文化に、逆にやすらぎを覚えたのかもしれません。

また、アメリカは**移民社会がその基盤**であることから、新しい移民によってもたらされるアジア文化の流入が、アメリカ社会をさらに多様でダイナミックなものにしてゆきます。日本文化も、そうした新しいアメリカ社会の底辺にしみ込んだエキスの一つとなったのです。

80年代以降、音楽からファッションまで、多様な分野で日本のアーティストが世界で活躍します。特に、90年代以降、日本のビジュアル文化が世界に浸透し、戦後日本で子供から大人まで親しんだマンガが英文で紹介されると、たちまち支持を受け、今では**マンガ**は世界語となっているほどです。

現在では日本の若者の**オタク文化**も、世界で市民権を得ています。日の丸を意識せず、自然体で日本文化が世界に流れ出ている現在、日本文化は海外の若者に率直に受け入れられ、彼らのライフスタイルの一部となっているようです。

98 Heisei

Emperor Shōwa passed away in January 1989, marking the end of an era. And in November the same year, the Cold War ended as the Berlin Wall came down.

The end of the Cold War meant that east and west were no longer divided into two camps. This led to a surge in nationalism, with conflicts breaking out in various places. Along with the chaos of the Palestinian issue in the Middle East, anti-Americanism in the Islamic world has also gathered pace and become a destabilizing force in the world.

In Asia, China recovered from the chaos caused by the outrages committed on them by Japan and the West, and their balloon was again expanding as they sought to expand their territory to the level it had been under the Qing dynasty. Also, Korea continued to democratize and became one of the great economic powers of the Far East.

Yet though the world had become more diverse and chaotic, people were more connected than before. This was thanks to a new industrial revolution: information technology.

In the 1990s, Japan was still floundering in the economic crisis caused by the bursting of the bubble and was unable to lead the IT revolution.

Land prices inflated by speculation suddenly dropped and asset values nosedived, with many firms going bankrupt. The sluggish economy was the advent of the first serious recession in Japan since the economic miracle. The Kobe earthquake in the winter of 1995, and then in March

平成とは？

　昭和天皇は、1989 年 1 月に他界し、昭和という時代が
終わります。そして同じ年の 11 月に、ベルリンの壁が崩壊
し、**冷戦**が終了します。

　東西冷戦の終了は、国家が所属するグループの崩壊を
意味します。世界は新たな**民族主義**の時代に入り、各地
で戦争がおこり、民族運動が活発になりました。また、中
東ではパレスチナ問題の混沌とともに、イスラム圏での**反
米活動**が活発になり、それが世界の不安定要因となって
います。

　アジアでは、19 世紀から 20 世紀にかけて、欧米や日
本に蹂躙されていた中国が混乱から立ち直り、その風船
が再び膨張し、清以来の超大国になろうとしています。そ
して、韓国も民主化が進み、極東の経済大国の一員となっ
てきました。

　このように世界が多様で混沌としてきた中、人々のネット
ワークは以前とは比較できないほど活発になりました。新
たな産業革命ともいえる IT の発展です。

　日本は、90 年代におきたこれらの変化を見つめながら、
IT 産業を牽引できないままに、**バブルの崩壊**による**経済
危機**から立ち直れず、もがいていました。

　投機により高騰していた地価が一気に下落し、資産価
値が急降下する中で、多くの企業が倒産し、経済は低迷
します。それは、高度成長以来はじめて日本が経験した
本格的な**不況**の到来でした。1995 年の冬に起きた**阪神**

the same year the sarin gas attack on the Tokyo subway by the Aum Shinrikyō cult cast a further shadow on the recession, and the population was beset by anxiety. Japan's pride as an ecomomic power, and the myth of it being a safe country, had been shattered and the Japanese people experienced a loss of confidence.

Since the Kishi and Satō cabinets, the reins of government had been passed around factions of the Liberal Democratic Party and it gradually lost its unifying force. Added to this, successive corruption scandals, including Lockheed in the 1970s and Recruit in the 1980s, further undermined the people's trust in politics. People felt alienated by the backroom politicking by bureaucrats once considered excellent.

Japan had performed an economic miracle, but with the government unable to provide a strong remedy for the recession, the country's confidence plummeted. This recession is known as the "ten lost years."

In the same period, the IT industry was nurtured under Bill Clinton's administration, bringing the trade deficit under control and reviving the American economy. In contrast, Japan's government was clearly suffering from structural fatigue, and in the absence of any leadership the recession was becoming worse.

淡路大震災、そして同年3月におきた、カルト集団オウム真理教による地下鉄サリン事件は、不況にさらに影を落とし、国民を不安に陥れました。経済大国の自負に加え、安全な国日本という神話が崩壊し、日本人の自信喪失へと繋がったのです。

　自由民主党は、岸内閣、佐藤内閣以来、派閥による政権のたらい回しの中で、次第に求心力を失いつつありました。加えて、70年代におきたロッキード事件、80年代のリクルート事件など、相次ぐ汚職によって、国民の政治への不信感も払拭できずにいました。以前は優秀だとされていた官僚主導による密室での政治にも、国民は強い疎外感を感じていたのです。

　実際政府は、不況に対する強い処方箋を提示できないまま、高度成長の奇跡を演じた日本の信用が低下します。この不況は「失われた10年」とよばれます。

　同じ時代に、ビル・クリントン政権下でIT企業を育成し、財政赤字を克服し復活を遂げたアメリカ経済とは対照的に、日本政府には構造疲労が目立ち、リーダーシップがみられないままに、不況が深刻化していったのです。

ひとくちメモ
阪神・淡路大震災
1995年1月17日に発生した大地震。兵庫県南部を中心に多数の被害を出した

ひとくちメモ
ロッキード事件
1976年2月、アメリカの航空機製造大手のロッキード社による、旅客機の受注をめぐった大規模汚職事件

リクルート事件
1988年、リクルートコスモス社の未公開株を賄賂として受け取ったとして、政治家や官僚らが次々に逮捕された

99 Japan in the Twenty-First Century

The world was dramatically changed by the simultaneous terrorist attacks on New York in 2001.

When the wars in Afghanistan and Iraq started, the Koizumi government dispatched the Self Defence Forces to Iraq to provide reconstruction assistance, strongly aligning himself with America. On the other hand, he publicly visited Yasukuni Shrine where the war dead are enshrined, and which has a museum thought to endorse Japan's prewar actions. This invited protests from China and Korea, and relations especially with China cooled.

China's growth into a superpower poses an economic and military threat to Japan and the question of what kind of relationship the two countries should pursue to maintain peace is a major diplomatic issue for Japan from now on.

After the Koizumi administration, there have been three LDP prime ministers in as many years, and although Japan has somehow managed to come out of recession, it has not managed to regain the economic strength it once had.

Then in 2008, the Lehman Brothers' bankruptcy triggered by the subprime mortgage crisis in America spread into a global recession and Japan's economy again stalled. The national finances had for a long time relied on the issue of deficit-covering government bonds, but were now also extremely pressed due to the drop in tax revenue.

With many domestic problems, the government and people have tended towards excessive introspection, which some regard as a dangerous

21世紀になってからの日本は？

　2001年にニューヨークを襲った**同時多発テロ**は、世界のあり方を大きく変えました。

　アフガニスタン、そしてイラクとの戦争がはじまると、当時の小泉政権は、自衛隊をイラクに派遣し、復興支援を実施し、アメリカとの連携を強くアピールします。一方で、戦前の日本の行為を肯定しているともとられる資料館を有し、そこに戦没者が祀られている**靖国神社**を小泉首相が参拝したことが、中国や韓国の反発を招き、特に中国との関係が冷え込みます。

靖国神社

　中国が超大国として成長する中で、中国に**軍事経済的脅威**を日本が抱いていることは確かで、両国がどのように関係を維持し平和を守ってゆくかは、これからの日本にとっての大きな**外交課題**といえましょう。

　小泉政権の後、自由民主党は3年間で3人の首相が交代、不況からはなんとか抜け出したものの、以前ほどの力強い経済再生には及びません。

　そこに、2008年にアメリカでの低所得者向けの住宅ローンの破綻に端を発した**リーマンショック**が世界同時不況へと拡大すると、日本経済がまたも失速し、従来から**赤字国債**の発行に頼っていた国家財政も、**税収の落ち込み**などで極度に逼迫します。

　国内の課題の多い中、国民も政府も**内向き**に偏りがちで、そのことを右傾化と危険視する見方もあるほどです。

🔍 **ひとくちメモ**
リーマン・ブラザーズ
アメリカのニューヨークに本社を置いていた大手投資銀行及び証券会社。2008年9月15日に倒産して世界金融危機の引き金となった

swing to the right.

In fact, with the gap between rich and poor growing, disparity in education, the drop in the will to work amongst young people, and the loss of confidence of the people as Japan continued to flounder, there was an accelerating shift away from the Liberal Democratic Party.

Then in 2009, the shift in power was completed as the Democratic Party of Japan, which grew out of internal rifts in the LDP in the 1990s, won a landslide victory in the elections for the Lower House. However, the new administration failed to keep its election promises concerning Okinawa and other issues, lost popular support, and was further criticized for its slow response to the catastrophe brought on by the March 11, 2011, Great East Japan Earthquake and Tsunami as well as the complete breakdown of the nuclear plant in Fukushima Prefecture. As a result, at the end of 2012 the Liberal Democratic Party led by Shinzo Abe once more came into power. The Abe administration attracted criticism, but also growing support, for its controversial views on Japan's responsibility for the Pacific War, its desire for a greater voice in world affairs, and its aspirations for a strong military that could contribute to world stability.

Since the bubble burst, Japanese people have displayed doubts about the past "convoy system" whereby the government has protected weak companies from collapsing, and what used to be common sense is now viewed with skepticism. Meanwhile, Japanese people are beginning to place more value on individualism, and ideas have become more diversified. On the other hand, there is a marked movement toward creating a society that has parted with past history and possesses national pride, as can be seen in the efforts to revise the constitution. The number of people who see this as a movement toward the right has also increased. Do the current contradictions in the economy and society represent the birth pains of a new society for the future? Time will tell.

実際、貧富の差の拡大、教育格差、若者の勤労意欲の低下、低迷する日本というイメージが定着することによる国民の自信喪失など、難問が山積する中で、国民の自由民主党離れが加速します。

　そして、2009年の衆議院選挙で、90年代の自由民主党の内部分裂から成長した**民主党**が圧勝し、政権交代を実現します。しかし、この政権も沖縄の基地問題などでの公約を守れず、支持を失い、さらに2011年3月11日に東北地方を見舞った**東日本大震災**での巨大津波による未曾有の被害と、機能不全に陥った福島県にある**原子力発電所**への対応の遅れなどによる批判にさらされます。その結果、2012年暮れからは再び自由民主党の安倍政権が成立しました。戦後の課題を清算し、世界に対して発言力があり、軍事貢献もできる日本を目指そうという新しい政権の主張は、論議を呼びながらも支持を集めています。

　バブル経済の崩壊以来、日本人は、過去の政財官一帯となった**護送船団方式**の国家運営に疑問を呈し、過去の常識に懐疑的になりました。そうした中で、日本人は以前より個性を重んじ、趣向も**多様化して**きました。反面、**改憲**の動きなどに代表される、過去と訣別した日本人としての誇りをもった社会を築こうとする動きも顕著で、それが右傾化だと懸念する人もまた増えています。現在の経済と社会の矛盾が、この新しい日本人による未来型社会を創造するための産みの苦しみなのかどうか。まさに今、そのことが問われているのです。

Japan and the Future

Since 2020, the world has been confronted with what is said to be the biggest global challenge since World War II. In December 2019, the outbreak of COVID-19 in China spread around the world in a matter of months, becoming a pandemic. Due to this unprecedented virus epidemic, global economic activity slumped, and international travel became almost impossible for a while. During the coronavirus outbreak, people went online to work and study, and lifestyles changed dramatically.

In the midst of this turmoil, the Russian invasion of Ukraine began, triggered by territorial and ethnic disputes. This was the first full-scale military invasion of a European country since World War II, and there are fears that a nuclear war could break out. This was a tragedy that resulted from the division between authoritarian states such as Russia and China, which attempted to lead their societies by controlling speech, and democratic states such as Japan, the US, and Western Europe. And if we look around Japan, the situation is by no means stable, with missile provocations by North Korea, conflicts between China and Taiwan and its neighboring regions, and a persistent anti-Japanese movement in South Korea that questions Japan's responsibility for World War II.

On the other hand, Japanese animation, which already known around the world, has become even more established as a form of expression for the future, riding the trends of AI and IT since the

未来に向かう日本とは？

　2020 年以降、世界は第二次世界大戦以降最大ともい
われるグローバルな課題をつきつけられました。2019 年
12 月、中国で発生した**コロナウイルス**は、わずか数カ月
ほどの間に**パンデミック**と言われるほど世界に拡大しまし
た。この人類が経験したことのないウイルスの流行で、世
界の経済活動は低迷し、国際間の行き来も一時ほとんど
できなくなりました。コロナウイルス感染拡大の間、人々
はオンラインで仕事や学習をし、そのライフスタイルは大き
く変化しました。

　そうした混乱の中で、領土や民族の帰属問題に端を発
した**ロシアによるウクライナへの侵攻**がはじまったので
す。これは第二次世界大戦以降はじめてのヨーロッパ地域
での本格的な軍事侵攻であり、核戦争の勃発まで懸念さ
れています。これは、ロシアや中国など、いわゆる言論を
統制して社会を牽引しようとする**権威主義の国家**と、日本
やアメリカ、そして西欧などの**民主主義の国家**とに分断さ
れた結果が招いた悲劇でもありました。そして日本周辺に
目を向けると、北朝鮮による**ミサイルの挑発**、中国と台湾
やその周辺地域との対立、韓国での日本の戦争責任を問
う根強い**反日運動**など、その状況も決して安定したもので
はありません。

　一方で、すでに世界的に知られていた日本のアニメは、
21 世紀にはいって以降、AI や IT の時流に乗って、未来
に向けた表現形式としてさらに定着していきました。そして、

beginning of the 21st century. And after a one-year postponement, the Olympics were held in Tokyo in 2021 for the first time in 57 years. Even now, the number of foreign visitors to Japan has not returned to the level before the coronavirus, but it is also true that the number of foreign residents in urban areas such as Tokyo has increased significantly. On the other hand, it is also true that the inward-looking orientation of young people, the withdrawal of young people who cannot stand on their own feet, and the aging of society have made the problems of social alienation and loneliness even more serious.

In addition, the government's debt, which has been serious for a long time, has expanded further due to economic aid in the wake of the coronavirus and remains a major issue for the Japanese economy. The economic and political stagnation is perhaps the biggest challenge Japan must overcome today.

And, after Russia invaded Ukraine in 2022, Prime Minister Kishida, who succeeded the Abe and then Kan administrations, has also brought to a boil the debate over whether Japan should build up its defense capability, leading some to express the fear that Japan may be on the same path that led to the Second World War.

The world is becoming more and more chaotic. In the midst of this, Japan stands at a major crossroads that will determine what role it should play in the world. The question is whether the island nation of Japan has the courage and determination in all aspects of domestic politics and diplomacy to coexist with the rest of the world without repeating the mistakes of the past.

1年の延期の後、2021年には57年ぶりに東京でオリンピックも開催されました。今だにコロナ感染前ほどは訪日外国人の数は戻っていませんが、東京などの都市部では外国人の在住者も目立って多くなってきたのも事実です。反面、若者の**内向き志向**、自立できない若者の**引きこも**りや、高齢化社会が進む中で、人々の**社会からの疎外**や孤独の問題が、さらに深刻になっているのも事実です。

　さらに、以前から深刻であった政府の負債はコロナウイルスでの経済支援などでさらに膨張し、日本経済の大きな課題として残っています。**経済と政治の低迷**は、いま日本が乗り越えなければならない最も大きな課題でしょう。

　そして、2022年に、ロシアがウクライナに侵攻した後、安倍政権とその後の菅政権を引き継いだ岸田総理大臣になって、日本でも防衛力を増強するかどうかという議論も沸騰し、第二次世界大戦への道と同じ、戦争への歩みをはじめているのではないかという危惧を表明する人もいます。

　世界は一層、混沌としてきています。そんな中、日本は世界に対し、どのような役割を担うべきなのかを決める大きな岐路に日本は立たされています。過去の失敗を繰り返すことなく、島国の日本が世界と共存してゆくための勇気と決断が、内政外交の全てにおいて、今、問い直されているのです。

Index
索引

れ

ろ

わ

English Conversational Ability Test
国際英語会話能力検定

● E-CATとは…
英語が話せるようになるための
テストです。インターネット
ベースで、30分であなたの発
話力をチェックします。

www.ecatexam.com

● iTEP®とは…
世界各国の企業、政府機関、アメリカの大学
300校以上が、英語能力判定テストとして採用。
オンラインによる90分のテストで文法、リー
ディング、リスニング、ライティング、スピー
キングの5技能をスコア化。iTEP®は、留学、就
職、海外赴任などに必要な、世界に通用する英
語力を総合的に評価する画期的なテストです。

www.itepexamjapan.com

日英対訳 日本の歴史

2023 年 3 月 1 日　第1刷発行
2024 年 5 月 9 日　第2刷発行

著　者　　西海コエン

発行者　　賀 川　　洋

発行所　　IBCパブリッシング株式会社
　　　　　〒162-0804 東京都新宿区中里町29番3号 菱秀神楽坂ビル
　　　　　Tel. 03-3513-4511　Fax. 03-3513-4512
　　　　　www.ibcpub.co.jp

印刷所　　株式会社シナノパブリッシングプレス

ISBN978-4-7946-0753-9